8.95

Political issues in
America today

For Ros and Edie

Political issues in America today

Edited by
Philip John Davies *and* Fredric A. Waldstein

Manchester University Press

Published by Manchester University Press Oxford Road,
Manchester M13 9PL, UK

Distributed exclusively in the USA and Canada by
St. Martin's Press Inc.,
175 Fifth Avenue, New York 10010, USA

British Library cataloguing in publication data
Political issues in America today.—(Politics today).
  1. United States—Social conditions.—1980–
  I. Davies, Philip   II. Waldstein, Frederic A.
A. III. Series
  973.927   HN59.2

Library of Congress cataloging in publication data

ISBN 0 7190 1496 4 *paperback*

Typeset in Great Britain
by Alan Sutton Publishing Ltd

Printed in Great Britain
by Biddles Ltd, Guildford and King's Lynn

Contents

Acknowledgements   *page* vi

Introduction: American politics in the 1980s   1
    Fredric A. Waldstein and Philip John Davies

I   Leadership: changing styles and roles

1   The resurgence of the presidency *Philip John Davies*   6
2   The new Congress *George Goodwin, Jr*   27
3   Judicial appointment and change on the federal   41
    bench *Fredric A. Waldstein*

II   Representation: a changing political environment

4   Money in elections: the age of campaign finance   56
    reform *Philip John Davies*

5   Shifting sands: developments in party politics   75
    Philip John Davies

III Emerging influences: the changing cast of characters

6   The rising stars? Neoliberalism and neoconservatism   92
    Kenneth M. Dolbeare and Linda J. Medcalf

7   Religion and politics: the rise of the new Christian   106
    right *Paul Watanabe*

8   Women's issues in American politics *Gillian Peele*   122

IV Economic and social policy issues

9   The economics of health care policy   138
    Fredric A. Waldstein

10 Education: crisis, challenge and commitment   154
    Sandra E. Elman

11 Crime and criminal justice *Fredric A. Waldstein*   168

12 Environmental politics *Fredric. A. Waldstein*   184

V   Foreign policy issues

13 The banana republics revolt: the US and Central   200
    America *Jack Spence*

14 Giving peace a chance: the anti-nuclear movement   215
    Paul Watanabe

15 The new Cold War: foreign policy and Soviet-American   228
    relations *Paul Watanabe*

The authors   239

Acknowledgements

The editors wish to acknowledge the considerable support received during the preparation of this volume. The year that Philip Davies spent away from Manchester University as Visiting Associate Professor of Political Science at the University of Massachusetts at Boston and Visiting Fellow of the John W. McCormack Institute of Public Affairs provided the opportunity for the Waldstein/Davies partnership to develop, and led to this volume of essays. Thanks, therefore, to the Universities of Manchester and Massachusetts at Boston for their co-operation, to the British Academy for its support, and to Ed Beard, Director of the McCormack Institute, for friendship and help beyond the call of duty. Fredric Waldstein also has good reason to thank the McCormack Institute, and in addition Bentley College for their generous support of this project.

In Manchester Andrew and Carolyn were patient with Phil on condition that they were allowed an occasional go on the new word-processor, while in Boston Lauren developed a transatlantic telephone-answering style that belied her two and half years, and Eric delayed his arrival just long enough for the book to be finished. Ros and Edie remained calm through all of this, at the same time as pursuing their own professional lives with consummate skill. At Manchester University Press Alec McAulay's restrained impatience propelled us to completion, and we are grateful for that, too.

Fredric A. Waldstein and Philip John Davies

Introduction: American politics in the 1980s

The United States has spent the last decade or so apparently moving from self-doubt to self-congratulation. As the nation was preparing for its bicentennial festivities Watergate struck. The man who all had expected to preside gloriously over the 1976 celebration instead became the first president to resign from office. The shadow cast over the Nixon presidency seemed to affect the entire country. A few years later President Carter was talking about a 'malaise' in the nation. Others called it a crisis of leadership. With the economy weakening, and a group of Iranian fanatics threatening the country's sense of self-esteem by holding hostage part of the US diplomatic mission to Iran, Americans opted for a leader who promised optimism and good times ahead. By 1984 the voters were so convinced that the economy, the international reputation of the US and the promise of the future had been restored by President Reagan that he was re-elected by a landslide majority. The country even discovered its joy for parties – adding a Disneyesque glitz to the Olympics and the Statue of Liberty centenary celebration. The Supreme Court Chief Justice retired by his own admission to oversee the celebration for the bicentennial of the Constitution. But has Ronald Reagan, as his critics claim, merely brought Hollywood to Washington? If one strips away the tinsel is there any substantive policy initiative left? By examining the debates behind some of the major issues affecting US politics and political institutions perhaps we can get a better idea of the roots, direction, and future of American politics.

The following collection of essays is designed to serve two ends. First, it examines specific policy issues and how they have been addressed, and changes within the traditional political institutions that have occurred during the Reagan presidency. Each essay focuses on a topic of particular substantive importance. Second, we intend this collection, taken as a whole, to contribute to the reader's understanding of the American socio-political experience during the 1980s. We have attempted to address topics that have attained a level of prominence to be justly identified as characteristic of this crucial decade. This is based on the assumption that the Reagan agenda has shaped and been shaped by a socio-political context which constrains public policy options and institutional alternatives in a manner that we can at least partly identify.

Not unexpectedly there is disagreement on several fronts among students of politics concerning the impact on contemporary American political life of the so-called 'Reagan Revolution'. Is the rise of Reagan and the political philosophy he endorses the result of a strong leader with a clear vision capturing the imagination of the American people, and in the process fundamentally altering the future of American politics? Or did Ronald Reagan simply come along at the right time to enjoy riding the crest of a conservative but ephemeral wave moving opposite to the general tide of American politics? Is the Reagan philosophy as the basis for public policy going to produce results that are highly constructive, disastrous, or inconsequential? Is there indeed substance behind the style? These are some of the broad questions that social scientists and historians are asking as they attempt to analyse and evaluate the political landscape of the 1980s.

Recognising that consensus may never be reached within the community of scholars who address these questions, we nevertheless hope some insight can be gained by comparing different policy initiatives and institutional changes with their philosophical underpinnings; and, in turn, compare these with their historical antecedents. A useful place to begin this exercise may be to focus attention at the outset on the concept of 'federalism' since liberals and conservatives over the past 50 years or more have divided as consistently on what it is or should imply about the relations among the national, state and local governments as any other concept.

Franklin Roosevelt's *New Deal* fundamentally altered the relationship between the national, state and local governments with its emphasis on Co-operative Federalism, which meant that in 'such areas as public housing, highway construction, and aid to poor children and their families the national government instituted large programs that depended, for their implementation, on the financial and administrative co-operation of officials at the state or local levels.'[1]

Ronald Reagan has explicitly set for himself the task of making structural changes in federal, state, and local relations that reverse what he perceives to be the intrusion of federal government into matters best decided by states and localities. Dubbed 'New Federalism', the proponents of this idea believe 'that there should be a strict separation of federal from state and local program responsibilities and financing'.[2] Or, as the President's Task Force on Regulatory Relief puts it, 'Federal regulations should not preempt state laws or regulations, except to guarantee rights of national citizenship or to avoid significant burdens on interstate commerce.'[3] New Federalism was to be brought about through budget cuts in federal government programs and the 'swap and turn back' of federal programs to the states.

> The essence of this plan was that responsibility for welfare (Aid to Families with Dependent Children and food stamps) would be turned over to the states, in exchange for which the federal government would assume responsibility for medicaid programs currently being run by the state. All of this would be combined with an elaborate restructuring of taxes and grants.[4]

Attempts to determine the success of implementing New Federalism are complicated by several factors. One of these is the need to disentangle New Federalism from Reagan's economic policies, free enterprise, and other philosophical positions of the conservative movement. The degree to which these are consistent either in the abstract or when contemplating substantive policy changes is variable. Richard S. Williams, Special Assistant to the President for Intergovernmental Relations during Reagan's first term, concludes that the 'accomplishments passed reasonable expectations when he took office'.[5] This assessment is based on budget trends, the restructuring of block grants and other initiatives as well as the administration's rhetoric.

Timothy J. Conlan, on the other hand, argues that the goals of New Federalism have not fared that well when in competition with other aspects of Reagan's agenda, and he questions the level of commitment to them.

> Policies consistent with the president's definition of federal reform have

repeatedly lost out in the Reagan administration when they have conflicted with the sometimes competing goals of reducing the federal budget,
regulating the private sector, and advancing the conservative social
agenda. A full listing would embody administration policies and actions
across the broad expanse of federal activities, from restricting local
regulation of cable television to preempting state usury laws.[6]

The renewal of interest in the meaning of a concept as fundamental to the study of American politics as federalism is indicative
of how much influence Ronald Reagan has had on the academic
community at least. Much of the 'conventional wisdom' about
American politics in the 1970s does not hold for the 1980s. We are
given the opportunity to rethink the state of American politics in an
environment less encumbered by 'accepted truths'. Thus, it is an
especially exciting time to examine the issues which help define this
decade. We believe this enthusiasm is reflected in the following
essays, and hope the reader will be moved to think anew about the
issues and institutions discussed, and how they contribute to the
current political milieu.

Notes

1 Jeffrey R. Henig, *Public Policy and Federalism: Issues in State and Local
   Politics,* St Martin's Press, New York, 1985, p 15.
2 George E. Peterson, 'The State and Local Sector', *The Reagan Experi-
   ment,* J. L. Palmer & I. V. Sawhill (eds), The Urban Institute Press,
   Washington, DC, 1982, p 167.
3 President's Task Force on Regulatory Relief, 'Reagan Administration
   Regulatory Achievements', US Government Printing Office, Washington, DC, 11 August 1983, p 19.
4 Richard P. Nathan & Fred C. Doolittle, 'The Untold Story of Reagan's
   New Federalism', *The Public Interest,* no. 77, Fall 1984, p 96.
5 Richard S. Williamson, 'A New Federalism: Proposals and Achievement
   of President Reagan's First Three Years', *Publius,* XVI, 1986, p 26.
6 Timothy J. Conlan, 'Federalism and Competing Values in the Reagan
   Administration', *Publius* XVI, 1986, p 30.

I
Leadership: changing styles and roles

Philip John Davies

The resurgence of the Presidency

The apparent failure of Presidential leadership

For the past twenty years presidential candidates have promised the electorate leadership. 'Leadership for the 60s' was John F. Kennedy's slogan; then in 1964 the voters agreed to go 'All the way with LBJ'. A classic campaign design of 1968 showed Nixon leading a pack of runners, giving a double meaning to the slogan 'Nixon's the one'. Jimmy Carter promised to be 'A leader, for a change'. But the public have felt consistently disappointed with the presidential leadership they have seen, and for twenty years there has been a declining confidence in the ability of any man to manage successfully the office of President. Leaders have been seen to fail dramatically. Whilst Kennedy is widely remembered with affection, his brief term of office saw the disastrous Bay of Pigs excursion, and also few legislative victories, as a conservative Congress baulked when faced with his plans. The protracted agonies of the Vietnam War undermined Johnson's authority and personal morale. The excesses of Watergate sank Nixon into resignation via a humiliating and unavailing last few months spent assuring the public that 'your President is not a crook'. Carter claimed there was 'a malaise' in America, but the public was not used to leaders who blamed failure on them, and when inflation and unemployment rose, the USSR invaded Afghanistan, and American hostages were taken in Iran, the failure of leaders, rather than followers, seemed to be confirmed.

Nevertheless there has been little agreement on the correct response to this problem of Presidents being apparently unable to grasp firmly the reins of leadership. Indeed, both the public and the analysts have seemed undecided as to just how much leadership is enough, and when it becomes too much. In the early 1960s it was often claimed that Presidential power was too limited and the office-holder too restricted in his potential for action. Kennedy, for all the debate on his effectiveness, brought a sense of aggressive problem-oriented direction to the executive. That the Kennedy administration became known as *Camelot* was as much a fond acknowledgement of its despotic self-confidence as its romantic style. But this adulation of centralised power was not to last. Johnson and Nixon adopted an approach that was seen as domineering and 'imperial', and *The Imperial Presidency*[1] became reviled and feared. That such an executive approach gained notoriety seems, however, to have depended as much on the political environment of the times as on any underlying dislike of tough-minded leaders. The 'imperial presidency' was associated with the disastrously-failed foreign venture into South-East-Asia. It was also associated with Richard Nixon, a president who surrounded himself with an uncritical and cynically loyal staff, who made a risible attempt to increase the status of of the presidency by introducing Ruritanian dress uniforms for White House guards, whose lack of judgement led him deeper and deeper into the morass of Watergate, and who was faced with a very antagonistic, Democratic-controlled Congress, full of members delighted to find a weapon against the Republican White House.

The anti-government President and the anti-President government

Public trust in government declined precipitately during this period. In a 1964 survey 76 per cent of the public said they trusted the government 'most of the time' or 'always'. By 1972 this was down to 53 per cent, and the Bicentennial, and Presidential Election, year of 1976 saw this measure of public trust down to 33 per cent. Congress reacted to Watergate by trying to limit presidential power at home with new budgeting processes, and abroad through the War Powers Act, but in the public eye all politicians were suspect; they had no more confidence in Congress than in any other branch. The stage was set for the emergence of someone pledged to clean out Washington's Augean stables. The increasingly entrepreneurial nature of the political candidacies, especially in primary elections, allowed the freedom to try independent approaches to winning the party nomination, and ultimately the presidency. Candidates at all levels began running campaigns that distanced them from the 'politicians'. The political waters had become very disturbed, and bobbing to the surface came Jimmy Carter.

The Carter campaign took the politically shrewd route of painting their candidate as a 'non-politician'. Governor of Georgia he may have been once, but the campaign emphasised the managerial and organisational skills he brought to that role. Furthermore, his experience in office, whilst of an executive nature, was not tainted with the stain of Washington DC. For a self-proclaimed political outsider, Carter ran a brilliant campaign. He had the early disadvantage of very low name recognition, but hard work in the generally overlooked state of Iowa gave him a primary season victory that meant little in terms of convention delegates but attracted a huge amount of free publicity. Having once been established as a viable candidate Carter plodded steadily through his campaign timetable, outlasting and outflanking all the other Democratic candidates. In the wake of Watergate it was felt that the Democratic candidate would be assured of victory at the general election. This makes Carter's primary victory all the more remarkable, since Democratic party leaders, certain of the availability of the White House, were unhappy at the prospect of this maverick candidacy. While the public appeal of the outsider candidate, not 'of' Washington, but apparently with the ability to take Washington on, was ambivalent, it remained enough to take Carter to the Democratic nomination, and on to the White House.

If evidence is needed that the qualities tested by the presidential election are not necessarily those needed to run a successful presidential administration, then Jimmy Carter could serve as exhibit A. Foisted on his Democratic colleagues by a primary system they could no longer control, in Washington he faced hostility on all sides. His great campaigning asset, that icy disregard he held for the mores of the capital, became a major liability once he was himself in residence. Without the binding of rigid political parties, and with the 1970s erosion of traditional political hierarchies such as Congressional seniority, informal and flexible contact has become increasingly significant in Washington. Policy success depends on the building and constant tending of a political coalition which may itself shift over time, and between issues. Any potential political leader in Washington has to be thoroughly aware of the persuasive arsenal at his disposal, the assets that may be used developing and maintaining support, and the people who must be courted in order to garner the power fundamental to the successful passage of policy. Carter, entering the White House with none of the assets of familiarity or acceptability that an 'insider' candidate would have had, never seemed to grasp that he needed to make up for this deficiency. His liaison with Congress was poor on both personal and professional levels. He put little effort into massaging the egos of the Congressional leadership, and his congressional liaison staff approached the Capitol as though they were bringing the tablets down from the mountain, rather than supplicating for the support of powerful and firmly-installed political leaders. To some extent this non-traditional executive approach to Washington's movers and shakers may have been a fair interpretation of the public mandate Carter had received, but inexperience also played its part. The Carter administration opened its term with a broad perception of the fields in which initiatives were needed. Proposals across a broad policy spectrum were sprung on Congress without consultation and before the depth of support had been gauged. This approach did not result in the overthrow of the established order. Presidential authority is real, but limited, and the flexing of executive muscle in Washington without careful attention to circumstances, may prove no more than decorative. Carter faced Democrats who felt that he was not of their choosing and Republicans looking for revenge after the humiliation of Watergate, and attempted to impose his will by merely calling them into line. It was an approach doomed to failure, and by the time the Carter White House showed signs of learning from its mistakes external events were taking their toll. Rising energy costs stalled any chances of economic recovery, but the most major domestic problem to emerge was the national shock and shame felt after the American embassy in Tehran was overrun, and the staff taken hostage.

Carter had failed to take Washington by the scruff of the neck. The public impression was of a good, well-meaning man who was not competent to meet the demands of the job, and who had finally failed to either maintain his independence from the Washington establishment, or to impose his will upon the government. The public demand for a president who was not a Washington insider was tempered by the public demand for a strong president; and the only way a president could be strong was by using those tricks available to the Washington insider. There was an increasing feeling that the presidency was, in any case, too big a job for any single person to manage. The public appeal of the anti-Washington candidacy had not faded, however, and a skilled practitioner was waiting to take the mantle. Indeed, 1976 had almost seen a presidential election battle between two self-styled outsiders, as Ronald Reagan had failed by a whisker to wrest the Republican nomination from incumbent President Gerald Ford. In 1980 Reagan raced to the nomination against a broad field of well-established Republicans. Reagan's strong base in the west gave his campaign an image of 'sage-brush rebellion' which was a valuable symbol of the honest outsider, frontier candidate, ready to take on the eastern politicians. This time Carter, tied to the White House, an administration of slow economic growth, and continuing crisis in Iran, could not run an outsider campaign. Carter tried for some time to run a 'rose garden' campaign, identifying himself even more closely with Washington, while Reagan emphasised the distinction between them by studiously avoiding any Washington appearances during the campaign that took him to election victory in 1980.

Reagan takes the reins

Early in the 1980 campaign, so the story went, the candidate and his wife approached a potential voter who was relaxing on the stoop of his home. 'I'm running for President and would appreciate your support', the politician began. 'What's your name?', came the response. 'Well, the initials are R.R., and my wife and I used to be in the movies.' 'Mabel,' called the now animated voter, 'come here, Roy Rogers and Dale Evans are running for President!' The story underlines the degree to which Reagan had been underestimated. Commentators consistently portrayed him as a retired actor of easily forgettable talent and over-simple, even if sincerely held, beliefs, rather than a man who had shown political leanings even when in Hollywood, and who had fostered a full-time political career for 20 years or more. This underestimation has been a double-edged sword. Being known as a political light-weight was a liability at times, but the commentators' apparent willingness to overlook his second career acted to confirm Reagan's adopted position as a political outsider – no small asset in 1980. The fact that his term of office has seen substantial changes in the policy agenda and in the style of the Presidency has come as a surprise to many, but the earlier-received wisdoms about Reagan provided such a low level of expectation that these successes have reflected all the more favourably on the President. Reagan, while never adopting Carter's intense and dedicated commitment to the details of the job, made a convincing case in his first six years in office that the executive may, after all, be manageable.

The new administration learned well from the experience of Jimmy Carter. While Reagan had run as an outsider, he had a clear conception of the political etiquette of the capital. He and his appointees worked hard to avoid ruffling the feathers of potential enemies, and to encourage the loyalty of supporters. The Reagan White House had an initial advantage in the scale of Reagan's electoral victory. Defeating an incumbent President by a clear 10 per cent of the vote (albeit it with the intervention of a popular independent candidate, John B. Anderson) was in itself a remarkable feat. But the significance of that victory was heightened by the Republican Party's legislative gains, especially the victories, some by very slim margins, that brought a Republican majority to the Senate for the first time in a quarter of a century. Those Republicans newly elected to Congress in 1980 generally shared Reagan's conservative opinions. Republicans in Congress felt that they owed their new strength in part at least to the electoral appeal of their new President. Consequently Republican Party loyalty and internal cohesion in Congress was unusually high in the early days of the Reagan administration. Meanwhile the Democrats were in turmoil. Used to Congressional domination, they were shocked and disoriented by the loss of Senate control. The 'sage brush rebellion' seemed to some Democrats, as well as to ideological Republicans, to be part of a nationwide shift to the right. The unstable ideological coalition that makes up the Democratic Party was thoroughly shaken, and conservative Democrats, especially those from the South, felt politically comfortable and electorally safe in supporting the policy initiatives of a popular president.

A new president generally has the advantage of a brief 'honeymoon' period, when criticism is muted and co-operation available. Given the electoral victories of 1980, and the end of the Iranian hostage crisis simultaneous with Reagan's 1981 inauguration, the auspices were even better than usual for an incoming president. The Reagan White House was quick to take advantage of these political assets when it approached Congress with immediate, clearly stated, sweeping proposals to cut domestic spending and taxes in line with Reagan's perception of his mandate. The Republican majority in Senate gave the administration's initiatives a favourable hearing, while the Democratic majority in the House was in disarray. Reagan's 'Program for Economic Recovery', proposed in February 1981, capitalised well on this situation. Budget legislation in the United States takes a long and tortuous route, as executive proposals are segmented, dealt with by a variety of committees and sub-committees in both House and Senate, debated, adjusted, enacted in disparate parts, and often passed extremely late in the legislative day. Even then there will often be a delay between the legislation and the implementation, so that new presidents may have to live with the effects of the budgetary policies of their predecessors for some considerable time. Such a waiting game was unpalatable to the Reagan administration, and the initial proposals were pressed with an urgency rarely seen in Washington.

Domestic austerity was not new – per capita federal aid to state and local governments had peaked in 1978 – but Reagan's demand for substantial cut-backs, and a less regulated federalism built on fewer, more broadly-defined block grants, was a major deviation from the direction taken by federal government domestic policy ever since the New Deal. The Omnibus Budget Reconciliation Act passed in July 1981 gave Reagan much that he had requested. Cuts agreed to the 1982 Fiscal Year Budget amounted to $35.2 billion, mostly from domestic programmes. In response to Reagan's request that 85 categorical grant programmes be consolidated into 7 block grants, Congress agreed to the slightly less dramatic folding of 57 categorical grants into 9 block grants, while allowing a number of other grants to lapse as they came due for renewal – not quite what the doctor ordered, but close enough for House Budget Chairman James R. Jones to call it 'clearly the most monumental and historic turnaround in fiscal policy that has ever occurred'. Quite apart from the immediate and continuing economic effect of Reagan's initial budgetary success, it also contributed to the growing wisdom in Washington that the President was riding such a strong tide of public opinion as to become almost invincible. A widespread perception of this kind can serve to undermine opposition, thereby perpetuating the imbalance of power, but some observers felt that the initial Reagan victories were built on assets of timing and popularity that would not survive a serious challenge.

Reagan's persuasive Presidency: the Teflon years

Even prior to the first Iran/Contra disclosures of late 1986 Reagan did not enjoy unwavering public support. The economic recession of 1982 was accompanied by a steady decline in the public's approval of his presidency. In January 1983 the opinion polls showed only about 40 per cent of respondents approved the way Ronald Reagan was handling his job as President, while about 50 per cent disapproved. But Reagan bounced back, his approval ratings rose steadily to between 60 and 70 per cent by the time of the 1984 presidential election, and remained fairly steady until after the 1986 mid-term elections. This period saw no repeat of the sweeping legislative victories of Reagan's first year, and his administration was not without its problems or critics. However Reagan's stock rose even without major policy gains, and any difficulties faced by his administration appeared to leave him relatively unscathed.

While this public appeal may owe something to Reagan's stand on substantive issues, many observers believe that it depends a great deal on his style, hence he became known as 'The Great Communicator'. Certainly the skill with which he presents himself to any audience is remarkable, especially when compared with the efforts of other recent Presidents. The increased role of media coverage of US politics in recent years means that such skills are a great political asset. Nevertheless, it is too easy to write off his long period of success as being due to his ease with the media, and a heritage of 50 years' experience in front of one camera or another. Accepting such a simplified analysis protects Reagan's opponents from the self-examination and political soul-searching that might follow from a broader analysis of Reagan's success. It also protects the media from the accusation that they are a mere catspaw to the President, since if he is such a 'Great Communicator' there is nothing that their commentary can do about it. One suspects the administration's critics of having taken an ostrich-like approach in the hope that things will return to the status quo ante at the end of Reagan's term of office. This analysis, bolstered by accusations that Reagan is a leader without intellectual skills, bound by an overly simplistic vision of the world, indulging in sudden changes of political tactics, and who puts greater reliance on his personal optimism than on expert advice, threatens to turn liberal wishful thinking into a more broadly-accepted received wisdom. Each of these criticisms contains a clue to those political strategies that served Reagan well for almost six years.

The non-intellectual Presidency

Ronald Reagan embraces the comment that he is not an intellectual. Against the trend of contemporary visions of the Presidency, Reagan claims to see the personal role of the President as limited, firmly setting the direction of policy, but delegating control, relying on hierarchical decision-making, and sharing responsibility with trusted advisers.[2] There are dangers inherent in this approach. A president taking such a consciously limited role may fail to appreciate the complexity of situations, or be unaware of the strategic limitations on potential responses. The development of a management team of trusted, politically acceptable people can divorce a leader from broader political realities. One commentator felt that this was threatening to happen in Reagan's administration in 1986: 'Among those who work in the White House, the boss's infectious good humour is catching. If it isn't, they don't work there for long'.[3]

There are also real attractions in this approach to executive management. It can be compared favourably with the nit-picking intellectualism of Jimmy Carter, whose determination to master the details of government produced an immobilisation at the very centre of the White House. Its success relies on public approval. As long as the public accept the validity of a less-informed, but more free-wheeling, presidential style criticism may be deflected, since, if total knowledge is not necessary, then occasional public lapses are to be expected, and can be excused. It all becomes part of the essential 'humanity' of Ronald Reagan that is expected, and accepted, by his public. For the 'all-knowing' president, any slip is a fault. The part-time, managerial president, may be sadly let down by his organisation and may be baulked by his enemies in Congress, but as long as he maintains his publicly-stated firmness of purpose, he may be able to avoid the blame himself.

If Reagan is not an intellectual, he has on occasion shown himself politically shrewd. He does not undervalue the need to have access to political intelligence. His early appointments reflected this recognition as people acceptable to Republicans in the Washington political establishment were recruited to bolster the inside circle of

Reagan loyalists anxious to achieve important leadership and liaison positions. Led by Ed Meese, Reagan's Californian cadre displayed sensitivity in the transition period, assembling a staff that satisfied traditional Republican constituencies, while mollifying the far right and supply-side advocates. The development of a leadership group that could be moulded to Reagan's ideas, and were capable of projecting these ideas to the electorate, the bureaucracy, and the legislature, was an important part of the Reagan strategy. At the centre of this system. Reagan aimed to give the impression of somewhat regally detached, but firm, leadership.

However, management teams are not static. In February 1985 Reagan's trusted counsellor Ed Meese left the White House to become US Attorney-General. This came only a month after another major change, which saw White House Chief of Staff James Baker swap posts with Treasury Secretary Donald Regan. Regan's mode of operation brought to the executive a new air of hauteur and isolation. Autocratic and prime-ministerial while the administration bandwagon was rolling, Regan later discovered that he was ultimately dispensable when a sacrifice had to be made in response to 'Irangate' criticisms. With the replacement in March 1987 of Regan by the highly respected former Senator Howard Baker the Reagan White House again showed a skilful, if rather belated, response aimed at restoring public and institutional confidence in this administration's system of delegated management.

The simplistic Presidency

According to *New York Times* correspondent Leslie Gelb, 'Some critics see the President as being simple-minded. Rather, a number of his aides suggest, he is simplistic. That is, he reduces complications to simple symbols and images of good and bad, American and un-American. That allows him to cut through the complexities that bewilder and hold no interest for the general public, putting him squarely on the public's wavelength'.[4] Gelb believes that this straightforwardness comes from Reagan's unwavering commitment to certain principles throughout his political life, and dating particularly from his period as celebrity representative and speechmaker on behalf of General Electric. Reagan's favourite themes at that time included tax reform, school prayer, fervent anticommunism and getting 'Big Government' off the backs of the people. Simple though these ideas may be, they are shared by many of the American electorate, and they form a skeleton on which the body of Reagan's policy can be fitted.

Equipped with such a clear, if abbreviated, vision of the political agenda. Reagan rarely comes across an issue that cannot be decided quickly and without agonising. Taxes must be reduced, as must government spending (and 'interference'), traditional values deserve promoting, America must be militarily strong, and the Russians and fellow-travellers must not be appeased. It also provides the blueprint for responses to many issues of Reagan's term, such as reducing federal aid to states and localities or providing American aid for the Contras in Nicaragua. Complexity of analysis only serves to confuse matters, and anomalies that might arise can either be ignored, or dealt with on an *ad hoc* basis. Reagan's personal commitment to the broad outline of this agenda is so strong that opponents faced the possibility of being characterised as malign or naive 'enemies' of America. This combative style has served Reagan well. In 1980 he campaigned against 'big government', and 'big-spending liberals', as well as the failures of Jimmy Carter. In 1984 the Democratic nomination of Walter Mondale (Carter's Vice-President) allowed Reagan to run another campaign against the previous administration and 'old-style' politics. Until the Democratic Senate victories of 1986 Reagan was in the happy position of being able to rail against the recalcitrance of the Democratic House when his initiatives failed, while being protected against the more formidable opposition, and investigative powers, of the Senate by the loyalty of its Republican leaders. For example, when Democrats failed to approve all the domestic spending cuts he requested the President blamed bulging deficits on Congress, ignoring the fact that the Congressionally-imposed limits on defence spending more than made up for their domestic largesse. When Congress in 1986 proved slow to approve aid to the Contras in Nicaragua Reagan portrayed his opponents as naively playing into the hands of communists. Time and again the Reagan administration managed to couch its policy in terms which wrong-footed opponents, and which gave the impression of a President single-mindedly pursuing the policy aims mandated by the public, and protecting the nation from others more foolish or less committed than himself.

The zig-zagging Presidency

Reagan has not been immune to reverses, but on many occasions he has been able to manage an enforced change of position so as to minimise the long-term damage. In the words of Barry Sussman, public opinion analyst for the *Washington Post*, 'Jimmy Carter used to do flip flops, and they were regarded as a sign of weakness. Reagan not only gets by with his reversals, he uses them as a key to keeping a high level of pubic support, or, at least to hold down opposition'.[5] When Congress could not be persuaded, when the polls showed that public opinion was stirred actively to reject the administration's view of things, or when unforeseen disaster struck, the Reagan administration's skill at damage control has been severely tested.

In 1983 US Marines were sent to Beirut as a peace-keeping force. Reagan vowed to maintain an American presence until the job was done. When a terrorist attack killed 241 Marines in Beirut there was shock and disbelief in America, and faith in the nation's leaders was again shaken. Reagan appeared on television, and, at his most sombre, accepted responsibility for the failure to protect adequately the American soldiers. Shortly thereafter the Marines were summarily withdrawn from the Lebanon. At the height of American involvement in the Vietnam War Senator Aiken advised that the government should 'declare victory and withdraw'; in the Lebanon Reagan effectively did just that. His acceptance of 'responsibility' defused criticism without implying that the President should be punished, and the withdrawal, while leaving the Middle East much as it had been before, reassured the US public. The political damage was minimised, and the chance of a repeat disaster eliminated. Everything in the Rose Garden was back to normal well before the 1984 election campaign.

In 1986 the Phillipines provided Reagan with another foreign policy reverse. In the wake of a visibly corrupt election Reagan nevertheless maintained his support for the administration of Ferdinand Marcos. The opposing Aquino camp was as guilty of election fraud as the Marcos forces, claimed Reagan, contrary to the opinions of senior American political observers in the Philippines. Over the following few days Reagan attempted to deflect concern away from the Philippines – visiting Grenada on a publicity-oriented trip, and restricting foreign polic statements to attacks on Nicaragua. But public concern was not deflected, and opinion polls suggested that the tide would continue to shift against the President's position. Under such pressure Reagan withdrew his support for Marcos. Within days the administration was claiming much of the credit for the peaceful transfer of power to the democratically-elected leadership of Corazon Aquino. The administration's action came as public disquiet was mounting, and instead of allowing that disquiet to turn to outrage, America claimed the kudos of protecting democracy in the international arena.

If Reagan's foreign policy has been characterised by political pragmatism and adjustment, the same approach has been seen on the domestic front. Tax reform would not have passed without some tax-breaks being maintained, and the 1982 'New Federalism' proposals were virtually abandoned, finally traded off for a modest further step towards consolidation of categorical grants into block grants. Belying his die-hard image, Reagan has said '. . . . . . if I can get 70 or 80 per cent of what it is I'm trying to get, yes, I'll take that and then continue to try to get the rest in the future'. But here too one has seen the strategy of 'declaring victory', since, in the words of a former White House official, 'he'll take 40 per cent and call it 80'.[6]

The personalised Presidency

Reagan has perhaps shown his greatest skill in maintaining a distance between himself and 'politics'. In early November 1986 public opinion polls showed approval ratings well over 60 per cent for President Reagan, but trust in government had barely improved since its post-Watergate lows, with only 40 per cent expressing a trust in government all or most of the time. In part, this detachment has been a result of his impressive skill in the ceremonial role of the Presidency. As David Broder says, 'When it comes to a patriotic occasion, a memorial service or a religious observance, his words, his bearing, his expressions and gestures speak eloquently for the American people and nation'.[7] Reagan has on occasion been able to use this Head of State performance to his benefit. After the *Challenger* disaster it was Reagan the Head of State, humane spokesman of the nation, who publicly expressed the country's grief, not Reagan the Head of Government explaining how his campaign ploy of encouraging a teacher to travel on the space shuttle could go so disastrously wrong. Reagan, Head of State, was also in evidence at the 40th anniversary of the Normandy landings, showing military bearing, and being emotionally moved, all the while being filmed for home consumption, and for use in 1984 campaign ads. The ceremonial role has not always been solemn – indeed there was a Disneyesque quality to the Los Angeles Olympic ceremonies, the Presidential participation in launching the Superbowl on Inauguration Day 1985, and the Statue of Liberty centenary celebrations – but it is almost always fulfilled with an air of nationalistic pride that enhanced the Presidential stature as a common man's Head of State.

Reagan has consistently denied that he is a 'politician', preferring the view that he is only concerned with what is good or bad for the people, and that his political involvement is almost an accident of fate. This pose, whether it is sincere or just a political technique, appears to have been generally accepted by the electorate. Reagan's optimism for the future of America, notwithstanding signals that might suggest at least a degree of circumspection, has been shared by the public.[8] His ability to portray himself as defender of the people against Congress, the federal government, and the international forces of communism have made him appear the personal friend of middle Americans. In the 1986 election campaign the administration's farm policy spelled disaster for Republican Senators in North and South Dakota. But even in these states where farmers were demanding government action to ease their plight, and even after Reagan had made a speech claiming that the most frightening words in he English language were 'I'm from the government and I'm here to help', the standing of the President did not fall. Approval of Reagan apparently could not be easily transferred to other levels in spite of his best efforts – a phenomenon named 'Teflon coattails' in one newspaper report – but neither was Reagan's approval rating damaged in the face of criticism of some of his administration's policies.

The combination of regal demeanour and an intensely personal, concerned approach has not just been an asset when talking to the broad electorate, but also in negotiations in Washington. The six years of Republican control of Senate allowed Reagan to take a broadly confrontational line against the Democratic House, but Reagan never lost sight of the need for direct and intimate

intervention on his part. Larry Hopkins, a Republican congressman, was persuaded by Reagan to alter his position to support the
1986 aid package for the Nicaraguan Contras. Explaining his change
of mind, Hopkins said, 'I'm from Wingo, Kentucky. I never thought
I'd get to the Oval Office, much less get to meet a president. This
president puts you at ease. He jumps up, meets you at the door,
takes your hand, and he *winks* at you . . . It's like visiting with a
close personal friend that you have a lot of trust in . . . He's so
accommodating, so genuine and sincere. He's not fakey, and he's
not an actor . . . He's the kind of guy you just want to help, and I'm
proud to stand in his shadow.'[9]

The altered agenda

'Great Communicating' does not operate in a simple vacuum. Leslie
Gelb says, 'Time after time during his Presidency, Ronald Reagan
has demonstrated his unrelenting determination to have his way. In
the process he may outrage supporters, employ sophistry, totally
reverse his position while all the while denying it.'[10] Reagan's style
and optimism have attracted public support, but rhetorical
optimism would be unlikely to attract maintained personal support
for so long without there also being substantial public support for
many of his main policies. Reagan has impressed the electorate with
his sense of purpose, and his skill in pursuing that purpose. He has
employed these skills in a helpful environment. The oil price
collapse of the early 1980s underpinned a national economic boom
that rebounded to the benefit of a president who had always said
things would turn out right. The Democratic Party only began to
show its teeth after the 1986 election results put Democrats back in
charge of Senate. Even the media seemed cowed, and unable to
combat the careful management techniques employed by the White
House.

These circumstances set the scene for substantial changes to the
political agenda. Domestically there were cuts in spending by the
federal government. The details of the New Federalism proposal
may have been lost, but the greater use of block grants, and reduced
intergovernmental aid, pressed more responsibility onto the states
for a wide variety of domestic policies. The attempt, begun under
Carter, to improve the business environment by reducing the
government's role in economic and social regulation, was

expanded. Initial tax cuts were followed by sweeping tax reform – the fact was that although the final legislation was not in the precise form recommended by the White House, the Reagan administration created the political environment and direction without which such reform would have been very unlikely. Reagan has been accused of failing to deliver on his promises to those conservatives among his supporters who are most concerned with social issues. The issues of abortion rights, prayer in schools and such are dangerous ground for any politician, and for the most part Reagan has restricted himself to a rhetorical assault in favour of 'traditional values'. Nevertheless this administration's conscious and consistent commitment to conservatism in its appointments to the federal judiciary may be the most effective and long-term influence a modern president can have on such social issues.

The administration has not, as it initially promised, balanced the budget. Indeed the country's deficit has more than doubled under Reagan. The White House accuses the Democratic Congress of responsibility for much of this increased debt, while Democrats point to Reagan's extravagant defence plans. Wherever the blame lies, this has in its turn led to the passage of the Gramm-Rudman-Hollings Bill, aimed to enforce a balanced budget over a fixed timetable. As a long-time supporter of the theory of a balanced budget, Reagan can again claim the responsibility for creating the political environment in which such legislation could be passed. The 'big government', high-spending approach to domestic problems, already under challenge before Reagan entered the White House, has come under consistent attack from his administration, and while the Democratic victory in the 1986 Senate elections undermines almost any chance Reagan has of further successful domestic policy initiatives, the Democrats are unlikely to deviate far from the new conservatism seen under Reagan's leadership.

On the foreign affairs scene the illness and deaths in rapid succession of Soviet leaders Leonid Brezhnev, Yuri Andropov, and Konstanin Chernenko left the Kremlin in disarray throughout Reagan's first term of office, giving him virtual free rein in the superpowers' international public relations battle. In an atmosphere of combative rhetoric aimed against the Soviet Union, defence spending not only grew, but introduced prospects of enormous growth in the future by means of the Strategic Defence Initiative, or 'Star Wars' programme. Reagan's tough-talking approach to the

USSR attracted a good deal of public support. After the Reykjavik meeting with Mikhail Gorbachev in 1986 the generally-held 'expert' opinion was that the discussions had been a failure, but the American public were more willing to accept their president's version, that his unflinching commitment to American international strength was serving to keep the Soviet Union in order. Even in the close fights Reagan showed an ability to come out on top, as in June 1986, when initial Congressional opposition to his plans to sell $265 million worth of weapons to Saudi Arabia was overcome. Congress had passed a measure to block the sale, and looked ready override Reagan's veto of this blocking legislation. Personal lobbying by the President convinced eight Senators, two of them Democrats, to switch their position, thereby obtaining the minimum vote to uphold the veto. Given such a record, Reagan might have been expected to continue an aggressive and innovative foreign policy leadership role even after the 1986 election defeats, the President having a generally freer hand in foreign affairs, but the exposure of White House involvement in legally-dubious arms deals with Iran, the profits from which were used to subsidise the Contra forces in Nicaragua, was very damaging. Although well-tried damage control techniques were immediately put into action, even a President as popular and skilful as Ronald Reagan was bound to face severe criticism for making yet another ill-judged American move relating to Iran.

Acting Presidential: the flaw in Reagan's masterpiece

In November 1986 disclosures began to surface regarding the supply of arms by the US to Iran in an attempt to improve the likelihood of Western hostages in the Middle East being released. Such arms trading appeared on the surface to contravene US legislation, and to run directly counter to Reagan's public stance against 'trafficking with terrorists'. In an early attempt to defuse the situation Reagan said: 'Eighteen months ago . . . this administration began a secret initiative to the Islamic Republic of Iran . . . I considered the risks of failure and the rewards of success, and I decided to proceed, and the responsibility for the decision is mine and mine alone . . . It was a high-risk gamble . . . and I don't see that it has been a fiasco or a great failure of any kind.' The public and press were not so sure, as evidence emerged of former White House security adviser Robert

MacFarlane visiting Iran bearing gifts of a cake and an inscribed bible from the President; of a large-scale financial operation run by a National Security Council staff member, Lt-Col Oliver North, using profits from the Iranian sale, and funds solicited from private donors to support the activities of Nicaraguan anti-government Contra forces; of millions of dollars being accidentally deposited in the wrong Swiss bank account. Aggravating under any circumstances, it was particularly galling that the US could be made to look so foolish by Iran.

Reagan suffered the added disadvantage of these revelations coming after Republican legislative losses. When the Democrats gained control of Senate in early November 1986 there had been a distinctly conciliatory mood – they were, after all, dealing with a very popular President, and the election results had not gone entirely their way, with substantial Republican victories at the gubernatorial level. Looking forward to 1988 the Democratic Party would have to concentrate on finding a powerful presidential candidate, and could not really afford the opprobrium that a head-to-head clash with Reagan might produce. The difficulty presented for the White House by the Iran exposures changed this scenario somewhat, allowing the new Democratic majority to take the moral high ground, and giving them an opportunity to berate the President.

Time honoured damage-control tactics were deployed. Press conferences, never regular under Reagan, ceased altogether for months. Access to the President was carefully controlled as the White House tried at least to manage that part of the information system under its control. In a statement repeating his tactics after the Beirut killings of 1983, Reagan accepted at least a limited degree of responsibility in his State of the Union Speech on January 27, 1987: 'I took a risk with regard to our action in Iran. It did not work, and for that I assume full responsibility.' Personnel changes began quickly with the November 1986 transfer of National Security Adviser Admiral John Poindexter, and NSC staff member Lt-Col North, out of the White House. And in an attempt to pre-empt criticism from outside, Reagan appointed his own blue ribbon commission, chaired by former Senator John Tower, who, with the aid of former Secretary of State Edmund Muskie, and former National Security Advisor General Brent Scowcroft, was asked to investigate the operations of the National Security Counvil.

The February 1987 Tower Commission Report found NSC staff avoiding interagency review, ignoring official procedures, and dodging Congressional restraints in their dogged pursuit of a flawed policy in Iran, and a continuing civil war in Nacaragua. The report had particularly sharp words for Reagan's 'casual' and 'informal' approach to the NSC decision-making system. But the commission stopped short of identifying Reagan as the main culprit. Reagan's memory failed him when questioned about particular meetings, and in the absence of concrete evidence the most that could be said was that the President did not have his hand firmly on the tiller.

With the publication of this report Reagan again tried to put the issue behind him. White House Chief of Staff Donald Regan was replaced by former Senator Howard Baker, and, having been implicated in the Iran/Contra affair, CIA chief William J. Casey was replaced by FBI Director William H. Webster. In an address to the nation Reagan made his fullest, though still circumscribed, apology so far.

> A few months ago, I told the American people I did not trade arms for hostages. My heart and my best intentions still tell me that it's true, but the facts and the evidence tell me it is not. As the Tower board reported, what began as a strategic opening to Iran deteriorated in its implementation into trading arms for hostages . . . It was a mistake.

This served to reassure many, but nevertheless the history of these disclosures exposed the limitations of some of the Reagan administration's strategies. Delegation of authority in a matter this important began to look ill-advised, or even suspect. Detached disregard for journalists' questions appeared evasive, rather than strong-willed. Televised affirmation of responsibility by the President did not stop public disquiet from mounting. Disclosure of the transfer of funds to Nicaragua and the sacrifice of those deemed to be responsible served to increase, rather than to quell, the demand for more information, and to feed the fear that the President should have known more about what was going on.

A hard act to follow

After the 1984 election thoughts turned to the prospects for 1988, and in many minds there was the accompanying thought that it would be difficult for any candidate to fill the place of a President who had resuscitated the idea of a manageable and successful Presidency. Reagan had taken the role of leadership seriously, had restored public confidence in the Presidency, had involved himself closely with attempts to accelerate his party's growth, and had shown a skill in combining brinkmanship and pragmatism which had engendered public support, and gained grudging admiration from all quarters. Certainly this was going to be a hard act to follow, but by late 1986 it looked as though it might even be a hard act to maintain.

Reagan's assets in Washington's political marketplace have been severely devalued, but he has not chosen to become inactive. His continued lobbying of Congress and further rhetorical swipes against his traditional enemies show an impressive willingness to fight, even if he no longer has control of the political agenda. In January 1987 66 per cent of respondents to an opinion poll agreed that 'Reagan may have made mistakes in this particular instance, but it doesn't raise major questions about his ability to run the country overall', and in May 1987 the polls still found 65 per cent of respondents saying they trusted the President, even though 65 per cent had doubts about his version of Irangate.[11] Investigations by the House of Representatives, the Senate, and Special Prosecutor Lawrence Walsh will continue through 1987, and with key witnesses Admiral Poindexter and Lt-Col North still to testify at the time of writing it is impossible to predict whether more revelations will further damage the Reagan presidency.

Whatever the problems faced by Reagan during his last months in office, the public demand for national, party, and executive leadership from the succeeding president will be real, and will have the example of Reagan's successful years for comparison. But not all leaders can manage such a convincing public show of optimism and national boosterism. Reagan's Iranian crisis has still to be resolved. If it very substantially undermines the air of Presidential authority that Reagan has nurtured, any successor will again face the problem of restoring public confidence in the office. This may be especially difficult given the severe limitation on a successor's initiatives that is a likely consequence of the doubled national debt. Increasing debt inevitably ties up a large proportion of the budget, deficit spending is made more difficult by Gramm-Rudman-Hollings, and tax increases are likely to be unpopular in a nation only just getting used to Reagan-inspired tax reforms. A successor is unlikely to be the beneficiary of an unforeseen windfall as helpful to him as the oil-price collapse has been to Reagan, while it is possible that social problems, neglected in the Reagan agenda, could re-emerge as urgent demands. While leaders and supporters of both parties will be carefully sifting through the lists of Presidential hopefuls, there is no guarantee that the recently nurtured confidence in Presidential leadership can be maintained.

Notes

1 Arthur M. Schlesinger, Jr., *The Imperial Presidency,* Houghton Mifflin, New York, 1984.
2 Paul J. Quirk, 'What must a president know?', *Society,* XX, no. 2, 1983; reprinted in *American Government 86/7* (ed. Bruce Stinebrickner), The Dushkin Publishing Group, Guildford, Conn., 1986, pp. 77–85.
3 Dick Kirschtein, 'Reagan's 'feel good' strategy can't mask the country's woes', *National Journal,* XVIII, 1986, pp 1898–9.
4 Leslie H. Gelb, The mind of the president', *The New York Times Magazine,* 6 Oct. 1986; reprinted in *American Government 86/7,* p 91.
5 Barry Sussman, 'Another presidential zigzag', *The Washington Post National Weekly Edition,* 17 March 1986.
6 Gelb, pp 87, 90.
7 David Broder, 'A tough act to swallow', *The Washington Post National Weekly Edition,* 30 June 1986.
8 Barry Sussman, 'Their minds are made up; don't confuse them with facts', *The Washington Post National Weekly Edition,* 15 Sept 1986.
9 Heidi Landecker, 'The politics of disinformation', *The Boston Sunday Globe,* 12 Oct. 1986.
10 Gelb, p 87.
11 'Reagan and Iran', *Public Opinion,* IX, Mar/April 1987, pp 34–7; Alex Brummer, 'World passes by the caretaker of the marginal White House', *The Guardian,* 16 May 1987.

George Goodwin, Jr.

The new Congress

Congress versus the Executive: the axe analogy[1]

The United state Constitution requires that the American voters select a new chief executive at least every eight years. A new President brings his own Cabinet and White House team with him – almost always members of his own political party – to control the bureaucracy under him. In other words, change and hierarchy are mandated for this branch.

Congress, on the other hand, never experiences a sharp break in its continuity; there are always more old timers than newly-elected members. The Constitution, which provides for a single leader for the Executive Branch, discourages unified leadership of the Legislative Branch by dividing it into the Senate and the House. There are further divisions, into two political parties and into some forty subject matter committees. In the final analysis, legislators are beholden to the constituents in the districts from which they are elected. Congress is an institution that features continuity and resists hierarchy.

Each new head of the Executive Branch brings a brand new axe, and takes it with him when he leaves office. A new Congress keeps a great-grandfather's axe – one that has had many new handles inserted and a few new heads attached over the years. A change of party control could be thought of as a new handle; a change in the way by which Congress organises itself could be though of as a new head.

On those occasions on which Congress has attempted to change the way in which it organises itself, it has steered a course somewhere between anarchy and autocracy, between total freedom for each Member, which is likely to produce no results, and total subordination of each Member, which is likely to produce the wrong results. At various times the Members have placed leadership in the hands of party heads, in the hands of committee chairs, even in the hands of sub-committee chairs. And they have experimented with a variety of means of holding each set of leaders accountable.

Organisation is particularly important in the operations of the House, which is more than four times as large as the Senate, and a number of differing organising patterns have been tried in this century. During the first decade, that chamber acceded to party leadership that bordered on the autocratic. When it rebelled against Speaker Joseph Cannon, it moved to a decade in which party leaders dominated, but they were checked by a number of participatory mechanisms, such as a Steering and Policy Committee and the Caucus. The 1920s saw a decline in party fervour and a gradual move toward placing power in the hands of committee chairs who, as the result of the growth of a seniority system, had time to develop expertise in their subject matter areas and to operate largely free of party control. The 1970s saw somewhat contradictory thrusts on the part of reformers. The predominant drive was to make committees more responsive to the membership by decreasing the powers of chairmen; almost coincidentally, the Members took steps in the direction of greater party control.

Space does not allow a discussion of the developments within each chamber and each party. Here I will concentrate on the House of Representatives, as this is more organisationally complex than the Senate, and on the Democratic party, which was the major source of the Congressional reforms of the 1970s.

Congressional reforms of the 1970s

Speaker John McCormack told the newly elected Members of the United States House of Representatives early in 1965, 'When you pass a committee chairman in the hall, bow from the waist – I always do.'[2] One of those freshman legislators, Richard Ottinger, recalled these words when he returned to the House in 1974, after an absence of two terms. The way the House operated had changed a good deal during that intervening decade, and Ottinger was to play a part in changing it even more.

The so-called 'Class of 1974' had ninety-one members (though five, including Ottinger, had served previous non-consecutive terms). It was one of the largest freshman classes ever to hit the House, and four-fifths of them were Democrats. Generally speaking, they were early products of the World War II baby boom. Opposition to the Vietnam War had turned them to politics. The Watergate scandals had helped shape in them a more cynical attitude toward government than that of their predecessors. Their activist experiences and their public relations skills, frequently employed on television, had allowed many of them to by-pass or cut short an apprenticeship in local party and government office. These were people who had been movers and shakers in American colleges in the 1960s, and they were fully prepared to move and shake the legislative way of life when they reached Capitol Hill.

Ottinger brought a knowledge of the ways of the House to the reformist tendencies of the members of this new Democratic class. The newcomers were helped by the fact that a recent reform had provided that Members should meet for organisational purposes in December, shortly after the election, rather than crowding all such activity into the first days of January. They formed an unusually active freshman party caucus under Ottinger's tutelage, even securing funds from a foundation to enable them to hire a temporary professional staff.

The activities of these Members were summarised in a 1976 fund-raising brochure entitled 'The Class of 1974', stating, among other things, that 'toppling the seniority system was the first no-nonsense act of this new breed of Congressman'. To this end, they had interviewed all those people who would be chairmen if the seniority system were to hold, to determine whether or not to give them their support. (It is not difficult to believe that they took a particular dislike to W. R. Poague, who had served as Chairman of Agriculture for eight years, because he addressed them as 'boys and girls'). They played a central role in the unseating of three chairmen. The 'feudal barons' got the message. Power relationships were drastically altered; no longer would either a Speaker or a freshman Member have to bow from the waist to a committee Chairman.

To broaden the discussion beyond the freshman class, the decade of the 1970s saw an extraordinary number of changes in Congress, in the form of statutes (the Legislative Reorganization Act of 1970 and the Budget and Impoundment Act of 1974, in particular), of House and Senate resolutions, and of rules of the four party caucuses. As might be expected from a body as complex as Congress, these reforms attempted to move the legislature in a number of different and sometimes conflicting directions. They sought:

– to open up the legislative process to greater public scrutiny ('sunshine reforms'),

– to favour sub-committees and thus the more junior members of Congress, at the expense of committee chairmen,

– to strengthen legislative party mechanisms, and

– to decrease Congress's dependence on the Executive Branch (especially the Budget and Impoundment Act of 1974).

By the start of the 1980s, instructions to incoming freshmen would no longer be to bow from the waist to committee chairmen but closer to 'bow, but certainly not from the waist, to sub-committee chairmen, to party leaders and to lobbyists, and to try not to more than nod to the President'.

The 'reformed' Congress

More than a decade has passed since the major reforms of the 1970s were put in place. How has Congress changed? The returns are not all in by any means – but they never are in an institution as intricate and as changing as the United States Congress.

Sunshine reforms

The 'sunshine reforms' were part of Congress's reaction to the widespread distrust of all government. They called for committee meetings to be open to the public, and for Members to commit themselves more openly in both committee and floor voting.

Some years ago, a venerable committee clerk answered my request to be allowed to sit in on a closed mark-up session with 'We do not run the Congress for the benefit of political scientists'. Since the sunshine reforms, political scientists can poke around more, and so can lobbyists. Some in Congress are having second thoughts. A task force of the Select Committee on Committees that reported in 1980 concluded that these changes, especially as they applied to meetings of conference and standing committees, has tended to inhibit discussion, discourage compromise, make it more difficult for Members to change their positions, and subject them to greater lobbying pressures. It is never easy to undo ostensibly democratic reforms, and Congress is not likely to make major modifications in these sunshine regulations.

Subcommittee Reforms

Subcommittees were built up at the expense of full committees. All committees with over fifteen members were required to subdivide. Subcommittees were guaranteed both staff and financial support, and provision was made that matters which fell within their jurisdiction were automatically referred to them. To spread the gravy around, no Member was allowed to serve as chairmen of more than one committee or subcommittee. To be chosen as chair, members of a given committee were to request specific berths. They were to be voted on by the majority party caucus on the committee and their names taken up in order of their committee seniority. Reformers hoped that this control by the committee caucus would keep subcommittee chairs from obstructionism of the kind that had been exercised by full committee chairs in the past.

By almost any test, subcommittees have increased greatly in importance. Their numbers have grown. After Congress organised itself in 1985, 53 per cent of the Democratic Members of the House had chairmanships. Over 80 per cent of the total committee meeting time of the House was spent in subcommittees in the 1977-78 sessions of Congress. Full committee ratification of subcommittee work became increasingly automatic. Further, an increasing number of subcommittee chairs and their ranking Republican members handle measures when they come to the floor for debate, whereas this task used to fall almost entirely on the shoulders of the chair and the ranking member of the full committee.

A career in Congress has certainly become more attractive to a large number of well-educated and ambitious people. I got my clearest feel of this fact when I talked recently with a junior Congressman who had just received his first subcommittee chairmanship. He was very frank about his good fortune – a tripling of staff available to him, greatly increased political visibility and a new sense of being able to leave his mark on public policy.

How far has this decentralisation gone toward making Congress a more 'disparate ministry'? Surely, the tasks of the Leadership have become much more difficult, but the reformers provided some tools to help it tie the pieces together. In the first place, subcommittee chairmen cannot assume the autonomous 'feudal baron' role of the pre-reform full committee chairmen. The Speaker has been given the power to refer legislative proposals to two or more committees and to set a time limit for their consideration. He has begun to use the staff of the Steering and Policy Committee to keep track of subcommittee activities, and to use the Rules Committee to encourage the shaping of committee measures to make them more acceptable to the party.

Party reforms

The reforms which affected legislative parties empowered both the Caucus and its elected leadership in ways that could lead to serious internal party conflict. The new party relationships had to be tried out and adjusted over time. Of the three Speakers who have run the House in the period – John W. McCormack (1962–70), Carl Albert (1971–76), and Thomas P. O'Neill, Jr. (1977–86) – McCormack seemed the least friendly to the changes, Albert showed greater flexibility, and O'Neill was the most supportive. He, of course, had the advantage of succeeding to the Speakership after the bulk of the reforms were in place, and he showed considerable skill in making use of, and co-ordinating, three main party tools which came from the reform movement:- a new Steering and Policy Committee, a Rules Committee made sensitive to the Leadership, and a beefed-up Whip System.

The Speaker chairs the Steering and Policy Committee. Its membership includes the party Leadership and the chairs of the Appropriations, Budget, Rules and Ways and Means committees, *ex officio*. In addition, as of 1985, there were twelve members elected by regional party caucuses and eight appointed by the Speaker. It is not totally dependent on the Speaker, but it is on the other hand far from autonomous. The Committee was given the dual tasks of making committee assignments and making certain policy decisions.

Combining in one committee control over awards for Members and the opportunity to delineate party positions on issues is the sort of thing that appeals to reformers who believe in strong party organisations, with power to reward supporters and punish dissenters. The Steering and Policy Committee has not moved very far down that road, however. Initial committee assignments have been given out largely on the basis of Members' requests, though considerable care has been taken to seat only the more loyal on the money committees. Steering and Policy has done little to unseat dissident Members once they have received their committee assignments and started to move up the seniority ladder. In 1975, Steering and Policy did propose that two chairmen be replaced by those next in line (but the Caucus went farther than that, as is noted below). On the policy side of its assignment, the Committee and the Speaker have been feeling their way. Steering and Policy staff have monitored standing committee activities and kept their Committee members posted on controversial developments taking place. The Committee has met two or three times a month in recent years, acting as a sounding-board for policy proposals.

In 1981, when Ronald Reagan became President and the Democratic majority in the House was diminished, an increasing number of conservative Democrats gave their support to Republican budget- and tax-cutting proposals. Liberal Democrats demanded that the so-called 'Boll Weevils' be punished. The Leadership took no action at the time, but it issued a warning. Majority Leader James C. Wright Jr. announced that chairmanships and assignments on such committees as Appropriations, Budget, Rules and Ways and Means are rewards from the party and 'We expect some responsibility to the party and their colleagues' from those who receive them.[3] Steering and Policy has begun to designate some 'litmus test votes' for loyal party members. The most dramatic action by the Committee was its proposal in 1983 that Representative Phil Gramm be removed from the Budget Committee, after he had sided consistently with Republicans on budget matters. (Gramm resigned from Congress, ran in a special election as a Republican, and returned to the Budget Committee as a member of the opposite party.) Since then, perhaps chastened by the experience, the Steering and Policy Committee has not proposed any alterations in the working of the seniority system as the determinant of committee positions.

The reforms of the 1970s also gave the Speaker the power to appoint and remove Democratic members of the Rules Committee, without being governed by the seniority system or having to work through the Steering and Policy Committee. The Speaker has not yet found it necessary to exercise his right of removal. The existence of that power, plus the nature of his new appointment, has succeeded in turning what used to be a very independent committee into a useful tool of the Leadership.

The Rules Committee determines the conditions under which most important bills are brought to the floor of the House. These so-called rules allot time for debate and divide it among proponents and opponents. Rules may even limit the amendments that may be brought up on the floor. In performing its functions, the Committee tends to serve the Leadership in a variety of ways. When chairmen come to it requesting a rule that will govern the way the measure is handled on the floor, it provides a dress rehearsal of the arguments that are likely to be brought up when it reaches the full House – training which is particularly valuable to recently empowered subcommittee chairmen. Key members of the Rules Committee advise the Speaker on legislative matters, including pending committee proposals and the abilities of the people who will be in charge of them on the floor. The full Committee can expedite action for the Leadership; it can also encourage committee changes that will make a measure more acceptable to the party.

The Whip System, which is the major channel of communication between the Leadership and the party members, was strengthened considerably by the reforms of the 1970s. In the 99th Congress (1985–86) it consisted of a Chief Whip and forty-four Deputy Whips, all appointed by the Speaker and the Majority Leader. (Of this group, twelve also served on the Steering and Policy Committee and two on the Committee on Rules, so there was considerable overlapping). There were also twenty-one Assistant Whips elected by various regional caucuses.

Policy and strategy sessions are held by the Whips, meeting with the Speaker and the Majority Leader, on a weekly basis. Some twenty measures are singled out in a typical year for a canvas of the party membership. The elected regional Whips make the contacts, asking what position each Democratic Representative is going to take on a forthcoming measure. After a tally is made, the Whips try to persuade those who indicated that they were undecided or not strongly committed in either direction. In the process, they sometimes find that an amendment may attract the needed support. Whip Notices go out, informing Members of the nature of the upcoming measure, the amendments that are likely to be offered, and the proposed timing of the debate. When the bill is up for consideration, the organisation works to get Members on the floor for the vote. It is worth noting that the enlarged staff spends a good deal of effort attempting to assist the Members, providing them with speech cards on various issues and 'recess packets' that give information that is useful when they are in their home con-stituencies.

Finally, we come to the Party Caucus, which elects the Lead-ership, but cannot quite decide the extent of its power to supervise them once they are chosen. The Caucus consists of all members of a given party in a legislative chamber. Since Congress is both bipartisan and bicameral, there are four – though Republicans in the House and Democrats and Republicans in the Senate prefer the more genteel title of Conference. When called together, shortly after the biennial election of a new Congress, these gatherings play a central role in determining who will run the party for the next two years, thus setting the general direction it will take.

For most of this century, once the Leadership had been put in place, the Caucus had tended to take a back seat, delegating a great deal of power to party agencies, and coming together from time to time to ratify their decisions. The reformers of the 1970s, however, seized on the Caucus as a major vehicle for reform. To this end, they called for regular Caucus meetings and the ability of a percentage of the members to call special meetings without the consent of the Leadership. New procedures, worked out in Caucus, would be controlling. Party policy positions would be decided upon in Caucus, and all elements of the party would be called upon to support them. Committee chairmen, who had been rather impervious to party pressures under the old seniority system, would be made more responsive to these party policies.

Certainly, the new Democratic Caucus played a basic role in many of the procedural reforms of the period. Over the years, supporters of a strong Caucus – sometimes its majority, sometimes only its liberal members – have complained that the Leadership has been too slow in establishing clear policy positions, 'whipping' Members into line, and punishing them for disloyalty. In three instances, the Caucus has moved beyond the Leadership in discip-lining committee chairmen. In 1975, it disputed the Steering and Policy Committee proposals for replacement of two chairmen, and ended up replacing three. In 1977 it replaced an Appropriations Subcommittee chairman, and in 1985 it unseated the Chair of Armed Services, over the opposition of the Leadership and the Steering and Policy Committee.

With some exceptions, the Caucus has been least successful as a policy-making body. It has taken positions ranging from opposing the oil depletion allowance to favouring sanctions against South Africa. It tends to be most active when there is a large Democratic majority and a Republican President. Many Members, however, especially in more conservative times, look upon these meetings that discuss policies as primarily vehicles for liberals, and they tend to stay away, after the important work of organising the chamber has been completed.

Probably, the reformers expected too much of the Caucus. The United States seems to be too heterogeneous to produce responsible, highly centralised parties, particularly at this time when both voters and candidates are less influenced by party than they have been in the past. A Democratic leader once told me that whenever his party met in Caucus, he was reminded of the pervasive after-effects of the Civil War. Caucus meetings seemed to divide his members rather than to unite hem. There is a considerable body of opinion that believes that the Caucus can start the machinery going in a given direction, but that it is too quixotic a group to do much more than that. Certainly there is tension between the agencies of the Leadership and the Caucus.

The reform in legislative-executive relations: Congress and the budget

A further thrust of the reforms of the 1970s has been to strengthen the Congress in relation to the Executive Branch. Standing committee jurisdictions were shaped to parallel more closely the organisation of the Executive, and each committee was encouraged to organise and staff itself to improve the function of administrative oversight. The Budget and Impoundment Act of 1974 was another assertion of legislative power. It sought to organise Congress so that it could gain greater control over the budgetary process and over a President who refuses to spend (who impounds) money appropriated by Congress.

Congress has certainly improved the resources with which it seeks to exercise control. By its very disparate nature, however, it probably cannot develop these to the point where it can present a united front to the Executive. The difficulties it has had with the budget process are illustrative.

Shortly after the Civil War, both houses of Congress, responding to the heavy workload, separated the tasks of raising revenues and making appropriations. Since the Second World War, they have been trying to create some mechanisms which would assist them in recovering their ability to look at the total fiscal picture. In 1946, Congress voted to hold joint meetings of the revenue and appropriations committees of the House and the Senate for the purpose of setting a ceiling on expenditures in the light of the revenue and deficit situation. The two chambers found that they could not agree, however, and the reform was still-born. A more sophisticated procedure was adopted in 1974 by the Budget and Impoundment Act. While it has not operated entirely as expected, it remains essentially in place, and was amended in 1985. A major reason for its survival is undoubtedly related to the sea change in American public opinion – from particular concern about unemployment and widespread support for an active national government to primary concern for inflation and a decline in support for government intervention.

The 1974 Act sought to ensure that Congress considered an overall budget level and then related taxing and spending policies to this level. The law provided that newly created House and Senate Budget committees were to receive reports on the President's budget proposals from a number of relevant committees and the newly-created Congressional Budget Office. These Budget committees were to send Budget Target Resolutions to their respective chamber floors, to be adopted by 15 May. Congress was then to spend the summer enacting appropriations measures for the next fiscal year, based on these targets. In the early fall the Budget committees, adjusting to the political and economic developments of the intervening months, were to bring to the floor final Budget Ceilings, to be adopted by 15 September. These Ceilings were to be enforced by Reconciliation Procedures: congressional directives to authorising and appropriating committees indicating the changes necessary to keep the programmes within the Ceiling requirements. These changes were to be presented to Congress in a single budget-cutting bill, which was to be adopted prior to 1 October, the start of the new fiscal year.

The budgeting mechanism worked fairly well during the first few years, but then it came closer and closer to breaking down. One reason has been the decentralisation of the legislature, encouraged by the reforms of the 1970s. Subcommittee chairmen on the House Appropriations Committee were now voted on by the House Democratic Caucus rather than being selected by the chairmen of the full Committee. As a result, it became more difficult to co-ordinate Committee activities and enforce deadlines. Even more important, partisan and ideological differences within the government tended to increase delays.

Republican President Gerald Ford was a caretaker who did little to challenge the Democratic House and Senate, and Democratic President Jimmy Carter was in general agreement on budgetary matters with a Congress controlled by his party. When Republican Ronald Reagan took office in 1981, he helped carry in a Republican Senate, though the House remained in Democratic hands. Reagan had a very different view of the proper fiscal program for the country from any president since Franklin D. Roosevelt took control in the 1930s. He sought great increases in the defence budget and drastic reductions in domestic expenditures. A tax reduction in his first term aided him in capitalising on public concern over the deficit, and he used it with great skill as a weapon to force Congress into compliance with his proposals. In 1981, with the support of the Republican Senate and of Republicans and conservative Democrats in the House, he succeeded in having a draconian Reconciliation Agreement attached to the Early Target Resolution. He eventually succeeded in having some 35 billion dollars out from 250 domestic programmes. He was less dramatically successful in using the budget mechanism in later years and the process moved closer and closer to stalemate.

In December of 1985, Congress passed the Balanced Budget Emergency Control Act, popularly known as Gramm-Rudman. The focus of the new act was on the federal deficit, which it sought to reduce by approximately 36 billion dollars a year over the succeeding six annual Budgets. If Congress and the President could not agree on appropriation reductions and/or tax increases that would meet that schedule, a reduction was to be automatically applied to all government programmes not specifically excluded by the law itself, with the proviso that the defence and domestic sides of the budget should bear equal burdens. Conservatives in Congress had supported the proposal as a means of reducing the size of the national government; liberals, who had succeeded in placing a number of programmes beyond the reach of the budget axe, thought of the proposal as a way to force the President to compromise with Congress.

Senator Warren Rudman, one of the sponsors of the measure,

referred to it as 'a bad idea whose time has come'. Within less than a year. however, the Supreme Court merely said that it was a bad idea. It declared unconstitutional the procedure that empowered the Comptroller General to make automatic appropriations cuts. In effect, that court stated that budget decisions had to be made by officials who are held responsible to the voters by means of election.

Appraisals of Congress's budgetary process are mixed. Congress has certainly not been able to act quickly and decisively on the nation's priorities. It has seemed even more stumbling in the face of a President who has the clear goal of reducing the size of the national government. Congress after all, is an institution where varied economic, social and sectional interests of this continental democracy find expression, test their relative strengths, and work toward compromise. It does seem safe to say that the budgetary reforms have given Members of Congress a greater sense of the total financial situation and of the fact that there are limits to what the government can afford, however much they may differ on specific fiscal policy. It has encouraged them to weigh their preferences against the bottom line. Perhaps the most important conclusion is that the reform has survived more or less intact, except for the buck-passing provision of Gramm-Rudman. One commentator has suggested that it is not so remarkable in what it does as the fact that it does it at all, like the proverbial talking dog.

How's Congress?

A Congress-watcher should answer this question with the caution of a husband who, when asked 'How's your wife?', responded, 'Compared to what?'

A legislative body is not likely to act decisively, unless there is a unique national consensus. It provides, however, that link between the people and the government that is central to democracy. Congress examines the proposals of the more hierarchical, more nationally-oriented Executive Branch through the prisms of states and Congressional districts. It has the power to say 'No' and 'Yes' and, more commonly, 'OK, but with these modifications'. In the process it frequently succeeds in pointing out solutions that alienate fewer people and groups, and in educating the citizens to recognise and understand interests other than their own.

The reforms of the 1970s did a number of useful things, by

opening up the legislative process, encouraging greater specialised participation by younger members, experimenting with means of strengthening party organisation, and attempting to get legislators to consider the fiscal situation of the nation. The tuning was not perfect, but there is little clear agreement, either in Congress or in the country, as to what perfect tuning would be. One thing is certain: change is continuing, though not at the speed that it took place in the 1970s.

Perhaps the most important conclusions are that both houses of Congress have remained strong at a time which has seen many upper chambers decline, and that the whole Congress has survived as an important, independent branch of government in a century which has not been kind to legislatures. The cautious answer to 'How's Congress' might well be, 'Not so bad'.

Notes

1   My major sources for this chapter have been: Arthur Maass, *Congress and the Common Good,* Basic Books, New York, 1983; Frank H. Mackaman, Editor, *Understanding Congressional Leadership,* Congressional Quarterly Press, Washington, DC, 1981 (especially chapters by Joseph Cooper and David Brady, Christopher Deering and Steven Smith, Lawrence Dodd and Terry Sullivan, Bruce Oppenheimer, and Barbara Sinclair); W. Thomas Wander, Ted Hebert and Gary Copeland, Editors, *Congressional Budgeting,* John Hopkins U.P., Baltimore, 1984. *Congressional Quarterly Weekly Report* has been my means of keeping up to date.
2   *The New York Times,* 22 January 1975.
3   Randall E. Ripley, *Congress: Process and Policy,* 3rd Edition, W. W. Norton, New York, 1983 p 206.

Fredric A. Waldstein

Judicial appointment and change on the federal bench

The judiciary as a political institution.

As a political institution the judiciary is perhaps the least understood of the three branches of the federal government. Indeed, attempts to place the judiciary within a political context have met with opposition from members of the legal profession, and there are strong sentiments in the public at large that courts should be 'above politics'. But courts are political institutions in the most fundamental sense, for they serve as the focal point of conflict resolution concerning the distribution and redistribution of finite resources. Whether it is the Supreme Court ruling on mandatory bussing, or a judge ruling on bail in a criminal case, these actions have direct consequences on how resources – both personal and public – will be allocated in society.

Yet there exists general agreement that decisions made by the courts, even though they may be political, ought to be reached through a framework that is distinct from other political institutions, and that these procedures emphasise a tradition independent of crass partisan politics. Or, as James Eisenstein puts it:

> Many citizens believe that the typical mechanism for translating resources and influence into practical advantage are absent from the legal process. The belief that principles of due process, impartial judgement by judge and jury, equal justice, and the like govern its operation precludes the possibility that politics sticks its sleazy fingers into the legal pie.[1]

Thus, Americans have come to expect judicial decisions to reflect non-partisan judgements by men and women based upon rules of law according to principles of Anglo-American legal norms.

There has existed disagreement throughout American history about how well the courts have conformed to these expectations. In the early years of the republic the judiciary was staffed primarily by Federalists who were constantly at odds with the Jeffersonian Democrats over basic questions about the supremacy of federal *versus* state authority. The Dred Scott decision (19 Howard 393) in 1857 was rendered by a Supreme Court divided strictly according to regional loyalties, and there are those who argue that decision, more than any other act, helped precipitate the Civil War. President Grant filled two vacancies on the Supreme Court with men he knew would support a coalition of justices to reverse a specific decision of which he disapproved. Thus, there have been periods when, as Judge Irving Kaufman states, 'In the public mind, the Court became a blunt instrument in the hands of whatever ideological bloc held control of it at a given time'.[2]

Judicial power

The power of the judiciary is not static, and in some respects its influence is more dependent upon the esteem in which it is held by the public than the other branches of government. This is so because the judiciary has no independent means to enforce its decisions, and must rely on the executive and legislative branches to carry out its mandates. The willingness of the President and Congress to enforce judicial decisions is, in turn, at least somewhat dependent upon the legitimacy and prestige which the judiciary enjoys in the eyes of the public. Politicians have been much less willing to challenge court decisions when the judiciary enjoys widespread respect, for fear of risking damage to their personal and institutional powers. For example, the prestige of the federal judiciary was relatively high compared to the presidency during the 1970s as the Watergate affair unfolded in the courtroom of Judge John Sirica. A classic confrontation of executive versus judicial power took place when Sirica ordered President Nixon to turn over to the court tape recordings as material evidence in a criminal trial, and the President refused on grounds of executive privilege. A unanimous Supreme Court ruled in 1974 that Nixon had to comply with the judge's order (*US v Nixon,* 418 US 683), and he did so knowing that to disobey would almost certainly mean impeachment.

But the power and legitimacy of the judiciary is also dependent upon the types of decisions rendered by courts, and especially the

Supreme Court. When the judiciary confines itself to issues of dispute resolution within a well-established legal context, it runs little risk of losing public support. However, when the judiciary ventures into areas that are perceived to be more appropriately within the realm of politicians and other traditional policy-makers, the courts can become the focal point for public dissatisfaction that may harm judicial legitimacy and power. This has happened in some areas of the US where court-ordered bussing was used as a tool to end segregated schools. In cities such as Boston massive white flight from public to parochial schools has led to bitterness towards the courts, and a school system that remains largely segregated – a public system for minority students and a private system for whites. At least some of the failure of the court's policy in this instance has been attributed to the belief among a large percentage of the local population that federal courts had no business interfering in the operation of local schools.

Reagan and the federal judiciary

Predictions that Ronald Reagan, by the end of his second term, will have appointed a majority of judges sitting on the federal bench have created quite a stir among journalists, academics, and politicians. Had the rate of appointment established during his first term continued throughout his second, this would have occurred. Although the rate has slowed, it remains true that no President since Franklin D. Roosevelt has had the opportunity to appoint such a large proportion of federal judges, and this alone makes the topic worthy of attention. But it is the overt desire of the Reagan administration to refashion the federal judiciary in its own ideological image that has caused much of the attention, and led to speculation about the impact of Reagan's impact on the courts well into the next century. The remainder of this chapter will be devoted to factors which affect the ability of the President to influence the judiciary, to examining Reagan's goals and his efforts to maximise them and to speculate briefly about his potential impact on the judiciary.

Judicial selection and Presidential impact.

By the middle of the 1980s there were slightly more than 750 federal judgeships, including the nine seats on the US Supreme Court.

During the same period, the number of cases filed in US district courts has been approximately 300,000 per year, and the number filed in the US courts of appeal is approaching 35,000. The total docket for the Supreme Court, on the other hand, consists of about 5,000 cases, and it acts on approximately 1500 of these. Thus the lower federal courts determine a tremendous amount of federal law, only a relatively small fraction of which is reviewed by the Supreme Court. Therefore, the opportunity for a President to appoint a majority of judges to the federal bench, even if he does not appoint any Supreme Court justices, offers the possibility of influencing the judiciary fundamentally.

A number of factors must, however, be considered when attempting to measure the degree of influence over the judiciary that a President may exercise through the appointments at his disposal. The first and most obvious factor is the position to be filled. A position on the Supreme Court is more important because of the broader scope of the policy horizon, in addition to the fact that it is the final forum for review. Moreover, a Supreme Court justice is one of only nine, whereas a district judge is one of several hundred. By appointing Sandra Day O'Connor and Antonin Scalia to the Supreme Court and elevating Associate Justice William Rehnquist to the position of Chief Justice, Reagan has had greater opportunities to influence the Court than his two predecessors.

But the relative worth of an appointment to the federal bench is dependent upon factors other than its position in the judicial hierarchy. Of some importance is the individual being replaced, and the extent to which he or she deviates from the President's political agenda. The opportunity to exercise influence will increase as the disparity between the President's position and the position of the judge being replaced increases. For example, Antonin Scalia will likely align himself with the conservative wing of the Court as did the departed Chief Justice, Warren Burger. Consequently, the Court will not be realigned to the extent it probably would have been had Scalia taken the place of liberals William Brennan or Thurgood Marshall.

A related factor to consider in attempting to determine the significance of judicial appointments is the range of judicial perspectives exhibited by members of a court, and the degree of polarisation among the judges within that range. Recently the Supreme Court has contained a broad range of judicial perspectives, and the justices holding them were highly polarised as reflected by the large number of 5–4 decisions, with Lewis Powell frequently casting the deciding vote. The pivotal role played by Powell becomes clear when one observes that in recent years he has only rarely decided with the minority. And in several cases during the 1984 term when he did not participate due to illness, the Court found itself deadlocked 4–4. Thus, Powell's position became more significant than when he was first appointed in 1972 because the orientation of the Court has changed significantly since that time. When Powell resigned in June 1987 Reagan tried to give the Court a decidedly conservative tilt, by nominating Judge Robert Bork for the vacant seat. At the time of writing this nomination has yet to be considered by Senate.

Reagan's judicial philosophy.

The appropriate role of the judiciary in the government of the United States has been discussed extensively, at least since debates over ratification of the Constitution. In general terms the two positions in this debate have come to be labelled as one of 'judicial activism' and one of 'judicial self-restraint'. Just what characterises each position and distinguishes one from the other in practical terms is far from clear. But in the abstract the judge who practises judicial self-restraint is perceived as one who normally attempts to limit the scope of his or her decision to the narrow parameters of the case at hand, relies heavily on judicial precedent, and demonstrates a propensity to defer to the policy choices of elected officials except when they are contrary to the Constitution. The judicial activist is perceived to be philosophically less committed to these goals, but the deviation appears to be one more of degree than of kind.

The inadequacy of this dichotomy as an analytical framework is apparent when considering two points. First, judicial activists are frequently identified as those who 'make the law', whereas the jurist who practises judicial self-restraint is merely interpreting it. Because legislators, not judges, are supposed to make laws, the term 'judicial activism' is implicitly, if not explicitly, pejorative. Second, statutory language is more often than not vague and imprecise, and requires judges, when adjudicating a dispute, to make substantive decisions about legislative content, and whether or not it conforms to the law. This is inevitable in a system where judges have the power of judicial review. Thus, one's judgement about the degree of judicial activism or judicial self-restraint practised is dependent upon one's position in a given dispute. As retired California judge Bernard Jefferson has put it, '(You) call it judicial activism if you disagree with the court's decision. If you agree with it then the court is doing what it is supposed to do.'[3]

The Reagan administration, like others before it, nevertheless uses this dichotomy as justification for the nominations it makes to the federal bench. During the 1984 campaign the President stated that his administration was looking for judges 'who share the same sense about the judiciary . . . envisioned by our founding fathers . . . an approach that seeks to interpret rather than 'make' the law'.[4]

Presidential proclamations asserting a desire to appoint nominees who will exhibit judicial self-restraint may not be new, but implied knowledge about what the founding fathers envisioned as an appropriate judicial role is a rather novel notion. Reagan's Attorney General, Edwin Meese, has been the administration's point man in advocating this position. In a July 1985 address to an American Bar Association meeting, Meese, speaking about the role of the Supreme Court, said its proper function was to 'resurrect the original meaning of constitutional provisions and statutes as the only reliable guide to judgement'.[5] Meese then went on to suggest that Court decisions involving prayer in the public schools would have struck the founding generation as 'bizarre'.

This is an extraordinary position for an Attorney General to take, and it has prompted an extraordinary response from the bench. Justice Brennan has criticised Meese's attitude as reflecting extreme arrogance, noting that it is 'arrogant to pretend that from our vantage we can gauge accurately the intent of the framers on application of principle to specific, contemporary questions'.[6] Justice Stevens joined the fray by criticising the Attorney General by name. Even Justice Rehnquist, a staunch conservative whose position is similar to the President's on most issues, implied that the administration's interests would be served better if it toned down its criticism of the Court.

One problem faced by the Reagan administration when it attempts to invoke the intent of the founding fathers in support of its position is that even by contemporary standards it is difficult to fathom philosophical consistency among the positions it takes on various cases before the Supreme Court. For example, on the one hand the administration's position with respect to abortion is that the federal government should not interfere with a state's right to decide whether or not it will permit abortion. On the other hand, the Justice Department actively opposed an affirmative action agreement reached between the school board and teachers' union in a Michigan community, and argued that the Court should not let it stand because it discriminates against whites purely on the basis of race. In the words of Laurance Tribe, '[The administration] favours lifting the constitutional limits on states when the subject is abortion, but lowering the constitutional boom when the subject is affirmative action'.[7] Attorney General Edwin Meese and William Bradford Reynolds, the Assistant Attorney General for Civil Rights, have been among the most vociferous critics of affirmative action. Because of their positions in the Justice Department, their view has been the one most forcefully articulated before the federal courts.[8]

In nominating individuals to the federal bench the administration has not limited its selections to those with reputations for advocating or practising judicial self-restraint. For example, recognised conservative legal scholars Robert Bork and Richard Posner, two former law professors elevated to the circuit courts of appeal under Reagan, are not noted for practising judicial self-restraint. Bork is considered somewhat more cautious than Posner in his willingness to overturn judicial precedent, and the former has been somewhat critical of the latter for being too much of an activist. But Bork too has been criticised for judicial activism. In short, there is very little evidence to suggest the existence of a philosophy of judicial self-restraint which guides consistently the administration's position in the judicial arena. This pattern of behaviour is consistent with that of previous Presidents. The Reagan administration, like its predecessors, attempts to utilise the judiciary as a political instrument both to change policy with which it disagrees, and to prevent judicial interference with those policies it favours. And appointment to the federal bench of individuals who share the President's policy preferences is potentially an effective means to create a judiciary that is sympathetic to the administration's goals. From this perspective, every appointment to the bench is political because the President, whoever he may be, will attempt to seat someone who shares his political agenda. To do otherwise would not be rational.

Nonetheless, Reagan's federal court appointments have been perceived by some observers as more 'ideological' or 'political' than those of his immediate predecessors. Senator Edward Kennedy reflected this sentiment when he stated that he was 'concerned about the administration's scheme to stack the courts with right-wing ideologues'.[9] This perception has been fuelled by Reagan's repeated public pronouncements of his intention to move the perspective of the federal judiciary, through appointments, in a direction consistent with his brand of conservative politics. Much of the increased concern over Reagan's appointments compared to previous Presidents may be attributed partially to his distance on the right from the traditional centre of the Washington political spectrum. In the words of Mark Goodin, spokesperson for the Senate Judiciary Committee when it was chaired by Strom Thurmond, 'Every President appoints judges and individuals of like-minded philosophy and [the Democrats] simply don't like Reagan's philosophy'.[10]

The Reagan administration's desire to alter the perspective of the judiciary in a direction more consistent with its political agenda poses potential risk in that public trust in the judiciary may be undermined. If there is a widespread public perception that the courts are a mere extension of the partisan political process, then the judiciary may lose the legitimacy and credibility it needs to be an effective, equal partner in the federal system. Thus, even if the administration appointed a majority or some other significant proportion of federal judges, it still might produce an overall net loss of influence if the public perceived that crude partisan politics motivated the selection process. As Irving Kaufman has stated, in politicising the judiciary a 'President may dull the independent and nonpartisan lustre essential to its vitality'.[11]

Some criticism has been levelled at the administration's nominees not so much for their ideological perspective, but for the process used to select and appoint them.

Criteria and process for selecting judges under Reagan.

The Reagan administration relies heavily on the traditional practice of senatorial courtesy for the names of potential nominees to the federal bench, particularly to fill district court vacancies. Under this practice the senator from the President's party is customarily given the opportunity to recommend a nominee to the district court located in his or her state. If the President does not follow the recommendation the senator may block the nomination during confirmation proceedings in the Senate by simply requesting that his colleagues not approve the nomination, and normally they would comply. Thus, senatorial courtesy is used to protect a venue for dispensing patronage. But, compared to previous administrations, an elaborate screening mechanism has been devised which allows close scrutiny of potential nominees by a cross-section of administration personnel from both the White House and the Justice Department.[12] Potential nominees are reviewed by the Office of Legal Policy within the Justice Department. Evaluations are forwarded to a 'Judicial Selection Working Group' within the Department chaired by the Attorney General. Recommendations from this committee are sent to the nine-member Presidential Committee on Judicial Selection, which is the centrepiece of the screening mechanism. It consists of two presidential counsellors, the White House Chief of Staff, the Assistant to the President for Personnel, the Assistant to the President for Legislative Affairs, the Attorney General, the Associate Attorney General, and the Assistant Attorney General for Legislative Policy. It is this committee which makes a final recommendation to the President. The traditionally dominant role of the Justice Department has been reduced, and the American Bar Association Standing Committee on the Federal Judiciary has not been invited to participate actively in the prenomination stage, as had been the case under recent previous administrations. This has led Sheldon Goldman to conclude:

> It is perhaps not an overstatement to observe that the formal mechanism of the committee has resulted in the most consistent ideological or policy-orientation screening of judicial candidates since the first term of Franklin D. Roosevelt.[13]

It is this apparent search for ideological purity which has caused some to question the methods used both within and without the formal mechanism to find appropriate candidates, and weed out the inappropriate. In particular, questions have been raised about the use of ideological 'litmus' tests for selecting nominees, in part because both the 1980 and 1984 Republican party platforms called upon the President to appoint 'judges at all levels of the judiciary who respect traditional family values and the sanctity of human life'

– a phrase that many interpret as a code word for opposition to the 1973 decision in *Roe v. Wade* (410 US 113) which permits abortions.

Attempts to solicit specific opinions from prospective judges on issues that are likely to be raised in a judicial setting are considered to be highly inappropriate and unethical as undue political interference in the judicial branch of government. White House and Justice Department officials deny that any litmus test is applied to judicial candidates, but concede that they are looking for individuals who believe in 'the sanctity of human life' as promised by the Republican platform. Given the administration's commitment to changing abortion, school prayer, affirmative action, and other court decisions, it seems highly probable that it would quite explicitly elicit pertinent information to determine the suitability of individual candidates. One avenue around this potential conflict between propriety and the desire to choose the candidate most sympathetic to the administration's position is to select those who have taken explicit stands on the issues in some other context. This may help explain why the administration has nominated a high proportion of individuals with previous judicial experience.

The alleged use of litmus tests has also been a source of controversy during the confirmation process in the Senate. A Reagan nominee to the district bench in New Jersey was asked to complete a questionnaire on his views concerning such issues as abortion, school prayer, the right to bear arms, and the proposed Equal Rights Amendment by three conservative senators on the Judiciary Committee. Democrats on the Committee described it as an improper attempt to predetermine a judicial candidate's potential rulings. Democratic Senator Howard Metzenbaum stated, 'that whatever your position is on [the Equal Rights Amendment] has nothing to do with your qualifications to be an able jurist'.[14] Committee chair at the time, Strom Thurmond, and the Reagan administration were also unhappy about the questionnaire which they perceived to be a renegade effort which delayed the nomination for eight months.

In most instances nominations forwarded to the Republican-controlled Senate by the White House have been confirmed quickly. Many go through the confirmation process in a matter of a few weeks. This contrasts sharply with claims by Senator Edward Kennedy, who says that when he chaired the Judiciary Committee in 1979 and 1980, a procedure was instituted which allowed an average of sixty days for background checks alone. Indeed, a number of Senate Democrats have complained that the Republicans ought to slow down the confirmation process so they can examine nominees more carefully. According to Kennedy, 'The issue is whether the administration should be permitted to railroad its judicial nominees ... without adequate scrutiny ...'.[15] Republicans countered that Democrats simply wanted to delay the confirmation process so that fewer judges could be appointed prior to the convening of the 100th Congress in 1987 when the Democrats regained the majority in the Senate. This event makes it more difficult for Reagan to appoint the type of conservative he has tried to place on the bench during his first six years in office.

There seems to be little doubt that during Reagan's presidency there has been a shift toward increasing the role of the administration and decreasing the role of the Senate, in selecting federal judges. There is a perception among senior judges and members of Congress – both Democrats and Republicans – that the formal and informal mechanism used by the administration to ensure close scrutiny of potential nominees has created longer delays in the nomination and confirmation process than under previous administrations. Delay may prove to be costly to the administration if a number of vacancies exist after the Democrats regain control of the Senate. But this potential cost may be offset by ensuring that judges who are selected are highly compatible with Reagan's position on the appropriate role for the judiciary in American politics.

Reagan's impact on the federal judiciary.

Given the high priority the administration gives to selecting judges who share the President's political agenda, it is not surprising that his nominees reflect socio-economic backgrounds from that segment of the population where Reagan has enjoyed his strongest political support: wealthy, white, male Republicans. In addition, Reagan has exhibited a propensity to select nominees with proven track records by elevating to the federal bench state judges and law professors who have demonstrated a strong commitment to positions held by the President. This is particularly true with respect to the twelve courts of appeal, where the administration has greater discretion in judicial selection because senatorial courtesy plays a smaller role. These are some of the conclusions reached by Sheldon

Goldman, who has published the most thorough study of the background characteristics of individuals nominated to the federal bench by Presidents Reagan, Carter, Ford, Nixon, and Johnson.[16] His study reveals an extraordinary commitment to and diligence in ensuring the existence of a body of ideologically conservative judges. He claims it is the most determined commitment since the first Franklin Roosevelt administration to mould a judiciary to its liking. While it is too early to determine the administration's success in moving towards this end, there is some evidence that conservatives are generally satisfied thus far. For example, a survey of published decisions by every Reagan appointee during his first two years in office, conducted by the conservative Center for Judicial Studies, led the Center to conclude that the overwhelming majority of appointees demonstrated behaviour consistent with the President's judicial agenda.

Summary

It is evident, from an examination of its actions and pronouncements, that the Reagan administration hopes to tilt the federal judiciary in a direction consistent with its conservative political perspective. How substantial and lasting its impact will be in the long term remains to be determined, but given the meticulous attention to the nomination process, the characteristics of the judges Reagan has appointed, and early evaluations of the decisions those judges have handed down, it seems that the administration may well be accomplishing its goal. To the extent that the administration can continue to do this without damaging the credibility of the judiciary as an independent, nonpartisan body governed by the rules of the legal culture, the probability is high that it will have a greater impact than any administration since Roosevelt. However, much more work needs to be done, and time must pass, before one can determine whether or not the judiciary will stand as a legacy to the 'Reagan Revolution' well into the 21st century.

Notes

1   James Eisenstein, *Politics and the Legal Process,* Harper & Row, New York, 1973, p 338.

2   I. Kaufman, 'Keeping politics out of the courts', *New York Times Sunday Magazine,* 12 Dec 1984, p 81.

3   'Symposium: politicization of the courts', *Harvard Journal of Law and Public Policy,* VI, 1983, p 295.

4   'The candidates answer', *American Bar Association Journal,* LXX, 6 November 1984, p 54.

5   'Brennan opposes legal view urged by administration', *New York Times,* 13 Oct 1985, p 36.

6   'Brennan opposes legal view', *New York Times,* p 36.

7   L. Tribe, 'A revealing look at the Meese philosophy', *Boston Globe,* 14 Nov 1985, p 23.

8   But there has been substantial disagreement within the administration at cabinet level regarding the propriety of abandoning long-standing affirmative action policies.

9   'Partisan battle joined over court appointments', *Boston Globe,* 1 Dec 1985, p 3.

10 'Partisan battle joined', *Boston Globe,* p 3.

11 Kaufman, *New York Times Sunday Magazine,* p 87.

12 W. Fowler, 'Judicial selection under Reagan and Carter: a comparison of their initial recommendation procedures', *Judicature,* LXVII, 9–10, p 313.

13 S. Goldman, 'Reaganizing the judiciary: the first term appointments', *Judicature,* LXVIII, 6, p 315.

14 'Public advocate awaits judgeship', *New York Times,* 28 April 1985, p 16.

15 'Partisan battle joined', *Boston Globe,* p 3.

16 Goldman, *Judicature,* p 313.

Part II

Representation: a changing political environment

Philip John Davies

Money in elections: the age of campaign finance reform

The push for reform

The first million-dollar presidential campaign was that of Republican candidate James A. Garfield in 1880, and expenditure has been in the millions ever since. With the exception of occasional high-spending elections. expenditure rose gradually until the last thirty years. In 1948 the Republican and Democratic campaigns together spent less than $5 million. But spending doubled in 1952, and had doubled again by 1960, when the John F. Kennedy and Richard Nixon campaigns cost around $10 million each. In 1968 Richard Nixon's successful presidential bid cost $25 million. There was a good deal of concern about this rise in spending. Some blamed it on the development of new and expensive campaign technology – particularly the use of paid television advertising. Others saw in it the sinister hand of those corporations, combines, and individuals capable of putting millions into a campaign – 'big business', 'organised labour', and 'fat cats' – and thereby threatening the public accountability of the elected official. Candidates at all levels wondered where they were to get the money to compete in such an inflationary business. And Democrats worried particularly, as Republican presidential candidates seemed to find money much easier to raise than their opponents.

These concerns contributed to a new era of election campaign regulation, beginning with the Revenue Act of 1971, and the Federal Election Campaign Act of 1971. But almost before the ink was dry on this legislation there was serious consideration being given to passing more stringent reforms. The Democrats appeared to lever themselves into the election-spending ball-game when they raised $30 million for the 1972 McGovern campaign, but the Nixon re-election campaign spent more than $60 million. Some of this money was channelled into a number of illicit activities that became known jointly as 'Watergate', after the building which housed Democratic campaign headquarters, broken into by a Republican-financed team of operatives. These excesses, culminating in the resignation of President Nixon, created a political environment favourable to those pressing for further control, limitation, and general regulation of campaign donations and expenditures. In this atmosphere the 1974 Amendments expanding the coverage of the Federal Election Campaign Act were passed even before many of the clauses of the original Act had taken effect. The adaptations did not finish there. Laws in action do not always have the effects intended by the legislators, and more Amendments were passed in 1976, and again in 1979. Legal challenges to the laws have also altered their effect.

The new campaign regulations

The 1971 Federal Election Campaign Act tackled the questions of disclosure of political contributions, limitation of campaign spending on media advertising, and limitation of the use of personal fortunes for campaign spending. Additionally, the Revenue Act of the same year introduced tax deductions for small political contributions, and a 'check off' provision whereby tax payers could divert $1 per person to a fund to subsidise the expenses of presidential election campaigns. These Acts, however vestigial their remnants today, set the agenda for campaign regulation in the 1970s and 80s. The issues of prompt financial disclosure, limited campaign contributions, campaign-spending ceilings, and public-funding of election campaigns were repeatedly addressed in legal challenges to the legislation, and in subsequent legislative adjustments to the regulations.

Disclosure

It has long been a tenet of the public interest lobby in the United States that 'information is power'. 'Sunshine laws', opening up the process of government committees to public scrutiny, and the Freedom of Information Act, giving public access to a wide variety of government documents, are just part of the new arsenal of groups such as Common Cause. At the same time the demand for public accountability by making political actions widely visible sounds eminently reasonable in a political system often praised by self-congratulatory participants for its pluralist characteristics. The pressure for disclosure of campaign contributions fits easily into this general concern that political participants and organisations be open to public examination.

The 1971 Campaign Act required candidates for House, Senate and the Presidency to file reports on the funding of their campaigns, and political parties were required to disclose the accounts of presidential convention costs. Reports by political committees and candidates had to identify the donors of all contributions or loans exceeding $100 a year. The 1974 amendments insisted that federal candidates report all contributions and spending through a single campaign committee, and established the Federal Election Commission (FEC) with responsibility for operation of the law. The attempt to regulate campaign finances met with some opposition, and various aspects of the law were challenged in a court case, *Buckley v. Valeo*. In January 1976 the Supreme Court upheld the plaintiffs' case in part, including the claim that the FEC was improperly constituted. The Commission had only been in operation for a year, but this Supreme Court decision forced Congress to amend the law once again in order to maintain campaign finance regulation. After a hiatus of some months the Commission was reconstituted in a constitutionally satisfactory way as part of the 1976 FECA amendments. There were more amendments in 1979, by which time some observers and participants felt that the regulations on disclosure were excessively burdensome. The number of reports to be filed was reduced for Congressional candidates; campaigns receiving or spending less than $5,000 were exempted from filing; donors to a campaign only had to be identified, or expenditures itemised, if they reached $200; and other thresholds for disclosure were similarly raised.

Though the disclosure parameters have been changed, and the FEC reconstituted, the original intent on disclosure of the early regulations seems not to have altered fundamentally. In so far as the new campaign law was supposed to disperse the shadows around candidate funding and spending, the mechanisms are still there. All those pursuing federal office have to file their reports and the possibility that an inquisitive reporter, or opponent, will examine the returns for evidence of any campaign finance indiscretion complements the other regulations of the 1970s laws.

Regulating donations

Among the concerns of the reformers was the potentially undemocratic effect of very large campaign contributions by rich individuals or organisations. The 1971 Federal Election Campaign Act went no further than a section limiting the amount that could be spent on an election campaign by the candidate and his/her close family. The 1972 election, however, saw massive individual contributions continue in the presidential campaign, headed by donations in excess of $2 million given by W. Clement Stone (this continued his largesse of 1968, when he had donated nearly $3 million to the Nixon campaign). Public anger and political revenge after Watergate gave reformers the opportunity to curtail such obvious exercise of financial clout. 1974 saw the introduction of a limit on individuals' political donations of $1,000 per candidate per election, up to a total amount donated in any one year by any one person of $25,000. The law also introduced separate regulations covering the Political Action Committees (PACs), formed by a wide variety of labour, business, ideological and lobbying organisations, and charged with the responsibility of disbursing funds in pursuance of the political objectives of the organisation. PAC contributions were limited to $5,000 per candidate per election, with no ceiling on overall campaign contributions. Contributions to political parties were limited to $20,000 per annum for individuals, and $15,000 for PACs. The limitations on donations were intended to broaden political participation and to reduce the real or apparent debt that some candidates might otherwise have to particularly generous supporters. However, the regulation of donations also suffered from the attentions of the Supreme Court, when, as part of the *Buckley v. Valeo* decision the blanket limitation on donations to his/her own campaign by a candidate and his/her immediate family were declared unconstitutional infringements of free speech.

Regulating expenditure

The Supreme Court decision in *Buckley v. Valeo* affected all aspects of campaign law, but possibly influenced expenditure regulation more than anything else. The 1971 law addressed the most inflationary, and what was considered the most manipulative, area of campaign spending, by putting limits on candidate spending on media advertising. By 1974 Congressional resolve to limit spending had been further strengthened, and overall spending limits were imposed for all candidates for federal office. Furthermore independent spending – money spent by individuals independent of the official election campaign, but in an attempt to influence the outcome – was limited to $1,000. All of these regulations were struck down by the Supreme Court. The loss of the particular regulations is not so significant as the general reasoning behind the legal decision which, in its apparent equation between freedom to spend on getting a message across and freedom of speech, makes spending limits very difficult to impose without falling foul of the first amendment to the Constitution of the United States. Consequently, little remains of the attempt to limit federal campaign spending across the board. Only in cases of presidential candidates accepting public funds have spending limits been maintained, the Court perceiving such limits as conditions of the grant, rather than blanket limits on speech. Even so, these conditions can only be imposed on the official campaign organisation of the presidential candidate. The Presidential Election Campaign Fund Act (which governs the operation of the election fund financed by the $1 tax check-off) included a clause limiting to $1,000 any single independent expenditure aimed at influencing the presidential election. In March 1985 the Supreme Court's decision, *Federal Election Commission v. The National Conservative Political Action Committee,* declared this limit unconstitutional even in the case of the fully-funded presidential election. This decision appeared finally to lay to rest the potential for anything other than the most narrow of spending limits.

Rules were imposed in 1974 governing the amount which the political parties could spend in support of candidates for House, Senate, and the presidency according to a formula depending in part on the size of the constituency, but for the most part subsequent action on spending appears to have eased those limits that do exist. State and local parties in particular have been given new freedoms in the 1979 amendments, which allow unlimited spending on traditional campaign materials (eg. leaflets, stickers), and unlimited spending on efforts to register voters and encourage them to exercise their franchise, as long as these projects are manned by volunteer labour.

Public funding

The Revenue Act of 1971 created a fund for the public financing of presidential campaigns. Campaign law as amended in 1974 set qualifying thresholds beyond which candidates for the presidency were eligible for public funding. In the primaries, candidates have to display a degree of widespread public support by collecting at least $5,000 in each of 20 states. This having been done, the candidate qualifies for federal funds matching all contributions up to a maximum of $250 per contributor.

These matching funds are only available on condition that the campaign be governed by spending limits. Limits were written into the law, to rise in dollar value according to a cost-of-living index, covering spending on the campaign in individual states, and an overall limit on all spending. The state limits total more than the overall limit, leaving space for strategic spending decisions by the campaign. For the 1984 presidential primary season the overall spending limit reached $20,200,000 for a candidate. This phase of public funding gets the candidates for nomination as far as the party convention. The 1974 law included a provision giving a grant towards the costs of each major party convention. Once endorsed by one of the major political parties the nominees qualify for further federal funds. This index-linked grant reached $40,400,000 in 1984. Having accepted public funding, the official campaign may not spend any money on campaigning after the convention other than that received from the federal election fund.

State-level regulation

In addition to federal efforts at regulation, many states have considered reforms in the field of election finance. The federal legislation applies only to federal offices. State action is required if campaign finance regulation is to reach the parts federal law cannot reach. States have reacted with widely varying combinations of laws covering disclosure, spending, donations and public funding. According to Herbert Alexander's codification of state laws all states require some form of disclosure, but only half attempt to put any limit on donations. About half the states have selective restrictions on corporate contributions, while 10 states prohibit direct contributions from unions. Following the federal lead, PACs are generally accepted as legitimate political participants. About one-third of states have instituted some form of public funding, generally financed by optional provisions in the state income tax system. The operation of this funding varies considerably, but in a handful of states fairly sizeable funds have been channelled either to the parties (for example $600,000 distributed in Minnesota, $240,000 in Iowa in 1980), or to the candidates (especially in New Jersey, where the maximum subsidy is calculated on the basis of the previous presidential vote, and now exceeds $1,000,000 for a major party gubernatorial candidate). A handful of these state subsidies have attached conditional spending limits.

The post-reform experience

It may be argued that the legislative and judicial activity of the 1970s has created a false impression about the regulation of campaign finances. While much of the legislation was premised on the belief that there should be effective spending limits on campaigns, that has not been the final result. The 1974 Act imposed spending limits on all candidates for federal office, but the Supreme Court has made it clear that it considers such limits illegitimate except where they are conditions of public funding. It is only the presidential election, therefore, that has been subject to the broadest regulation of campaign spending. Even then the limits are so full of holes as to be porous.

Delivering a message to a large constituency is an expensive business. Election campaigns are often compared with commercial advertising campaigns, but while a business is aiming for market share, in politics shares of the vote count for nothing unless you top the poll on election day. The professional advisers to a campaign are obliged to find every way within the law to maximise their clients' electioneering resources. They now practise in an environment dominated by the regulations introduced in the 1970s. The reforms were intended to minimise the influence of single, large donations, to encourage a broader participation in financing elections, to reduce the overall cost of elections, and to increase political competition. But if some things change, some stay the same as ever, and campaign spending continues to escalate.

Political Action Committees

There were 608 Political Action Committees registered in 1974. In 1985 the FEC recorded spending by 4,345 PACs. This massive growth is entirely attributable to the campaign reform legislation of the 1970s, and is the most visible institutional response to the new finance laws. A Political Action Committee collects funds from donors to distribute for political purposes. The committee may be closely associated with a particular organisation, for example, a single corporation, union, or professional association – or may be organised to promote a single policy issue or ideological stance. The money collected may be spent independently to support the PAC's objectives, or used to finance contributions up to the limit of $5,000 per candidate per campaign.

The inclusion of PACs in the campaign reforms was a Democratic ploy to protect and enhance the role of labour unions in elections. Republicans insisted that the legislation allowed the establishment of corporate PACs too, and in 1975 the FEC confirmed the legality of the Sun Oil Company's PAC, setting the stage for any company to use this new channel of political influence. Sponsoring organisations are allowed to use their own corporate or union funds to set up, operate and solicit funds for their Political Action Committees. Labour union PACs approximately doubled in number from 1974 to total 380 in 1982, but corporate PACs increased more than 16 times to almost 1,500.

Many PACs represent broad commercial or union interests. For example the American Federation of Labor and Congress of Industrial Organisation's Committee on Political Education (AFL/CIO-COPE) has a long history of campaigning on behalf of union members, while the National Association of Realtors' PAC supported the general trade interests of its 661,000 members. In the 1984 congressional elections the Realtors donated $2,500,000 to candidates, funded registration drives that put 415,000 voters on the electoral rolls, and claims to have put in $10 million worth of volunteer work for candidates. Using its freedom to spend independently, the Association spent $49,000 on last-minute television advertisements aimed at unseating incumbent Congressman Clarence Long of Maryland. He lost by 6,000 votes.

The ideological PACs have been highly visible. Conservative committees such as the National Conservative PAC seized the initative, establishing an early lead in collecting and distributing funds, and organising independent spending, to support conservative candidates and oppose liberals. These conservative PACs claimed much of the credit for defeating four liberal Democratic Senators in 1980 (Bayh of Indiana, Church of Idaho, Culver of Iowa, McGovern of South Dakota), and in 1982 spent about $1,000,000 futilely opposing Senator Edward Kennedy's re-election in what may rather have been an effort to weaken any future Presidential aspirations.

Lobbying groups on individual issues, such as abortion, or gay rights, have formed PACs, as well as those with a broader agenda, for example on environmental or public interest matters. Officeholders and candidates have also formed their own PACs, aimed at promoting issues, or with the intention of raising funds for distribution to other candidates for different office, thus building up a constituency of beholden political colleagues.

Political Action Committees have changed the political environment, and their impact continues to grow. In 1979/80 PACs collected about $138 million, in 1983/4 the amount collected rose to $288.7 million. They have provided an increasing proportion of campaign funds at all levels, and some observers claim that the growing financial power of PACs has served to accelerate the decline of partisan politics in America.

Political parties

If, as Jesse Unruh said, 'Money is the mother's milk of politics', then the ability to donate, and then to track and assess the effectiveness of those donations is significant. It has been the argument of some critics of contemporary campaign finance laws that the reforms have put more power into the hands of the private contributors, and have undermined the role of the parties. Besides the weakening effect of PACs on parties, public funding for presidential candidates is accused of increasing intra-party competition by subsidising challengers for the nomination, limiting the spending of leading candidates, and maintaining the primary conflict longer than private financing alone would be likely to.

In some ways, though, the law favours the political parties. Individuals and committees are allowed to donate larger amounts to parties than to individual candidates. In their turn, the national party committees may contribute substantial amounts to Senate and House candidates. The amounts were set in 1974 at $10,000 for most House seats, $20,000 plus 2c per voting-age person for Senate races – inflation-indexing had doubled these standards by 1984. The state party committees can double party expenditure on any race by co-ordinated spending, which may be organised in co-operation with the national committee. State and local party committees can spend freely on the traditional campaign paraphernalia, and they can organise voter registration and motivation efforts in parallel with presidential campaigns. The major parties also receive funds for their quadrennial national conventions.

The political parties took some time to encompass the reforms. Candidates were forced to raise funds in a changed environment, yet when they looked to the parties there was little help available. The Republican party was first to respond to the new demands. Sophisticated direct-mail solicitation has been used by the Republicans to develop huge lists of reliable small contributors who, in addition to organised groups of larger contributors, produce a large, steady income for the Republican National Committee, and for the party's House and Senate campaign committees. While the Democrats have come lately to recognise the importance of such efforts, they still lag far behind their opponents.

Apart from contributing and spending in individual campaigns, the parties have invested in other activities. The Republicans have again been the groundbreakers, using their wealth to organise the recruitment and training of potential candidates for office, and fostering talent at all levels. It has used national advertising to generally improve the political environment for Republicans, while targeting marginal seats for special campaign efforts. Centralised technical services have been set up. The party's staff can help by designing low-cost opinion polls and providing survey analysis for candidates. The party's media team provide candidates with low-cost television and print services, enabling them to produce a professional media campaign at minimum cost.

In the wake of the campaign finance reforms parties have found themselves in competition with PACs. While the parties remain the biggest single financial and organisational force in election campaigns the combined giving of PACs outstrips party activity. PACs are many and various, but while it is unreasonable to see them as monolithic, they are nevertheless a considerable force. PACs can offer services, generalised promotional campaigns, and candidate training, trespassing on the traditional turf of the party. In reacting to the challenge of finance reform the national party committees have expanded their activities, and one detects a trend toward centralisation. If a generation of office-holders results whose members have benefited from party encouragement, recruitment, training, donations, co-ordinated spending, and service-provision there may be potential for greater party cohesion on policy, and loyalty in the legislatures. But this all depends on the way the entrepreneurial candidate reacts in the long-term to the reformed environment.

The candidate as entrepreneur

The relatively weak American political party system has always demanded that participants be very self-motivated. The wide use of primaries demands that candidates go through a gruelling, expensive and revealing selection process, during which they must establish their individual appeal to the electorate. Once nominated, candidates may still be unable to depend on the party for very much financial or strategic support. The public intra-party conflict of the primary process demands organisation based on loyalty to candidate rather than to party, and it is this organisation which tends to remain around the candidate throughout the candidacy and into office. Once elected, a politician may find it advantageous to carve out a particular niche in which to establish a personal reputation, rather than risking the anonymity of being a team player. While this is not a new development, the financial reforms have further encouraged this entrepreneurial style. The campaign has become a professional exercise based on the most successful exploitation of the candidate's personal assets.

Fundraising

The campaign finance reforms have had some entirely intended results – such as increasing public involvement in financing through the tax check-off – and some unintended – such as encouraging the massive expansion in PAC activity. But a common feature of these developments has been greatly to increase the complexity of the fundraising and financial management of the campaign, thereby encouraging its professionalisation.

The limitations have reduced the possibility of candidates depending on a handful of large contributors. The ability to organise large numbers of contributors is now the benchmark of successful campaign organisation. Direct mail fundraising has been a popular approach. Party, PAC, or candidate fundraisers identify potential supporters by their known record of political giving, or by demographic factors, and direct fundraising 'mailshots' to these people. It may be that over time this technique will suffer from diminishing returns. Known contributors appear on more and more lists, so that the number of solicitations arriving through the mail becomes a flood. Mail fundraisers attempt to identify ways of overcoming consumer immunity to such mass appeals – the letters are printed to look handwritten, or even typed with apparently handwritten notes added to enhance the personal appeal; the envelopes are stamped rather than business-machine franked, the stamps affixed crookedly, again to create the feeling that this solicitation came from a human, not a machine. The techniques become more gimmicky (and more expensive) in the face of increasing competition for the electorate's political dollars.

The 'fat cat' has not disappeared from American politics. Political entrepreneurs have been busy seeing that such potential does not go to waste. Candidates, PACs, and party committees offer contributors ways of directing the regulation $25,000 per annum into federal campaigns. Given that this is a per person limit, the opportunity exists for a wealthy family to co-ordinate campaign donations for maximum effect. Since the same limits do not apply at state level, arrangements can be made for money to be shifted around the country into campaigns where it may legally be used. The logistics of these efforts are considerable, especially as all the fundraising participants attempt to find ways to exploit any loopholes in the finance laws.

Candidates raise money directly from the electorate, but also wish to attract support from PACs and party committees. PAC support is most likely to be available to a sitting candidate or to a candidate making an effective challenge in a marginal or vacant constituency. PACs want their money to result in access to policymakers, and are unlikely to waste it in futile gestures of support for doomed candidacies. Sitting, powerful Congressmen can be quite belligerent in their solicitation of PAC funds. Congressmen on prestigious committees dealing with significant issues can attract large war chests from PACs concerned with maintaining a sympathetic hearing for their cause in Congress. In the 1985 run-up to the consideration of tax reform the 36 Representatives on the House Ways and Means Committee, and the 20 Senators on the Finance Committee found no shortage of takers at their $500 and $1,000-a-plate breakfasts, lunches, and dinners. Business PACs donated $11.4 million to the 1984 campaigns of these committee members, including $1.4 million from banking and financial services PACs, $1.28 million from real estate and construction PACs, and $1.27 million from insurance PACs. Union PACs wanted to pay for their share of access too, donating $2 million. In fact almost everyone felt that these congressmen deserved pampering, with a further $1.2 million coming from ideological PACs, almost $1 million from health interest PACs, and over half a million dollars each from farm interests and professional PACs. This PAC concern to invest in access to known, sitting, lawmakers adds financial muscle to the already considerable electoral advantage of incumbency.

Congressional candidates have become increasingly dependent on PAC money, and less dependent on small contributors, in recent years. In the 1981/2 election cycle 94 House members received at least half of their campaign cash from PACs while in the elections two years later 156 House members reported getting at least half of their campaign contributions from PACs. There are limits on PAC donations, but at the same time as candidates are attempting to raise funds from sympathetic PACs, the PACs are looking for ways of increasing their campaign contributions to favoured candidates above the $5,000 per candidate per election limit. 'Bundling', for example, entails collecting contributions made out directly to a favoured candidate, and passing them on. This saves the candidate the expense of solicitation, allows the PAC to handle more campaign money, and may reach audiences otherwise unavailable to the candidate campaign.

Wealthy candidates are significant in this reformed political environment. There are no limits on the amount a candidate may loan or donate to his/her own campaign. Lew Lehrman ran a multi-million dollar campaign in an unsuccessful bid for the governorship of New York in 1982. Jay Rockefeller spent $12 million of his own money switching from the Governorship of West Virginia to the US Senate, having already spent $13 million of his own money on three previous state-wide campaigns. Money does not guarantee victory, but the availability of large-scale funds early in the campaign gives the wealthy candidate a logistical advantage in a system where the non-monied candidate must rely on relatively small donations collected from many sources.

At the presidential level one might expect fundraising to be a less important factor, given the existence of public funding. Candidates have to get to the starting gate, however, and the 'pre-campaign' stage is getting longer and more expensive. Hopefuls need to establish their credibility as presidential candidates. A strategy may involve extensive national appearances, especially in those states with early or significant caucuses or primary elections. There are ways of funding such efforts without invoking federal campaign limits. In the run-up to 1988 potential presidential candidates have discovered that by forming non-profit political foundations (for example, Jack Kemp's 'Fund for an American Renaissance', and Gary Hart's 'Center for New Democracy'), and then acting as the spokesman for the new foundations, they may begin the campaign untrammelled by regulations on donations, spending, or disclosure. The individual PACs of various undeclared 1988 candidates have also spent considerable amounts on 'party-building' exercises, thereby avoiding financial regulation while gaining visibility and laying the campaign groundwork in various strategic states. Any candidate has to raise sufficient funds to qualify for the federal grants, so fundraising remains important to the presidential candidate into the primary season, and as the timing of expenditure can be crucial, so early success in fundraising is important.

Spending

There remain many ways to spend money in federal elections, and the total amount involved continues to rise. Some spending is subject to limits; the public funds awarded to presidential nominees; the funds collected and spent to fulfil the compliance regulations of campaign finance law; the federal grants for national party conventions; the limited expenditure that may be made by the national parties in support of presidential candidates; and the limited party funds that may be spent by national and state party committees in support of congressional and senatorial candidates. Additionally, 'normal' national party expenditure (which would include generalised 'vote Republican' or 'vote Democrat' campaigns) is virtually unlimited. Traditional 'get out the vote' and grass roots activities by local parties are exempt from limits. State party spending on generalised party campaigning only counts against presidential limits in proportion to the total number of party candidates on the whole ballot, a limit which can serve to broaden the impact of spending considerably. Labour Unions, Trade Associations and Corporations can spend funds on internal communications to their memberships without regulation. Individuals and groups can spend unlimited amounts promoting or attacking any candidate, as long as this is done entirely independently, involving no collusion with the official campaign organisation of the candidate. All of these methods of spending are in addition to the sums raised and spent by the official campaign organisations of candidates throughout the system.

Effective spending in this complex system has become as professionalised as has the collection of contributions. Since the presidential elections do have spending limits for all those accepting public funds it is here perhaps that campaign strategy has been most affected. Public funding may have the effect of keeping marginal candidates in the primary race for a longer period, and spending limits restrict the ability of the front-runner to swamp the opposition. Indeed, the timing of spending becomes a crucial strategic decision. Early victories may create a bandwagon effect, but they may also exhaust the allowed spending allocation, and leave a candidate vulnerable to the emergence of a late challenge. Walter Mondale's 1984 strategy involved high spending in the early rounds. When this failed to wipe out the opposition, he was fighting off the challenge of Gary Hart, and the continuing campaign of Jesse Jackson, with few funds left. Hart, bursting from the pack in the early contests, found money flowing in, but without a substantial war chest in the beginning, the ground had not been adequately prepared in many states to mount effective campaigns nationwide. Jackson managed to maintain results strong enough to keep the pipeline of federal subsidy open, and the campaign going. Meanwhile Ronald Reagan, unchallenged for the Republican nomination, had the luxury of being able to use all his allowed pre-nomination funds to put in place the foundation of his subsequent general election campaign. All the main candidates found the new legislation affecting their strategy, and their chances of victory.

Minor party candidates found the legislation no help, since they could only qualify for federal funding after the election if in receipt of 5 per cent of the vote.

After the nominating conventions presidential candidates again make strategic decisions based on their reliance on a fixed fund of money. Recently major party candidates have concentrated more of their funds into the mass media, especially television advertising. Not only is this a reasonable per capita way of spending the campaign's dollars, it also makes the best use of the alternative channels of spending. Since national, state and local parties may spend extensively on generalised party campaigns, 'get out the vote' efforts, and other traditional forms of canvassing, the cost of such efforts are left to them, while the application of these efforts is co-ordinated with the presidential campaign. Additionally, the major party candidates can expect substantial independent spending on their behalf by sympathetic PACs or individuals. Democratic candidates gain overwhelmingly from organised labour's spending efforts, but in recent elections the Republican presidential candidate, Ronald Reagan, has benefited from a huge lead in other independent spending. In 1980 the federal grant to the two major party nominees was $29.4 million each, but with the addition of party, labour, corporate, independent, and other spending directly on the presidential general election campaign, the total spent came to over $118 million ($64.1 million on Reagan, $53.93 million on Carter). Herbert Alexander, the leading expert on campaign finance, further calculates that the total cost of electing the president in 1980, including the prenomination campaign, was $275 million.

Spending strategy may have been most affected at the presidential level, but there are other consequences for the system. Apart from donating to and raising funds for candidates, any political committee may act independently. Campaign literature is distributed by PACs both in favour of and against particular candidates. Television time may be bought and used independently to the same end. Some PACs have found 'negative advertising' a particularly effective method of undermining a candidate they oppose. This is a technique only to be used with care, as it risks being labelled unfair. Since the PAC campaigns are not under the control of the supported candidate, however, he/she can benefit from them while nevertheless being able to deny any responsibility for the potentially unsavoury 'mud-slinging' tactics that might be used. Individuals also have the right to sink their funds into independent campaigning, and while such expenditure is generally small-scale, along the lines of a displayed 'open letter to the electorate' put as a paid newspaper advertisement, there are examples of citizens willing to put substantial amounts of their personal fortune into a campaign. For example one Michael Goland, a Californian businessman, was so deeply opposed to Senator Charles Percy of Illinois that he spent a sum reported as between $1 million and $1.6 million for anti-Percy billboard, television, radio and newspaper advertising, that may have contributed to Percy's 1984 election defeat.

In non-federal elections it is impossible to generalise about the effects of the finance reforms since they have been adopted in the haphazard way that a federal system encourages. Nevertheless some similarities can be seen. PACs have become fashionable even in states where·there are no restrictions on corporate or labour spending. The effort to comply with state and federal regulation in those states with strict laws has further increased the professionalisation of the campaign organisations. State and local parties are expected to use the leeway afforded them to become ancillary support vehicles for the presidential candidates in the relevant years. And those states where regulation is lax have become the recipients of 'soft money' – funds channelled by enterprising organisers from contributors wishing to give freely to the least restrictive political environments. State legislative campaign costs vary widely, but they are rising nationwide. Estimates of average spending in 1986 were as low as $300 for New Hampshire, up to $70,000 in Michigan, and as high as $750,000 in some California districts.

The professionals

So complex has campaigning become that it can no longer be left to the party, the committed and the electorate. Every stage involves lawyers, fundraisers, political consultants, pollsters, media experts, strategists. The jobs are exciting, the stakes high, and the pay good. This is a multi-million dollar business, with election year expenditure at all levels estimated as $1.8 billion in 1984. A candidate must be able to attract to himself a skilful team of supporters which may include loyal friends from campaigns past, but will rely on the purchased expertise of professionals to maximise the campaign's effect, and to make sure it stays within the letter of the law. The credibility of a candidate's campaign can be bolstered by the stature of the professional staff who agree to be associated with the effort. This professionalisation would develop without the finance laws, but in so far as these laws have failed to limit spending, while making the political environment more complex, the laws have promoted this tendency. The candidate is increasingly the centre of a personal organisation forging links of personal loyalty, depending on purchased professional services, gathering funds and arranging support in a regulated but highly manipulable market, promising access in return for donations. The route to office in this high-spending environment is more entrepreneurial than ever.

Conclusion and prospects

There continues to be substantial growth in total national campaign spending. This growth may have happened without the reform legislation, but it is possible that the reforms helped promote this inflation. The encouragement of PACs together with the inability to impose blanket spending limits created a new impetus for the manipulation of campaign funds. Money freed from the presidential race because of the public funding provisions was invested at other levels where expenditure might result in a reasonable political payoff. Coinciding with the decentralisation of power in Congress, it became reasonable to spend widely and well in contributing to Congressional campaigns in order to maintain access to policy makers throughout the system. Fundraising entrepreneurs searched for new reserves of political money to feed into the electoral system, and when their efforts did overstep the boundaries of the law the FEC imposed penalties so light as to be unlikely to deter further innovation.

Once growth of this kind begins it can become self-sustaining. Candidates know that sustained campaign spending is generally necessary to win office, and concentrate on raising the funds. PACs, parties and candidates are now skilled at attracting funds for marginal or vacant constituencies. Incumbents never want to be caught off-guard, so make sure that they are fundraising at all times. The campaign becomes longer and the costs increase. Even at presidential level, the real expenditure is now increasing dramatically as campaigners discover ways around the limits. At the same time the whole procedure has become increasingly controlled by a myriad of election specialists, the professional, if peripatetic staff of a multi-million dollar industry.

Growing PAC influence has prompted concern. PAC contributions to House and Senate candidate tripled between 1978 and 1984, while the number of individual contributors declined. Resulting proposals have suggested a limit on the amount of PAC money a Congressional candidate could receive; tax incentives and higher contribution limits for individual contributors to encourage more citizen involvement; the abolition of 'bundling'; and the establishment of a candidate's right to free media time to reply to independently-sponsored negative advertisements. Legislation on these lines, proposed by Senator David Boren, received a degree of Senate support in August 1986 that surprised the pundits, but such suggestions merely tinker with the new political environment of campaign finance. The inability to restrain spending appears to lie at the root of any further effort to follow through on the aims of the 1970s reforms, and it is clear that the Supreme Court will not envisage imposing spending limits unless these are accompanied by public funding provisions, and neither Congress nor the public shows any enthusiasm for such a step.

Notes

The main sources used for this chapter were: Herbert Alexander's *Financing Politics: Money, Elections, and Political Reform, (Third Edition),* Congressional Quarterly Press, Washington DC, 1984; and *Financing the 1980 Election,* Lexington Books, Lexington, Mass., 1983; Elizabeth Drew, *Politics and Money: The New Road to Corruption,* Collier Books, New York, 1983; Joel Fleishman (ed.), *The Future of American Political Parties: the Challenge of Governance,* Prentice-Hall, Englewood Cliffs, NJ, 1982; Michael J. Malbin (ed.) *Money and Politics in the United States: Financing Elections in the 1980s,* Chatham House, Chatham, NJ, 1984; Michael Nelson (ed.), *The Elections of 1984,* Congressional Quarterly Press, Washington DC, 1985; Stephen J. Wayne, *The Road to the White House: The Politics of Presidential Elections, (Second edition),* St. Martin's Press, New York, 1984. Additional information was culled from the pages of *The New York Times, The Washington Post, National Journal,* and *The Washington Monthly.*

Philip John Davies

Shifting sands: developments in party politics

The changing party political environment

American political parties give an impression of concreteness in an often frantic political world. The parties' names have remained unchanged for lifetimes – the Republican Party is the junior partner, having been founded in 1854; the Democratic name has been around since the opening of the nineteenth century. However, the major American political parties are in a continuous state of flux. Any national, public institution in a country so large cannot help but change. The price of standing still while the country is growing, the needs of the population are changing, regional and group power is shifting, and policy agendas are altering would be to become redundant. An organisation that purports to represent the public as individuals and the nation as a whole must adapt or atrophy. The nature of that adaptation is the subject of heated debate among both political activists and political scientists. For more than a generation there has been a school of academics who have felt that American political parties have not been adapting in a politically healthy fashion. In 1954 the American Political Science Association published a report *Towards a More Responsible Two-Party System*,[1] promoting changes in the party system, but even as the original report's proposals were being outlined, party politics was entering an age in which the relationships between media and politics and money and politics were to undergo dramatic change.

The environment for party activity has been fundamentally transformed in recent years, and many feel the result has been a weakening of the traditional party role, by onerous regulation, by the development of other public institutions able to perform part of that role, and by an enthusiastic reaction of politicians to the independence that these changes apparently offer. While political parties act as a communicating mechanism between the electorate and government, institutionally organising public opinion into support for particular policy agendas, and the candidates sharing that agenda, there have always been other institutions replicating at least some parts of those functions. Recent developments have served to increase the opportunity for alternative channels of political communication, and to liberate both voters and candidates from dependence on the political party. The growing exploitation of television in politics has been the most remarked of these changes. Candidates for office naturally become the focus of groups of loyalists when they are competing for a place on the party ballot, and these cadres have not always easily fitted, or wanted to fit, into the party system. In some states legal regulations neuter the parties, reducing them to a mechanical role of organising primary elections without any real influence in them. Politicians have found that, using television, they can appeal direct to the electorate without relying on the political party to distribute their message. Using contemporary developments in public opinion polling and analysis, they can gauge the mood of the electorate (or at least of that part of the electorate relevant to their election) without relying on the political party. Using modern computerised direct-mail techniques, they can maintain a pseudo-personal contact with constituents and supporters.

This increasingly technological campaign and communications system, with its demand for media access, constant public opinion research and professional assistance, is expensive, but politicians, especially incumbents, have been able to attract the necessary financial support. Pressure groups have traditionally been mentioned in the same breath as parties, operating sometimes complementary to, sometimes competitively with, political parties in organising and communicating public opinion, but generally covering a much narrower spectrum of issues. The expense of campaigns gives the opportunity for organised interests to show their appreciation to a politician by making a contribution. While federal campaign laws have attempted to regulate such contributions, this legislation has encouraged the formation of thousands of political action committees, collecting and channelling funds from interests to candidates, but also in some cases providing a wide variety of publicity and training services traditionally within the purview of the political party. Business, labour, and issue-oriented groups are willing to contribute to a politician's war chest for the sake of access. They are not buying votes in the legislature, they argue, but they are trying to ensure that, should it become necessary, their side of an issue might get a hearing. Access is only useful if you have backed a winner, with the result that many interests express a bi-partisan concern for those already established in office, rather than investing more riskily in challengers. Incumbents already hold substantial advantages – name recognition, careful cultivation of constituents through government-financed 'newsletters', the office-holder's opportunity to have brought some tangible benefit to a constituency – and added to this is the power to attract considerable campaign contributions from special-interest groups in a system where campaign costs are escalating prohibitively, and where the accumulation of a substantial fund can itself prevent any serious opposition from emerging. No wonder, then, that in 1984 96 per cent of Congressional incumbents wishing to retain their seats managed to do so. And most of those assets that help them retain their seats do not depend on the political parties.

Reforms and the fears of party strength

Nevertheless the weakening of party structures may go back further than the impact of modern media and campaign techniques. Parties have always provoked an ambivalent response in the United States: many of the Founding Fathers did not want parties, and while they emerged as a necessary instrument of public power, they have often been viewed with circumspection, and the public temper widespread allegiance to one or other party with a general suspicion that political parties may somehow commit political excesses in the name of their supporters. 'Progressive Reform' was the by-word of the anti-party feeling of the late 19th and early 20th century. Convinced that the corruptions of 'machine politics', whereby small groups could gain and maintain control of the party machinery to use for their own profit, were in part a consequence of the tightly-organised leadership structures of the parties, these reformers sought to loosen the bonds of strong party leadership. The introduction of primaries, referenda, recall elections and nonpartisan local elections were part of an effort to widen public involvement, and reduce the party power of tightly organised cliques. The most sweeping consequences of these reforms were not immediate, however. Some corrupt leaders were overthrown, but other state and local party organisations managed to adapt to the reform era while losing little of their authority. During the Franklin Roosevelt administration the White House found well-organised and disciplined local parties to be valuable allies, and used the programmes of the New Deal to reward and bolster them. The tools of reform had been put in place, however, and when there erupted another crisis of faith in the leadership, in the turmoil of the 1960s, and especially inside the Democratic Party, a new generation of reformers could disinter some aspects of the Progressive urge, such as the primary election, and add extra rules of their own, again in an effort to achieve representative leadership.

It is not that reformers have always wanted to reduce the power of parties – indeed latter-day reforms such as those insuring access for women and minorities are aimed to strengthen them by making them more representative – but some of those reforms left over from the beginning of the century have recently expanded to weaken the parties' authority over both candidates and policy, and therefore hamstring any attempt to maintain a close connection between the party loyalist, the party candidate for office, and the policy outcome. The primary election, a fairly negligible influence until the late 1960s, has become over the last twenty years the only route to a presidential candidacy, and is almost universally used for other offices. This broadens participation in the candidate selection process, but effectively takes it out of the hands of party loyalists. It encourages further the balkanisation of party politics into the pushing and shoving of candidate-centred groups. Furthermore, it plays into the hands of single-issue interest groups since the primary electorate, though broad, is usually smaller than the general election electorate, so it is in this arena that well-organised and well-financed small groups have the best opportunity to make their presence felt.

'I don't vote for the party, I vote for the man or woman . . .'

The restraints on independence from all but a passing connection to the political parties have therefore been rapidly peeling away over the last 20 or 30 years. The candidates, office-holders and pressure groups are increasingly encouraged to become political entre-preneurs in this new environment. It is not so much a case of

candidates being chosen to represent the party line by party
loyalists, as it is of candidate organisations capturing the party
nomination, thereby eliminating some competitors, and gaining the
use of any party assets, on the way to a personal victory. The
advantages of incumbency, the exploitation of mass media's fasci-
nation with individuals rather than issues or parties, the candidate-
centred campaign, and the massive availability of funds from
non-party organisations make most politicians even less reliant on
the party once they are in office than during their initial candidacy.
Lately, activists have attempted to stem this tide of party decom-
position. the Democratic Party, more prone to dramatic reconstruction than the Republicans, has swung away from the wide-open
presidential nomination structure introduced by the McGovern/
Fraser Commission in the late 1960s and early 1970s, to the
moderately more party-activist orientation of the Hunt Commission's proposals. The aim now is to ensure that the party, when
gathering at the quadrennial convention to nominate a presidential
candidate and to compose a party platform, represents properly the
many groups in the population, but that these delegates are activists
truly sheltering under the party umbrella, and not just there for the
sake of temporary convenience. Simultaneously, there has been an
effort to strengthen the parties' hand in the nomination process at
the non-presidential level. For example, in Connecticut and Massachusetts candidates for statewide office now have to present their
case to state party conventions held prior to the primary elections,
where relatively committed party members vote on the candidates'
merits to represent the party. There is still a primary election, but
the party favourite emerges from the convention as having been
officially 'endorsed', while candidates failing to achieve a minimum
standard of support at the convention (set as high as 20 per cent for
Connecticut's Democrats) are required to withdraw from the race.
The endorsement does not ensure nomination, but it does effectively reduce the field to those candidates most acceptable to party
activists. On the other hand the introduction of yet another stage
into the election process makes candidature an even more expensive process than previously.

  While party reform and renewal efforts are under way to
strengthen the parties, not all officeholders are that enthusiastic
about the idea. Many enjoy their independence of movement, and
relish their role as brokers between the competing influences of

constituency, contributors, interest groups, and party. The fine-tuning of their personal coalition of support keeps them in office, and changes aimed at altering the balance of these influences introduce an element of instability unwelcome to those looking forward enthusiastically to re-election. State and regional political cultures differ enough that persons from different parts of the country who ostensibly support the same party may in fact have quite different ideas as to a reasonable political agenda for that party. It is not without a good deal of compromise that the Democratic Party can provide a home for conservatives such as former Governor George Wallace of Alabama as well as Congress-man Ronald Dellums, a member of the Democratic Socialist Alliance, or that the Republican political spectrum, if somewhat narrower, can nevertheless stretch from liberal Senator Lowell Weicker of Connecticut to the deeply conservative Senator Jesse Helms of North Carolina. A strong national party, especially one which began to impose policy discipline upon, as well as providing electoral services for, office holders, would inevitably threaten to hang some locally unpopular policies around the neck of some of its representatives. The weaker the party, the greater the opportunity for an entrepreneurial politician to tailor his image and per-formance in office to the demands of his personal coalition of supporters, rather than being pledged to support a coherent national policy manifesto.

If there has been a recent disintegration of internal party discipline, it has been paralleled by a decline in strong and lasting public support of one or other political party. Testifying before the Advisory Commission on Intergovernmental Relations, Colorado Republican Chairman Howard Callaway said, '. . . there has been a strong feeling of independence in the voter, combined with a negative image of party politicians that makes it fashionable for the average voter to say, "I don't vote for the party, I vote for the man or woman – I am independent, I make up my own mind, no one tells me how to vote." There is even an occasional apology from those who admit to belonging to or working for a particular party.' Politicians recognise this shift, and while they might rhetorically wish for a return to a more positive image of party politics, they are not willing to volunteer to have a millstone around their necks. Party identification has by no means disappeared, but an atmos-phere in which campaigners may feel there is a risk in stressing the party can benefit some candidates. In a 1985 special election for Texas' First Congressional District Edd Hargett, a telegenic, ex-college football quarterback, conservative Republican, appeared to have a fine chance of taking a traditionally Democratic seat. His campaign billboards urged: 'Vote for Edd Hargett, a Congressman in the East Texas Tradition'. It was the aggravated supporters of his Democratic opponent who went around adding bumper stickers saying 'Republican', to these personalised posters, and the Republicans who complained their billboards were thereby being 'defaced'.[2] This was a high-risk strategy for the Democrats, since the Hargett campaign hoped to capitalise not only on the apparent decline in public support for parties, or 'dealignment', but also on a possible long-term shift of public support between the parties, or 'realignment'.

The theory of realignment

The idea that electoral support for parties in the United States has gone through relatively regular periods of realignment is based mainly on the work of V.O. Key and W.D. Burnham.[3] Key hypothesised that certain national elections were the foci of political disruptions in which some groups of voters traditionally associated with one or other of the main parties shift their allegiance, thereby altering the balance of power between parties, and the nature of the base of that party power, for some time. Burnham, in *Critical Elections and the Mainsprings of American Politics,* identified five main party systems, each with a lifespan of about thirty to forty years. The latest of these systems dated from the 1930s, when the Republican party presided over the cataclysmic start to the Great Depression, the Democratic administration responded to the nation's need for dramatic policy and national pride with the New Deal and an upbeat, active approach, and Franklin Roosevelt forged a merger of ethnic voters, black voters, Northern urban voters, and Southern conservatives that gave his party a long-term electoral advantage. In view of the consistent historical cycle of realignment identified by Burnham, the late 1960s or early 1970s appeared the right time for a new electoral shift.

A number of political characteristics have appeared around the time of the earlier realignments. There is usually an associated weakening of party attachments, and growth of independence and split-ticket voting among the electorate. A rapid growth in the electorate, especially the extension of the franchise to new groups, can contribute to this periodic instability. Minor party activity might increase as disenchanted voters look for a permanent allegiance. Significant changes in party structure and general political style may be present. Highly salient issues may emerge which threaten to split the public along non-traditional lines. Ultimately these factors may signal the shift of significant voting groups between the main political parties. If this change is big enough one could claim that realignment has produced a new party system. Many of these signs have been present since the late 1960s. The proportion of self-identified 'independents' in the electorate grew from 19 per cent in 1958 to 36 per cent in 1976. Split-ticket voting (voting for the candidates of different parties for different offices) doubled between the 1950s and the early 1970s. Some minor party candidacies rose above their usual miniscule vote levels, the greatest impact being made by Democratic defector George Wallace (1968: 13.5 per cent), and Republican defector John Anderson (1980: 6.6 per cent), but with creditable performances by John Schmitz (American Party, 1972: 1.4 per cent), Eugene McCarthy (Independent, 1980: 1 per cent), and Ed Clark (Libertarian, 1980: 1.1 per cent). Changes in party structure and the political environment have been very evident. Issues such as the Vietnam War, civil rights, the conflict between the 'permissive society' and moral and religious traditionalism have emerged to exercise the electorate and their representatives. All this notwithstanding, and in spite of political scientists carefully examining the entrails of successive elections of the past twenty years, there exists little consensus as to whether a realignment can be declared.

1984: 'realignment is real'?

His landslide victory of 1984 prompted Ronald Reagan to announce 'realignment is real'.[4] One suspects that this was a partisan, rather than an intellectual, judgement on the President's part, but the same conclusion is shared by some analysts, who also conclude that the Democrat's New Deal coalition is finally splitting apart, to the distinct advantage of the Republican Party. Many Democrats, their judgements perhaps also coloured by wishful thinking, attributed the 1984 result to Reagan's immense (and for them, deeply frustrating) personal popularity. They take solace from the limited 'coat-tails' effect of Reagan's win – the Republican party gained only fourteen seats in the House, and actually lost two Senate seats, while their presidential candidate took forty-nine states. House Minority Leader Robert Michel was also unconvinced that this could be seen as a victory for his party, feeling that the President 'really never, in my opinion, joined the issue of what it really means to have those [Republican] numbers in the House . . . . Here the son of a buck ended up with 59 per cent [and brings in only fourteen] seats.'[5] This seems a harsh judgement on the President, however, as Reagan has taken his role as party leader seriously, supporting hundreds of Congressional candidates with personal appearances and specially-made advertisements.

Certainly party identification among voters has shifted in the Republicans' favour. Through the 1970s it was not unusual for Democratic supporters to outnumber Republicans by two to one. Some claimed that America had moved to a 'one-and-a-half party system'. Republican candidates won some notable election victories by persuading independents and wavering Democrats into voting for them, but failed to pull these crossover voters in wholehearted commitment to the Republican party. In 1980 Gallup polls found 46 per cent of respondents classifying themselves as Democrats, as opposed to 24 per cent self-identified Republicans, with the rest calling themselves 'independents'. By the end of 1984 the Democrats had slipped to 38 per cent, the Republicans had jumped to 35 per cent. As the enthusiasm of election year waned there was some slippage from both parties, but in May 1986 the figures still looked good for the Republicans in comparison to their generation of minority status:

Democrats			True Independents	Republicans		
Strong	Weak	Inds who lean to D		Inds who lean to R	Weak	Strong
21%	15%	13%	5%	17%	4%	25%
Total Dems: 49%				Total Reps: 46%		

If the Republican party can win the Presidency in 1968, 1972, and 1980 in spite of suffering considerable lag in party identification, then the party had reason to feel confident of its future having pulled up almost to parity in overall public support figures.

A Southern shift

Republican gains have been especially evident in the Southern States. Indeed, the received wisdom that there existed a 'solid Democratic South' moved from legend to myth years ago, with a consistent record in Presidential elections of defection by some Confederate states to Republican or third-party conservative candidates through more than thirty years. This was generally achieved, though, against an undisturbed background of strong Democratic party identification in this region, and exemplified most clearly the federal nature of American politics. Southern Democrats were conservative. Their conservative, Democratic Congressional, state and local politicians commanded the massive support of the region's voters. But in Presidential elections the nomination by the national party of a liberal candidate would provoke Southern defections. This political split personality of the South was clearly a fragile base for long-term Democratic prospects.

Issues associated with race have been a constantly recurring theme in Southern politics, and recently-published research supports the idea that a racially-motivated realignment occurred in the South in the late 1960s.[6] Southern blacks took advantage of the Voting Rights Act to begin to register and vote, and were attracted by the liberal civil rights messages of Democratic presidential candidates. This local expression of liberal Democracy further undermined Southern whites' faith in their traditional allegiance to the Democratic Party. A mass breakaway was slow in coming, but in 1984 71 per cent of Southern whites voted for Ronald Reagan, and 59 per cent voted for Republican Congressional candidates. For many this seems to have been a final realisation that their conservative beliefs fit as comfortably within the national Republican spectrum of ideas as they do within a regionally-based Democratic ideology. In a sense this is a personal victory for Reagan – the sincerity with which he displays his conservatism may have won the day – but his appeal would appear to be the final brick in the wall separating the majority of Southern whites from their old loyalties. Not all Southern whites have broken the Democratic habit, Southern Democrat office-holders have a self-protective tendency to distance themselves from locally unpopular national candidates, and the growth of the black Democratic turn out has replaced some of the defectors. Nevertheless, Democratic strength in the South has suffered severe erosion.

A Republican trend?

The general agreement that something has happened to party allegiance in the South points to some common threads in the discussion about realignment: namely, that if it is happening, there are regional, federal, demographic and timescale complications involved. One possible conclusion is that the South is not so much signalling a new realignment, as catching up with the New Deal realignment, more than a generation late. This has a certain appeal, given that, even within the broad ideological spectra of US political parties, there is something anomalous about an alliance between the traditionally very conservative Southern wing of the Democratic Party, and its much more liberal northern wing. Furthermore, while Ronald Reagan's victories showed that large portions of traditional Democratic voting groups could be persuaded into voting for a popular Republican President, in a time of economic boom, and apparent international strength, there have been no other wholesale inter-party defections similar to that of the South's whites. Democratic self-identification has declined among many groups. Those voting for Mondale (and against the Reagan tide) in 1984 form a litany of disadvantage – the poor, the unemployed, blacks, hispanics. The Jewish vote maintained a liberal history, with 68 per cent for Mondale, but the usually reliable union members only came through with 53 per cent. Potentially even more distressing for the Democrats, though, is the loss of the party's appeal to young voters – 66 per cent of 18–24-year-olds chose the oldest President in American history as the vehicle of their aspirations. The Democrats' New Deal coalition may still be the backbone of the party, but it is shrinking in numbers as loyal older voters die, and the large unionised industries decline; it is shrinking in impact, as the partisan commitment of these groups weakens; and it still contains the remnants of a fragile coalition of the most conservative and the most liberal groups in American politics.

If realignments are sometimes delayed, regionally or nationally, then one has to consider the possibility that current political shifts

are the culmination of movements stimulated in the late 1960s.
There were at the time many portents of realignment, and Richard
Nixon followed up a marginal first presidential victory with a
landslide re-election, in a similar way to Ronald Reagan. Nixon
neglected his responsibilities as a party leader, but the Republican
Party was slowly rebuilding a more centralised, more conservative
party structure. The catastrophe of Watergate cannot but have
damaged any emerging Republican appeal, but nonetheless this
caused only a brief interruption of Republican occupation of the
White House. Everett Carll Ladd has pointed out that in the five
presidential elections since 1968 23 states, with 202 Electoral
College votes, have been consistently for the Republican candidate,
while the Democratic nominee has only been able to place absolute
reliance in the support of the District of Columbia.[7] The West has
become a political bastion for Republican presidential candidates,
and the South appears to be following suit. Richard Wirthlin, a
Republican pollster, considers this to be evidence of a 'rolling
Republican realignment' – moving through the regions of the
country, and through the levels of the federal system, affecting each
at a different time as resistances peculiar to that part of the electoral
structure are overcome, but rolling relentlessly to a realignment
conclusion in favour of the Republicans. A Republican colleague,
V. Lance Tarrance, hypothesises that party identification has two
aspects – self-identification, and behaviour – with the identification
lagging somewhat behind the act of voting. Recent Republican
victories, therefore, seem to him the basis of an increasingly solid
Republican electoral coalition. A Democratic counterpart, Paul
Maslin, agrees up to a point: '. . . the country has fundamentally
gone Republican in national presidential elections . . .' but, he
points out, there is also '. . . a state and local system in which the
Democrats still prosper'.[8]

Party identification isn't what it used to be

There is little reliable evidence that recently-acquired party identifi-
cations will last the tests of time. If traditional alignments are
changed, but then do not form the basis of new long-term voting
traditions, can the realignment be said to have happened at all? In
an attempt to encompass this, contemporary trends towards
realignment have been characterised as real, but 'hollow', 'weak',

'casual', 'soft', and 'realignment by default'. The Reagan years seem not so much a new 'era of good feelings', as an 'era of weak feelings', at least as far as parties are concerned. While some expect this to mature into a hard and fast party realignment, Walter Dean Burnham considers that we are already in the sixth party system, that it does date from the late 1960s, and that the weakness of parties is a constant, and perhaps immutable, feature of it. The historic structure of party coalitions has given way to a state of 'Permanent Campaign' in which the new features of the political environment have become paramount.[9] Professionalised, personalised campaigns, the intervention of the electronic media, the financial obligations of running for office, are the defining characteristics of this party system. Its fundamental political division is between incumbents (with all the advantages) and challengers (with few), restricting effective electoral choice to elections where no incumbent stands. The Republicans have a growing advantage in this system, since they can beat the Democrats in any fundraising battle, and therefore purchase the channels of persuasion the system demands. The Democrats maintain their strength from their incumbency advantage in Congress, and are tooling up for the new system, if more slowly than their opponents. This system of decayed parties produces an ambiguous politics. Permanent campaigns win elections, but do not provide partisan bonding. Without partisan bonding there is little likelihood of coherent policy options being convincingly presented to the electorate, since those elected cannot be relied on to co-operate in pursuing any policy. Elections in this system take on an increasingly retrospective quality. Reagan's 'quality of leadership' was a major factor in the 1984 election. So was approval for the policy changes he had accomplished, but opinion polls suggest that, even given the massive majority, this is no reason to conclude that Reagan was given a mandate to pursue his political ideals much further. According to Merrill Shanks and Warren Miller, 'by the Fall of 1984, Reagan no longer enjoyed popular support for *more* conservative policies, but he benefitted from strong support for "current policies" . . .'.[10] This may indicate a realigning electorate's seal of approval for an altered policy agenda, or it may indicate the degree of electoral freedom enjoyed by popular leaders in Burnham's sixth system, of decomposing parties.

GOP leaders do not believe that theirs is a decaying party.

Greater centralisation of organisation, a remarkable fundraising effort which has been adapted to take advantage of the election laws, the provision of many of the technical services of the permanent campaign to candidates by the party, with all the political obligations that implies, are seen as evidence of re-emerging party strength. The Democrats are convinced, and are running hard to try to make up the advantage that their opponents have established on this route. For the moment, Republican leaders believe the pendulum is swinging in their favour, the disappointment of the 1986 results notwithstanding. The new record high survival rate among US Representatives indicated just how hard practical realignment will be at the House level, where incumbency, rather than the Democratic Party, is the enemy of Republican success. The loss of Senate control was to some extent counterbalanced by very good gains at the gubernatorial level, and reasonable state-level results, maintaining the prospect of some success for the '1991 Plan', a long-term effort aimed at maximising state-level representation in time for the redistricting battles that will follow the 1990 census. Republicans feel that their party may be capable of making gains in almost any voting group. The growing sectors of the population, in the South, in the West, among the economically comfortable, in non-unionised employment, may not automatically be Republican voters, but they are likely to include a high proportion of independents, and therefore be potential recruits. This recent Republican success has to be confirmed, however, before Democratic corrosion may be called Republican realignment.

Assuming Ronald Reagan survives his term of office, the presidential election of 1988 will be the first for twenty years where neither candidate is an incumbent. It gives the Republicans the chance to consolidate their party strength, and to extend it down into the lower levels of the federal system, and the Democrats the opportunity to find the candidate and message to stop the pendulum's swing. Perhaps in the light of that result there will be agreement over whether the realignment has happened.

Notes

1   American Political Science Association Committee on Political Parties, 'Toward a more responsible two-party system', *American Political Science Review*, XLIV, 1950 (supplement).

2 M. Ivins, 'The Gibber wins one and other news', *The Nation,* Nov. 23 1985, p 545.

3 V. O. Key Jr., 'A theory of critical elections', *Journal of Politics,* XVII, 1955, pp 3–18; W. D. Burnham, *Critical Elections and the Mainsprings of American Politics,* W. W. Norton, New York, 1970.

4 Cited in J. K. White, 'Partisanship in the 1984 presidential election: the rolling Republican realignment', paper delivered at the Northwestern Political Science Association Annual Meeting, Nov 1985, p 18.

5 Cited in White, 'Partisanship', pp 12–13.

6 H. Stanley, W. T. Bianco, and R. G. Niemi, 'Partisanship and group support over time: a multivariate analysis', *American Political Science Review,* LXXX, 1986, pp 969–76.

7 E. C. Ladd, 'On mandates, realignments, and the 1984 presidential election', *Political Science Quarterly,* C, 1985, p 17.

8 J. K. White, 'The party line: interviews with Richard B. Wirtlin, William R. Hamilton, and Paul Maslin', *Party Line: the Newsletter of the Committee for Party Renewal,* XIX, Winter 1985, pp 15–19; J. K. White, 'Interviews with V. Lance Tarrance and Peter D. Hart', *Party Line,* XXI, Fall 1985, pp 11–15.

9 S. Blumenthal, *The Permanent Campaign,* Simon and Schuster, New York, 1982. See also W. D. Burnham, 'The 1984 Election and the future of American politics,' in *Election 84: Landslide Without a Mandate?* (eds. E. Sandoz and C. V. Crabb, Jr.), New American Library, New York, 1985, pp 204–60.

10 J. M. Shanks and W. E. Miller, 'Policy direction and performance evaluation: complementary explanations of the Reagan elections', University of California, Berkeley, Survey Research Center Working Papers, August 1985, p 89.

III
Emerging influences: the changing cast of characters

Kenneth M. Dolbeare and Linda J. Medcalf

The rising stars? Neoliberalism and neoconservatism

Contemporary American liberalism was born in the New Deal and emerged from World War II at the peak of its strength. By the mid 1960s, its commitment to the attainment of equal opportunity for all Americans and governmental responsibility for economic growth and stability dominated both major political parties, all the institutions of the national government, and all but a handful of intellectuals and their journals. Two decades later, however, liberalism is widely perceived to be in total collapse, bereft of creative ideas and leaders, and unlikely to ever again mobilise popular support. Almost no thoughtful political leader accepts the characterisation of liberal without some exculpatory prefix or an extended qualifying explanation. At least for the moment, liberalism has lost its popular appeal, its major thinkers, and its political coalition.

The very success and strength of liberalism led to a radical variant, the 'New Left' of the late 1960s and 1970s. The perceived New Left successes then provoked a reaction, now the 'New Right'. Under attack from all sides, liberalism proved to be a system with almost as many exits as it had thinkers. Groups donned new labels and abandoned the sinking ship with sometimes unseemly alacrity. Many of liberalism's older stalwarts moved to the right as neoconservatives while its rising younger and technocratically-inclined leaders took the label of neoliberalism. Though many variants exist, we focus here on those two deserters – neoliberalism and neoconservatism.

Neoliberalism

Neoliberalism presents itself as a modernised, adapted version of all that was good in John F. Kennedy-style liberalism, and as the appropriate successor for the 1980s and beyond. The defining characteristic of neoliberalism is 'pragmatic idealism', a 'tough-minded' and 'non-ideological' approach that recognises fiscal and other limits while still seeking to promote social justice and equity. Sometimes defined as 'compassionate realism', neoliberalism purports to readily help those in real need but does not attempt to be all things to all people.

Most important, neoliberalism embraces economic growth as an absolute necessity. Since growth depends primarily on the expansion and profitability of the private sector, American entrepreneurs and risk-takers are enthusiastically encouraged. Government policies are crucial to private success in the rapidly changing world economy, however. Thus, major new policies and even institutional changes become necessary to enable the US economy to recover its leading role.

Neoliberals also believe that the Soviet Union remains a hostile and expansionist nation which has now built up its military power to a truly dangerous level. As a result, the US must make a major effort (but not the wastefully massive crash programme of the Reagan administration) to restore both its nuclear deterrent and conventional capabilities. These steps are necessary in order to fulfil the US's limited but decisive role as leader of the free world, and so that it can proceed with the urgently-needed arms limitation agreements from a position of parity.

Within the context set by these primary principles, neoliberalism remains true to the liberal commitment to a humane society. For example, minorities and women should be afforded full citizenship rights and enjoy genuine equality of opportunity. Scarce public funds will have to be conserved for the most needy. But a well-conceived government policy can go a long way toward assuring equity and social justice while maintaining progress toward a better society for all.

Neoliberals deny that they are really liberals who have merely yielded to the supposed rightward movement of American political thinking. They vigorously insist that their programme embodies new ideas synthesised with the humanitarian essence of liberalism to produce a realistic idealism capable of inspiring and satisfying Americans to the end of the century.

The US economy

Neoliberalism's distinguishing characteristic is the comprehensive approach it takes to economic renewal. Neoliberals are well provided with statistics showing the decline of the American economy in comparison with its own former productivity and achievements and with the performance of other industrial economies. American products are no longer competitive in world economic markets. They are more costly, not as well made, and not as aggressively marketed as those of other countries. Therefore they do not sell in the volume needed to make the American economy prosperous.

Neoliberals are also concerned about the scope of social dislocations sure to follow in the wake of the major economic transformation they see underway. The decline of heavy industries and the rise of new technologies – bringing with them the new knowledge society and its service occupations – mean widespread changes in who will be employed, where, and in what sorts of jobs. These problems add urgency to the necessity of thoughtful, long-term use of government to shape the society's adaptation to its inevitable future. All of this, of course, makes the current performance of government all the more in need of reversal.

In the context of their image of decline and transformation in the US economy, neoliberals believe government has multiple policy obligations. First, it must set up a system of incentives and financial assistance to enable the shift of capital from older, declining industries to the newer areas of future opportunity, principally in high-technology production and applications. This could mean national development banks or loan guarantee programmes, retraining and/or relocation assistance for workers, and various forms of aid to communities affected by the massive shifts of capital and jobs.

Next, government should articulate import restrictions with export promotion so that declining industries gain temporary protection and new producers are able to enter potential markets promptly. Declining industries should be helped only for the period it takes to modernise and return them to competitiveness or to accomplish an orderly shift of capital and workers to new uses. National government assistance should come with strings attached. Recipient companies may be required to make specific improvements in facilities or practices. Or the government may insist that workers or public representatives be given seats on the board of directors.

A related programme would consist of international financial policies to stabilise currency values, maintain export markets, and promote regular repayment of existing debts. The massive debts owed by Third World countries represent serious danger to the international banking system. If those countries cannot earn dollars by exporting their products, they cannot repay their debts.

Neoliberals propose a variety of new institutions for negotiating agreements between business, labour and government and for planning the implementation of these programmes. Some believe that a large new development bank run by leading bankers should do the job. Gary Hart urges a presidentially-focussed process in which all relevant interests are represented and work out agreements. Others prefer economic advisory councils of various kinds which, in most cases, report to the Congress. At stake is first whether, and then how, national economic planning of some kind is to be carried out. Secondly, and equally as important, is whether it should be an open, political process or one protected from politics and managed by insiders and experts.

Governmental capacity

Neoliberals frequently point to failures of governmental policy, as the foregoing suggests. But what concerns neoliberals even more is the government's *capacity* to accomplish whatever it undertakes. Neoliberals believe that the US government has been asked to do too many things on behalf of too many interests, the major loser being the national interest as a whole. A favourite line is, 'if you want the government off your back, take your hand out of its pocket'.

Though neoliberals agree that political pressures constitute a major problem for a government's capacity to make reasoned, public interest decisions, they have not resolved the question of how to fix it. Some would attempt to achieve agreement in an open, political process and thus advocate efforts to restore the participatory opportunities and bargaining, accommodating role of political parties. Still others would insulate government decisionmakers against politics and try to legitimate policy decisions some other way. Others urge cutting back civil service protections to provide greater appointment powers for newly-elected Presidents, thus breaking the backs of entrenched bureaucracies and providing expanded opportunities for public participation.

In virtually all cases, however, neoliberals are committed to finding a way to rise above the individual self-seeking, special interest powers, and adversary process of American politics. They decry the lack of performance standards in government, the emphasis on credentials, and the unwillingness to insist upon excellence. They seek a more decisive government with full capacity to act in the general public interest. Indeed, neoliberals can sound almost conservative when they talk about the need for decisive government action and a government of 'national unity', despite probable opposition from various sides.

International relations

The revitalisation of the American economy and the expansion of military power are linked to achieving a single neoliberal goal: restoring the United States to its world leadership position. No neoliberal sees these as separable. All are nearly as concerned with 'the growing Soviet threat' as they are with economic renewal. Their vision of US military buildup is heavy on new technological developments, enhanced managerial capabilities, and frugality – a summary of neoliberal principles. For example, most neoliberals oppose the MX missile and Star Wars as wasteful and inefficient. The goal is not superiority, but an enduring parity that provides the basis for mutually advantageous arms limitations agreements. Nuclear proliferation is so dangerous to the entire world that rational steps to control such weapons must be taken soon, before it is too late.

At the same time, major efforts must be made to help Third World countries toward economic stability and independence. Neoliberals recognize that the Soviet Union stands to gain from instability but refuse to see Soviet agitation behind most nationalist or economic justice movements in Third World countries. As disciples of JFK, they believe in economic assistance and support of indigenous nationalist movements. Once again, they stand against the hawkish Reagan policies, but see themselves as much more determined and 'realistic' than liberals of the last decade.

Summary

As neoliberals move from analysis of problems toward programmes to solve them, they see a world of general drift and decline that clearly calls for new kinds of government action. Neoliberals are almost as pro-business as the Reagan administration, but from an entirely different perspective. They deny that the Reagan combination of *laissez faire* reliance on the free market and favouritism for the rich will succeed in benefitting the many whose interests depend on renewed economic growth. No single business or industry, or even the entire business community, has the perspective or capacity to forgo immediate advantages and act in the long-range interest of the whole economy. Only a well-designed and comprehensive programme of government incentives, assistance and upgrading of both physical infrastructure and human resources will generate a period of sustained and widespread prosperity.

Neoconservatism

Neoconservatism is a quite self-conscious movement of a small but highly visible number of intellectuals who are well grounded in the universities, the media, and the governing establishment. Many of these leaders were once active supporters of the New Deal; some even thought of themselves as socialists. Their rupture with liberalism and coalescence in the neoconservative movement was both a reaction against what they saw as the excesses of the 1960s and an insistence on carrying forward some vital aspects of the older liberalism to which they were committed.

The beginnings of neoconservatism date from 1965 and 1966 but it did not reach its peak of visibility and strength until the early 1970s. The development of neoconservatism was rapid, in part because the media were so readily available for attacks on the left by people who seemed to have been former members of that very left. Most of the energies of neoconservatism in the early years were invested in vigorous polemics against individual radicals, their claims and actions, and the public policies of liberal government. The business community was generous in its praise and assistance. Established conservative think-tanks gained new legitimacy from supporting the neoconservatives in a variety of ways. By 1976, neoconservatism had become well established as a major force on the American political spectrum.

Neoconservatives believe liberals have lost sight of some basic American principles, i.e. concern for individual freedom and a necessary vigilant anticommunism. Freedom was being forced to give way before an egalitarian onslaught. It needed defenders

before it was smothered by government programmes and regulations. Also, most neoconservatives were marked in some way by
the Cold War and the struggles against domestic communist influence in the 1940s and 1950s. Liberals, they argue, have forgotten all
the lessons of that period. In particular, liberal American foreign
policy, in the aftermath of Vietnam, lacked firmness and political
will. Neoconservatives believe that the carefully nurtured system
containing communism is crumbling in the face of Soviet military
strength and boldness and a failure of American resolve.

But the problems that neoconservatism sees as most important
are not rooted in economic conditions or social structures. Rather,
they lie in the values and beliefs of leaders and followers in the
American social system. In other words, with the exception of
Soviet military strength and worldwide subversive activities, problems do not have objective content. They are quite real, but they
take the form of willfulness or error in people's minds.

Irving Kristol, a leading neoconservative, sums up the movement's 'consensus' as support for the welfare state but opposition to
bureaucratic intrusion and paternalism; respect for the economic
market; support for traditional values and religion against the
'counterculture' and its threats to order; opposition to egalitarian-
ism in which 'everyone ends up with equal shares of everything';
and insistence on a strong anticommunist foreign policy.[1]

The thrust toward equality

For neoconservatives, the key to the failures of American leadership and the decline of the American civilization is the rise of a
new class of middle-class professionals opposed to the basic values
of the society that nurtured them. This new class started at an
unprecedented level of affluence, encountered little in the way of
character-building hardship and had easy access to higher education. Its energies flowed into the effort to enable everybody to enjoy
the same opportunities, with little or no realization of how difficult
that would be or why many people might not desire such ends. Most
damaging of all, this class, whether in government positions or in
private life, was pro-egalitarian and anti-business.

Therefore, the United States is now faced with the problem of
firmly depressing public expectations and bringing about a return to
realism in the people's public aspirations. It must also replace or
reconstruct the governing élite so as to install a new sense of the

limits of government capabilities and a chastened vision of the importance of equality. This latter principle – equality – is really the heart of the problem. Giving it first priority, and trying to achieve it, is the death warrant of free society. Nothing is more important than controlling the thrust toward equality.

The false god of equality has combined with the rise of self-indulgence and the decline of religion to make for a basic cultural opposition to capitalist-liberal society. Some neoconservatives term this an 'adversary culture' whose basic source lies with the 'new class' of anti-business professionals. The exact composition and nature of this new class is not easy to pin down, in part because neoconservatives variously see it as consisting of intellectuals, or intellectuals and professionals, or government workers, or all college-educated people. But it is certainly clear that the problem lies with this new class, whether defined and located specifically or broadly – and, more particularly, with the egalitarian and anti-business beliefs that they hold.

The second major problem that neoconservatism identifies is located, by contrast, in mass publics. The dominant American cultural dynamic from the 1960s to the present is one of indulgence and self-gratification. This is the 'Me Decade', in which everyone's demands on the economy and society simply cannot be met. It is just this inclination that the new class has encouraged by means of its continuing emphasis on the right to equality. The decisive weakness of contemporary élites, in other words, has linked with the dominant inclination of masses of people in an incendiary mixture.

A society in which everyone seeks the maximum possible benefit for himself or herself without regard to others is not a pleasant, or even governable, society. Somehow, this basic cultural principle has to be controlled, so that the appetites unleashed do not tear the society apart. The civility of the future depends on solving this problem.

Moral regeneration.
The other half of the neoconservative programme is to revitalise the religious grounding of today's capitalist order. Michael Novak has led the way in trying to provide a new justification for capitalism.[2] He begins *The Spirit of Democratic Capitalism* with the premise that no system of political economy has so improved the quality of life,

or been so lacking in theological justification, as democratic capitalism.

What distinguishes Novak's argument is his premise that the combination of a capitalist market economy and political democracy is not an historical accident but rather a necessary relationship – in which democracy depends on the existence of capitalism. He declares that 'economic liberties without political liberties are inherently unstable. Citizens economically free soon demand political freedoms'.[3] Free markets are the necessary condition precedent to democracy; democracy does not occur without them. To have and to hold political democracy, one must protect and preserve capitalism.

The problem, Novak admits, is that 'throughout the world, capitalism evokes hatred. . . . Even at home, within the United States, . . . the Achilles' heel of democratic capitalism is that for two centuries now it has appealed so little to the human spirit'.[4] Mere acquisitiveness is not an uplifting principle of life. It has so many destructive consequences that most people turn away in revulsion when the moral basis of capitalism is seen to consist of little else. Novak takes as his task, then, the obligation to specify which genuinely uplifting moral values underlie capitalism. He finds that democratic capitalism is distinguished by pluralism, the multiplicity of sets of relationships that assure that no single set of authorities will make all the decisions in the society. It is this differentiation of systems that protects all against unitary (and therefore arbitrary) power.

The ideals of democratic capitalism, Novak insists, are the very bedrock ideals of Christianity itself. He concludes:

> Almighty God did not make creation coercive, but designed it as an arena of liberty. Within that arena, God has called for individuals and peoples to live according to His law and inspiration. Democratic capitalism has been designed to permit them, sinners all, to follow this free pattern. It creates a noncoercive society as an arena of liberty, within which individuals and people are called to realize, through democratic methods, the vocations to which they believe they are called.[5]

Novak adds that God will judge whether people have in fact accomplished their tasks. By implication, democratic capitalism should be judged in terms of whether or not it has permitted them to do so.

This argument is neoconservatism's best effort to revive capitalism's underlying moral basis. It is not a programme for new public policies. Rather it is a programme for wholesale moral regeneration of millions of people. Its appeal to conservative intellectuals, and perhaps to theologians, seems clear. But its capacity to gain acceptance at the level of mass culture remains to be seen.

International relations

There is one area, however, where neoconservatism has a very concrete programme for new public policy. This is the field of international relations, particularly relations with the Soviet Union. Neoconservatism stands for vigorous development of American military power and a readiness to use it around the world to counter continuing Soviet expansion. Close relations with Israel are the cornerstone of Middle East policy thinking. A generally hard line in any arms limitation negotiations fits this perspective as well. This adds up to a frank commitment to acting to serve American national interests throughout the world, in confidence that by doing so the cause of freedom and democracy, as defined by neoconservatives, will simultaneously be served.

Summary

Much of the neoconservatives' reputation has been built on the style and acerbity of their critique of the New Left and the liberal effort to propitiate all demands. It has not really proposed a programme for governing, but only outlined a critique of those who do. Neoconservatives see a need to turn around the underlying culture and return to traditional values. Thus, with the exception of the military, the policies that follow neoconservative principles mainly mean a tearing apart of those programmes and policies associated with the New Deal and beyond.

Impact and implications

Should either neoliberalism or neoconservatism become the dominant political belief long enough to enact and implement its programmes, the United States would be started down a new road. At this point, neither has either the dominance or the political power to do so. However, we can look to the implications of their proposed programmes and policies and speculate about where they might lead.

If neoliberalism were successful in gaining the willing involvement of business, labour, and government – and in constructing mechanisms that would permit agreements to be reached and implemented – it would create a government capability unprecedented in American experience. With this new government role would come a mageralism and technocratic role for experts that would exceed even that of the early New Deal or the most engineering-oriented days of the Great Society.

However, neoliberalism presently amounts to a still-inchoate set of beliefs in search of a solid constituency. It is in effect a transitional category not yet fully formed or located on the evolving American spectrum. The intriguing question is, transitional to what? We have suggested that the essence of neoliberalism may be its perception of the need for, and insistent justification of, a much more pervasive role for government in the economy and society. What neoliberalism sees as at stake is the adaptation of the society to the fast-changing future. What it is striving for is a decisive vehicle to facilitate that adaptation.

Neoliberals are increasingly clear in their understanding of what is at stake. They are searching for ways to communicate the urgency of the need for an instrument of adaptation. Lester Thurow, for example, states the scope of change needed:

> The time has come, however, to admit that the pursuit of equity and equal economic opportunity demands a fundamental restructuring of the economy. Everyone who wants to work should have a chance to work. But there is no way to achieve that situation by tinkering marginally with current economic policies. The only solution is to create a socialized sector of the economy designed to give work opportunities to everyone who wants them but cannot find them elsewhere.[6]

And Robert Reich bluntly states the long-term nature of the neoliberal perspective: 'We're building new frameworks. Administrations come and go. The frameworks can remain for generations'.[7]

What neoliberalism counts on is the capacity of this new programme to mobilise support from a large number of people who recognise the need to think freshly about the country's broad range of unprecedented problems. It is not just economic revitalisation that they seek, but social and political revitalisation as well.

Despite its respectable origins, neoliberalism seems to be caught in the classic American dilemma. It offers a plausible and not very threatening route to social and economic improvement. However, when it comes down to actual implementation, its programme seems too radical for more than a small portion of it to be carried out. Most difficult of all is mobilising a constituency around a programme designed to save capitalism when that very capitalism is demonstrably unenthusiastic. Only prolonged economic crisis, with more drastic solutions being urged from both left and right, can really provide the electoral context for neoliberalism to gain enough strength to be a decisive force. At that point, it could succeed to liberalism's centre role on the American spectrum.

It is easy to overestimate the importance and strength of neoconservatism. Its intellectuals are very prolific and occupy highly visible positions. But there is certainly no mass following behind neoconservatism. The Old Right and the New Right, particularly the latter, have all the troops that fill the ranks of conservatism today.

But just as certainly, there is a significant audience among American intellectuals and policy-oriented élites and technicians. Between the universities, semi-popular policy journals, business press, foundations, and conservative think-tanks, a ready platform and a powerful audience are assured neoconservatism in ways not yet approached by other forms of conservatism. Neoconservatism's opportunity is great. The question seems to be whether it can make good on that opportunity.

Neoconservatism is really an intra-élite argument over the criteria to be employed in shaping public policy. It arose in rejection of the radical-liberal equality-promoting approach. It argued the case for limits – limits to promises, expectations, and government expansion. Its images of the good society were developed in order to support these policy criteria. It purposefully addressed only, but very effectively, a policy-oriented audience. Its principal target was the 'new class' and its beliefs.

Neoconservatism arose from, and has taken as its mission, the imperative of replacing or converting the policymaking stratum of American society. In other words, neoconservatism is about the loyalties and beliefs of the new class – its reconstruction, in fundamental ways, so that it acts upon the correct (neoconservative) values and principles. This clearly points toward a continuing agenda and role for neoconservatism. Furthermore, this role does not depend at all on developing a mass following. Neoconservatism addresses only the governing class, because in its view of the world that is the only group that matters. And there is every reason to believe that it will continue to play an important role in educating that new class of policy-oriented leaders. In time it could come to serve as the rationale or ideology of governing in the United States.

This possibility carries quite mixed implications. Peter Steinfels expresses one side of this prospect:

> The great danger posed by and to neoconservatism is that it will become nothing more than the legitimating and lubricating ideology of an oligarchic America where essential decisions are made by corporate elites, where great inequalities are rationalized by straitened circumstances and a system of meritocratic hierarchy, and where democracy becomes an occasional, ritualistic gesture.[8]

The other side is that neoconservatism might reintegrate with a future version of liberalism in a reconstituted centre of the American political spectrum. With its self-limited focus on élite attitudes and behaviour, and almost deliberate avoidance of efforts to gain a mass following, neoconservatism must always take its stance from where governing élites seem to be heading. And that, in turn, depends at some point on what numbers of Americans believe and are willing to support. Working through the operational practices of governing élites seems to be neoconservatism's best hope for continued impact on American life.

Neoliberal and/or neoconservative beliefs, in some form, are highly likely to shape future political ideas and practice in the United States. However, if they self-destruct or default, old-fashioned liberalism may again arise to pick up the pieces and play its familiar rôle as the lesser evil of the middle ground. American liberalism has demonstrated amazing resilience throughout American history, and thus the news of its death may be somewhat exaggerated. If so, neoliberalism and neoconservatism may turn out to be not so much rising stars as momentary meteorites.

Notes

1   Irving Kristol, 'What is a Neoconservative'? *Newsweek,* January 19 1976, p 87.
2   Michael Novak, *The Spirit of Democratic Capitalism, (*Simon and Schuster, New York, 1982).

3 Novak, p 15.

4 Novak, p 31.

5 Novak, pp 359–60.

6 Lester Thurow, *The Zero Sum Society,* (Basic Books: New York, 1980), p 206.

7 Robert Reich, quoted in *The New York Times Magazine,* August 28 1983, p 63.

8 Peter Steinfels, *The Neoconservatives: The Men Who Are Changing America's Politics,* (Simon and Schuster: New York, 1979), p 294.

For further information on neoliberalism, see: Amitai Etzioni, *An Immodest Agenda: Rebuilding America Before the 21st Century,* McGraw-Hill, New York, 1983; Robert Reich and Ira Magaziner, *Minding America's Business: the Decline and Rise of the American Economy*, Harcourt, Brace & Jovanich, New York, 1982; Robert Reich, *The Next American Frontier*, Times Books, New York, 1983; Lester Thurow, *The Zero-Sum Society*, Basic Books, New York, 1980. For further information on neoconservatism, see: Daniel Bell, *the Cultural Contradictions of Capitalism*, Basic Books, New York, 1976; Philip Green, *The Pursuit of Inequality*, Pantheon Books, New York, 1981; Irving Kristol, *Two Cheers for Capitalism*, Basic Books, New York, 1978; George H. Nash, *The Conservative Intellectual Movement in America Since 1945*, Basic Books, New York, 1976; Michael Novak, *The Spirit of Democratic Capitalism*, Simon and Schuster, New York, 1972.

Paul Watanabe

Religion and politics: the rise of the new Christian right

Introduction

Thomas Jefferson regarded the struggle to erect a wall of separation between Church and State as one of the three important actions of his life, on a par with his founding of the University of Virginia and his authorship of the Declaration of Independence. The wall has been a sturdy one, particularly in preventing any significant tampering by government with the freedom of religious expression. Encroachments in the other direction, however, that is religious excesses impinging on the political realm, have been more common. The recent rise of political activism by the new Christian right constitutes the most formidable challenge yet to the principle that religion and politics should not mix.

A decade ago, Albert Menendez, in his book *Religion at the Polls,* described the evangelical and fundamentalist Christian vote as 'the sleeping giant of American politics'.[1] Within a few short years after Menendez's prediction the 'giant' had surely awakened. Large numbers of conservative Christians have jumped into the political arena at all levels of government and have pursued a broad political agenda ranging from concern over the content of elementary school textbooks to the size of the national defence budget.

The rise of the new Christian right

While it is difficult to determine precisely the number of Americans who can be characterised as evangelicals and fundamentalists, most observers agree that they comprise a substantial portion of the populace. The Gallup Organization, for example, has determined that about 20 per cent of the total adult population, or 30 million

Americans, could be categorised as evangelicals. Gallup defines evangelicals as individuals who display three characteristics: they describe themselves as 'born again Christians' or have had a 'born again' experience; they have encouraged other people to believe in Jesus Christ; and they believe in a literal interpretation of the Bible. A *New York Times*/CBS News poll applied a less rigorous definition of evangelicals and found that 42 per cent of those surveyed indicated that they had experienced a conversion to Christ as their saviour. Utilising this percentage, one can estimate that over 65 million adult Americans have had such a conversion.

Fundamentalist Protestants also constitute a considerable portion of the Christian right. Strictly speaking, evangelicals and fundamentalists share similar values and beliefs. Fundamentalists tend to be more doctrinaire and less flexible in their interpretations of the Bible, and less ecumenical in outlook. A conservative estimate of those who would be considered wholehearted fundamentalists is 10 million.

The most remarkable aspect of the rise of the new Christian right is the speed with which the activists have moved from the periphery of politics to centre stage. For conservative evangelicals and fundamentalists the immersion in politics represents the abrupt abandonment of the belief that politics is an undesirable and unworthy secular diversion that is incompatible with their faith. This stunning transformation has been described by Richard John Neuhaus, director of the Center for the Study of Society and Religion, in this fashion:

> Since the Scopes Trial, it has been assumed that the fundamentalist Christian community represented a declining, residual phenomenon. You started to get some rumblings of change . . . in the elections of 1976 and '80. Now the whole thing has reached a dangerous crescendo. The media and political elite are in culture shock. 'Where the hell are these people coming from?' they're asking . . . We have to face the fact that, whatever we think of their politics or theology, a group that's been out in the political wilderness now has an exultant sense of headiness about their new power.[2]

The politics of the new Christian activists are decidedly conservative. Unsurprisingly, the results of polling by Gallup indicate that the Christian right tends to be considerably more Republican and more pro-Reagan than the general population. Furthermore, the most politically active of the religious right tends to be the most staunchly ultraconservative element in American society. The widely shared ideological bent of the activists manifests itself in complaints about the alleged moral decay of America. 'The godless minority of treacherous individuals', Reverend Jerry Falwell, the major figure of the religious right, has declared, 'must now realize they do not represent the majority. They must be made to see that moral Americans will no longer permit them to destroy our country with their godless, liberal philosophies'.[3] An even more pointed expression of this outlook can be found in the statement of purpose of Christian Voice, a powerful Christian fundamentalist organis- ation. 'We believe that America, the last stronghold of faith on this planet, has come under increasing attack from Satanist forces in recent years, that the standards of Christian morality are now under the onslaught launched by the 'rulers of darkness of this world' and insiduously sustained under the ever more liberal ethic'.[4]

Positions such as these extend the boundaries of traditionally legitimate political discourse. 'What is alarming about these pronouncements', Seymour Lipset and Earl Raab have observed, 'is their fanaticism. If a political opponent is just wrong, or stupid, or misguided, he can presumably be dealt with in the marketplace of ideas. But when his political opinions arise from deliberate moral wickedness, as this kind of rhetoric implies, a case can be made that he does not deserve to be in the debate at all. It is only one step from here to a full-fledged conspiracy theory, wherein a cabal of evil men conspires secretly to thwart the popular will. This, of course, is the very model of political extremism'.[5]

The clash with modernity and the defense of activism

A compelling theme in many attempts to explain the cultural and political conservatism of the new religious right has been the clash between the traditionalism of the evangelicals and fundamentalists and the sweep of modernity. Faced with the forces of modernism – urbanisation, cosmopolitanism, industrialisation, and social and economic mobilisation – those with a stake in the past, those that seem to have been cast aside in the onrush, and those that were the least able to adjust to rapid change have found stability, strength, guidance, and a rallying point in their religion. For these people, progress has been viewed not as the search for truths but as the renunciation of Truth. Change has meant moral decay, not growth.

The outrage of the castaways has manifested itself in the rejection of liberal notions that linked the proliferation of individual rights and values with the sweep of social change. From here it is only a short step to identify intrusive government as the instrument of the old order's decline. The collision of forces representing secular change and traditional values has resulted in a tension that the devoutly religious have resolved by leaning more heavily on religious dogma and, ironically, by embracing politics.

The appeal of the church has been strong for those individuals who feel a great sense of separation between their private selves and public institutions and policies. The church, along with other agencies, has served as a convenient and logical bridge between the two realms. Theodore Kerrine and Richard John Neuhaus have called these linkages 'mediating structures', and they have applauded their emergence:

> Mediating structures are those institutions that stand between the individual in his private life and the large institutions of modern society. Examples include families, churches, voluntary associations, and neighbourhoods. . . . From the perspective of society, mediating structures provide a moral foundation in their ability to generate and sustain values where the megastructures offer mainly impersonal processes. Thus, mediating structures contribute to the well-being of the individual and the moral integrity of the larger society.[6]

This argument suggests that it is unrealistic and indeed harmful for mediating structures, including religious institutions, to remain apart from the determination of governmental policies. The requirement that churches play an active role in public discourse challenges the notion of the separation of religion and politics. Kerrine and Neuhaus have been cognisant of this challenge and have not backed down from their firm advocacy of religious activism:

> As the largest voluntary network in America churches need not be apologetic regarding their participation in public affairs. Churches can and do play an active rôle in public policy in a number of ways. they serve to inform and reinforce the values of their members and, indirectly, even of non-members. They function as advocacy groups on issues of social justice. . . . They serve as providers of services in ways that reflect and give meaning to their own world views.[7]

In response to this line of reasoning, detractors might wonder whether the support for religious penetration into political affairs should still hold when religious activists militate against the expansion of social justice and for the imposition of a decidedly narrow and intolerant world view? Must healthy scepticism about the performance of governmental structures and politicians necessarily require a firmer embrace of values and ideas generated by religious institutions?

Clearly one thing often absent from the arguments of proponents and opponents of religious encroachments into politics is consistency. Beliefs about the desirability of church intervention are dependent upon several factors, including one's own views on issues under consideration. When the church actively supports causes congenial to one's own interests, individuals tend to favour religious activism. On the other hand, those who oppose positions taken by churches or religious leaders are more inclined to support the maintenance of a high barrier between politics and religion. For their part, conservative Christians have railed against what they have perceived as the application of a double standard to evaluate their activities. They have argued that when liberal causes, such as the struggle to end the Vietnam War, support for nuclear arms control, and involvement in the civil rights movement, have been championed by various religious groups and leaders, there has been no torrent of criticism and worry about whether the line between church and state has been dangerously breeched. Howard Phillips, founder and chairman of the Conservative Caucus, has argued that the new Christian right has simply created an alternative to what he has described as 'an old boy liberal network' that has operated for years. According to Phillips, 'I'm delighted that religious conservatives and Christian conservatives have become active in the same way to try to get more people of a similar view into public service'[8]

Mobilising the faithful

The attack on modernity that Lipset and Raab and others have identified as behind the rise of the new religious right has ironically been aided consciously and adroitly by the mastery of modern communication technologies, most significantly television. It is not coincidental that the rise of the Christian right has been accompanied by the emergence of what has been dubbed 'the electric church'. The politics of the revival tent have been transformed by a network of some 1,300 radio and television stations that are devoted to religious programming and that touch every corner of the country. Television preachers with their sights set on shaping the political landscape and with their hands open to receive enormous sums of money to promote their causes have been the driving force behind the emergence of the religious right as a force to be reckoned with. Over half of the nation's population has listened to these programmes and 30 per cent of the public watch or listen to religious broadcasts regularly. The most successful television evangelists, like Jerry Falwell, Pat Robertson, and James Robison, have become celebraties, commanding large audiences and each generating over $1 million per week in contributions. Robertson's 'The 700 Club' programme, for example, is seen in over 16 million homes. His Christian Broadcasting Network operates with an annual budget of $230 million. Over 21 million persons see or hear Falwell's 'Old Time Gospel Hour', which appears on 681 television and radio stations. Another Falwell programme, 'Jerry Falwell Live', is transmitted to 34 million homes a week on Ted Turner's cable 'superstation' WTBS. It is not surprising given the skilful way in which the religious right has manipulated television to enhance its legions and fill its coffers that Robertson has described one of the most important turning points in his life as the moment when the Lord told him: 'Pat, I want you to have an RCA transmitter'.[9]

The new religious right is also characterised by a sophisticated network of organisations, both national and local, that are able to perform a number of functions – lobbying, education, voter registration and mobilisation, watchdogging, fund-raising, various legal services, and myriad of support-building tasks. The American Coalition for Traditional Values, Christian Voice, the Religious Roundtable, and Robertson's Freedom Council are among the most influential groups. The Liberty Federation (the name was recently changed from the Moral Majority) is the largest and best-known of these organisations. Founded in 1979 by Falwell, the organisation claims a nationwide membership of 6.5 million.

The political agenda

More important than the television and radio programmes and organisations of the religious right are the broad and ambitious political ends that these means are designed to serve. 'The Moral

Majority', William L. Miller of the University of Virginia has observed, 'is combining its conviction on certain more traditionally religious issues, like abortion and school prayer, with its support for general issues in public policy, such as a strong defense and strong economy, and claiming a moral grounding for the whole package. That combination is a new strain in our history'.[10] The agenda of the Christian right is wide-ranging because it does not acknowledge distinctions between moral and political issues. The core concerns involve family, school, church, and country. These concerns have been translated by significant segments of the religious right into stances such as opposition to the Equal Rights Amendment, gay rights, abortion, pornography, gun control, and the transfer of ownership of the Panama Canal, and support for the Strategic Defence Initiative ('Star Wars'), a constitutional amendment requiring a balanced federal budget, and aid to the anti-government rebels in Nicaragua. Two issues that are illustrative of the activism and concerns of the new Christian right are abortion and the conduct of public schools.

Abortion

The Supreme Court's 1973 decision in *Roe v. Wade* reaffirmed a woman's right to obtain an abortion. Advocates of every woman's right to control her own body and of a mother or couple's right to choose whether or not to abort a deformed or damaged foetus lauded the decision. For those in the so-called 'prolife' movement, the court's action meant the sanctioning of mass murder; since 1973, abortion has become the most widely-performed surgical procedure in the United States. Opponents of abortion generally agree that human life commences at conception, and, therefore, the destruction of foetuses is the sinful termination of unborn life. Opposition to abortion has become the single most important cause generating political activism from the religious right.

Until recently, the anti-abortion fight in the United States had been led by Catholics. Elements within the Catholic Church have not been shy about directly entering the political arena when they deemed it necessary. Vice-presidential candidate Geraldine Ferraro, for example, was publicly chastised on numerous occasions by Archbishop O'Connor of New York for her prochoice position. In a similar fashion, the Archbishop of Boston, Cardinal Humberto

Medeiros, once tried to influence voters by issuing a pastoral letter attempting to dissuade them from supporting Barney Frank, an aspirant for the United States House of Representatives, because of his abortion stand. The Cardinal wrote: 'Those who make abortions possible by law – such as legislators and those who promote, defend, and elect these same lawmakers – cannot separate themselves from that guilt which accompanies this horrendous crime. It is imperative that Catholics realize the law of God extends into the polling booth.'[11] Frank won the election decisively. It is interesting to note that the congressional seat that Frank secured became vacant only after the incumbent, Robert Drinan, a Jesuit priest, was instructed by his superiors in the church to retire from office partly because of his liberal views on abortion.

Although the Catholic Church still remains a driving force in the anti-abortion movement, the new Christian right has seized upon the issue with unmatched fervour. Lobbying activities and information campaigns have brought the issue of abortion to the forefront of American politics. Picketing of abortion clinics has been a common tactic. Recently, however, protests directed at these clinics have in many cases become much more violent. Women arriving at clinics in many locations have been taunted and harassed by angry lines of protesters. Fundamentalist activists have been linked with a disturbing trend of increased bombings of abortion centres. Although this violence has generally been condemned by most of the major anti-abortion organisations and leaders, many abortion opponents have been quick to point out that the destruction of helpless foetuses is in their view a much greater tragedy.

Christian activists have endeavoured to elect politicians at all levels of government who possess the 'right' position on abortion. Religious right organisations, for example, were an integral part of a collection of conservative groups that successfully engineered the unseating of several prochoice United States Senators, including Frank Church, Birch Bayh, John Culver, Dick Clark, and George McGovern. In 1978, legislative allies of the religious right were instrumental in securing passage of the Hyde Amendment, which stipulated that Medicaid money could no longer be used to fund abortions except in cases of rape or incest or when the life of the mother was seriously endangered. Many state legislators have also been persuaded to adopt laws restricting the use of state funds for abortions. Anti-abortionists have encountered more difficulty in

garnering enough support for passage of a constitutional measure
called 'the Human Life Amendment'. The language of the proposed
amendment deems life to exist from conception and, thereby, if
passed, would effectively outlaw abortions.

President Reagan has been a strong ally of the anti-abortionists.
In a statement marking the tenth anniversary of *Roe v. Wade,*
Reagan reaffirmed his position: 'I have always believed that God's
greatest gift is human life and that we have a duty to protect the life
of the unborn child. Until someone can prove the unborn child is
not a life, shouldn't we give it the benefit of the doubt and assume it
is? That's why I favoured legislation to end the practice of abortion
on demand and why I will continue to support it'.[12]

On the abortion question, as on many other issues that have
mobilised the new religious right, the courts have been regarded as
vital arenas. The support for Reagan granted by the anti-
abortionists is likely to yield a more favourable reception in the
courts for their position. By the end of Reagan's second term,
approximately 45 per cent of all federal judges would be Reagan
appointees. Reagan has noted that the long-range impact of this
shaping of the federal courts will be the establishment of a judicial
environment more receptive to his views on various issues including
abortion.

Public education

In 1925, a small, overheated courtroom in Dayton, Tennessee was
the setting for one of the most celebrated trials in American history.
Legal giants Clarence Darrow and William Jennings Bryan jousted
as schoolteacher John T. Scopes was tried for teaching the biological theory of evolution in defiance of a state law against teaching
doctrines deemed contrary to the Bible. Scopes was found guilty
and fined $100.00.

Forty-five years later, in Greenville, Tennessee, a few hours'
drive from Dayton, a group of fundamentalist Christian parents
sued their school board for subjecting their children to 'anti-
Christian' and 'heathen' textbooks. Complainants in the case, which
was dubbed 'Scopes II', testified that the assigned texts promul-
gated themes that conflicted with biblical teachings. Testimony
indicated that some of the allegedly contrary themes included an
improper suggestion of gender roles (e.g. a young boy in one of the

stories is said to 'have fun' while cooking); an attack on capitalism (e.g. a story questions the importance of defining worth chiefly in monetary terms); and the promotion of witchcraft (e.g. the story of 'the Three Little Pigs' ends with the pigs dancing joyfully as the big, bad wolf is consumed by fire). Also deemed objectionable were references to witches and wizards in King Arthur, Shakespeare, and *Cinderella,* and some dialogue from the programme *Sesame Street.*

The Greenville case and others like it reflect the importance that Christian activists have placed on the schools as arenas in the battle for children's minds. They have focused on issues such as textbooks and teaching methods, prayer in schools, sex education, and vouchers for private school students. School officials and politicians are blamed for promoting the sinister notion of 'secular humanism' and for contributing to the perceived breakdown of America's moral fabric. The liberalisation of education, the promotion of 'secular humanism' and 'situation ethics', the suppression of religious training, and the absence of stern classroom discipline have been identified by many conservative Christians as among the root causes of growing problems such as teenage pregnancy, pornography, drug and alcohol abuse, juvenile delinquency and youth suicide. Often cited as symbolic of the total breakdown of public education are the repeated failures of the courts to lift the ban on school prayer.

In many of the battles over the direction of the public schools, parents are locally-based and loosely-organised. Larger groups, however, do make available a number of services including educational and promotional materials, financial and organisational assistance, moral support, and legal advice. In the Greenville case, Concerned Women of America, a conservative Christian organisation, provided legal representation for the plaintiff families. Advice on textbooks is often sought from Texans Mel and Norma Gabler, who have gained fame for their critical assessments of standard school books. Heavy reliance is also placed on prominent conservative Phyllis Schlafly's book *Child Abuse in the Classroom* to guide troubled fundamentalist parents.

The political activities of the religious right in trying to control what goes on in the classroom have taken a variety of forms and met with mixed success. Isolated instances of public book-burnings have been staged, and censorship of some textbooks and libraries has occurred. The efforts to launch a massive drive to legislate prayer in the classroom and to establish a constitutional amendment lifting the ban on prayer are decidedly long-shots. The passage of laws allowing the establishment of tuition tax credits for the support of private schools is much more likely to succeed. School boards and administrators have been targeted for law suits, as in the Greenville case, or, more commonly and effectively, have been targeted for political punishment. Precious school resources have been drained in exhaustive legal skirmishes, and, in some instances, control of local school boards has been gained by aroused fundamentalists.

Perhaps the greatest impact of the right-wing Christian activists has been in the manner in which they have ensconsed themselves in their communities as watchdogs. Many school officials and teachers have been made aware in both subtle and overt ways that they will be held accountable for their conduct. Undoubtedly, in some cases, the mere presence of the activists has forced educators to modify their curriculum and methods for fear of having their patriotism or personal integrity called into question.

The fundamentalist cause was given a substantial boost when President Reagan appointed William Bennett to serve in his cabinet as Secretary of Education. Although both the religious right and Reagan have threatened to dismantle the Department of Education, for the time being at least, conservative Christians are satisfied that the secretary shares their views on the relationship between religion and politics. In one of his first speeches after being appointed, Bennett condemned the Supreme Court for 'misguided rulings that have removed religious influence from the public schools'.[13] In addition, he has stated: 'it is easier to repeat, like an incantation, the phrases 'wall of separation' or 'no entanglement of church and state', than to think seriously about such issues as the relationship of religious beliefs and self-government. The attitude that regards 'entanglement' with religion as something akin to entanglement with an infectious disease must be confronted broadly and directly'.[14]

To find a response to Bennett, one can turn back the clock almost 140 years to a time when some citizens of the state of Massachusetts were advocating the reintroduction of sectarian religious teaching into the public schools. Horace Mann, who was secretary of the Massachusetts Board of Education and was probably the nation's most prominent figure in the development of public education, was the target of most of the pressure. Mann, who was deeply religious and a strong believer in the importance of religious training, nevertheless felt that there was no place for that training in the public schools. Although addressing a mid-nineteenth century audience, Mann's words in his 1848 annual report on the schools remain germane:

> The old spirit of religious domination is adopting new measures to accomplish its work – measures which, if successful, will be as fatal to the liberties of mankind as those which were practised in bygone days of violence and terror. These new measures are aimed at children instead of men. They propose to supersede the necessity of subduing free thought *in the mind of the adult,* by forestalling the development of any capacity of free thought *in the mind of the child*. They expect to find it easier to subdue the free agency of children by binding them in fetters of bigotry than to subdue the free agency of men by binding them in fetters of iron.[15]

Candidates for Christ

At a conference sponsored by the American Coalition for Traditional Values, Jerry Falwell proclaimed that the only way to save an America 'going to hell' is for more Christians to seek and win public office. 'We are winning; it isn't a question of if, only when'.[16] Echoing the same theme as Falwell, Pat Robertson, in a letter soliciting support for his presidential delegate search in Michigan, began by announcing, 'the Christians have won'. Robertson went on to state: 'What a thrust for freedom. What a breakthrough for the Kingdom. . . . As believers become involved in this process, they will be able to turn this nation back to its traditional moral values'.[17]

These comments reflect the bold initiatives that evangelical and fundamentalist Christians have taken to involve Christian activists in the political decisionmaking process, either indirectly as delegates and voters or directly as candidates for office. The message is clear: the salvation of the society rests on the meshing of religion and politics; their separation spells doom.

The biggest political victories claimed so far by the religious right have been the election and re-election of Ronald Reagan. Reverend Falwell, on the night the Republican nominees were selected, told the delegates assembled in Dallas that Reagan and George Bush were 'God's instruments for rebuilding America'.[18] For the Christian right, Reagan pushed all the right buttons. He proclaimed the need to return to traditional values of family, home, and church. He was both deeply pained and angered by the alleged decline of morality in American society and the retreat from power abroad. And, just like the religious right, Reagan found a convenient and popular scapegoat in liberal policies and a government that had apparently lost touch with the people.

Although the claims by many in the new Christian right that they were chiefly responsible for Reagan's electoral successes are overstated, there can be little doubt that fundamentalists and evangelicals were enlisted in large numbers as soldiers in the Reagan revolution. The relationship between Reagan and the religious right has, therefore, been symbiotic. To the delight of Christian activists, Reagan has courted them unashamedly and, at least in his rhetoric, championed their treasured causes. Conservative Christians have, for their part, helped to deliver convincing victories for Reagan, demonstrating their strength in particular in the South, Midwest, and West. There have, of course, been some quarrels between Reagan and elements in the religious right. Bush's selection as the vice presidential standardbearer was vigorously opposed by some leaders, and, although Bush with his eye on the presidential nomination in 1988 has carefully strived to bolster his conservative credentials, the religious right still views him generally with some suspicion. The nomination of Sandra Day O'Connor to fill a vacancy on the Supreme Court was dismaying to many who found her too liberal. Some grumbling has also surfaced over the pace of Reagan's avowed goal of pursuing the religious right's political agenda. Pet projects like the introduction of constitutional amendments allowing school prayer and banning abortion have been placed on the back burner. Despite these disagreements, however, the relationship between Reagan and the conservative Christians has remained solid. Indeed, the political clout of the new religious right will certainly undergo a stern test when Reagan passes from the scene.

Conclusion

One might observe the current State and Church controversy in the United States and wonder what the fuss is all about. Politicians have never been shy about ritualistically asserting their religiosity. In this vein, one can recall the story of a British member of

Parliament, who, after the 1928 debate in the House of Commons on the Revised Book of Prayer, wondered why the discussion was so heated. 'Surely', said he, 'we all believe in some kind of something'.

The litmus test applied by the new Christian right for politicians and officials at various levels of government, however, has been a good deal stricter than simply asserting a belief in 'some kind of something'. The Christian fundamentalist organisation Christian Voice, for example, regularly issues 'morality ratings' of members of Congress. To score high, officeholders must support prayer in schools, a balanced budget, the dismantling of the Department of Education, and recognition of Taiwan as the legitimate government of China. They should oppose abortion rights, homosexual rights, the Equal Rights Amendment, and sanctions against Zimbabwe and South Africa. In short, virtually no major issue has escaped Christian Voice's ability to specify pro and anti-family and pro and anti-God positions. As Richard Jarmin, legislative director of *Christian Voice* and the religious right's most influential lobbyist, has asserted:

> The humanist trend denies there are any absolutes, any good or evil. It's okay to be gay; if it feels good, do it. That's a hedonistic mentality. There are absolutes and we have to make judgements about what is right or wrong. We don't call ourselves *the* Christian Voice, but we certainly believe ours is the correct one. The competing values right now are theistic and humanistic. You will have competition between them, but you cannot have peaceful coexistence because they are so totally opposite one another. This argument of pluralism is nonsense. You can have different political philosophies, but most in a society must agree with each other.[19]

A disturbing consequence of these religious tests is the growing spectre of divisiveness and factionalism. Spurious morality and treacherous acts of intolerance threaten to darken the political landscape. Pat Robertson, for example, has argued rather matter-of-factly that 'Christians feel more strongly about love of country, love of God, and support for the traditional family than do non-Christians'.[20]

A number of times throughout this chapter the leaders of the new Christian right have been quoted at length. Perhaps a good way to end, therefore, would be to include the thoughts of a critic of the rise of the religious right. A. Bartlett Giamatti, when he was president of Yale University, welcomed the new incoming class of students a few years ago with these words:

> A self-proclaimed 'Moral Majority' and its satellite or client groups, cunning in the use of a native blend of old intimidation and new technology, threaten the values I have named. Angry at change, rigid in the application of chauvinistic slogans, absolutistic in morality, they threaten through political pressure or public denunciation whoever dares to disagree with their authoritarian positions. Using television, direct mail, and economic boycott, they would sweep before them anyone who holds a different opinion.
>
> From the maw of this 'morality' come those who presume to know which books are fit to read, which television programmes are fit to watch, which textbooks will serve for all the young; come spilling those who presume to know what God alone knows, which is when human life begins. From the maw of this 'morality' rise the tax-exempt Savonarolas who believe they, and they alone, possess the truth. There is no debate, no discussion, no dissent. They know. There is only one set of overarching political, spiritual and social beliefs; whatever view does not conform to these views is by definition relativistic, negative, secular, immoral, against the family, anti-free enterprise, un-American. What nonsense . . .
>
> Those voices of coercion speak not for liberty but for license, the license to divide in the name of patriotism, the license to deny in the name of Christianity. And they have licensed a new meanness of spirit in our land, a resurgent bigotry that manifests itself in racist and discriminatory postures; in threats of political retaliation; in injunctions to censorship; in acts of violence.[21]

The thunder generated by the new religious right has unleashed a storm of controversy in the United States. Whether the new Christian activist movement is a temporary spasm or a more enduring feature of the political environment remains to be seen. The issues that it has raised, however, have been perennial ever since the founding of the nation: intimidation versus tolerance and absolutism versus pluralism.

Notes

1 Quoted in Dudley Clendinen, 'Reverend Falwell inspires evangelical vote', *New York Times*, 20 August 1980, p. B22.
2 Quoted in Richard Higgins, 'Is wall Jefferson built in danger?' *Boston Globe*, 9 September 1984, p. 89.

3 Jerry Falwell, *Listen America*, Doubleday, Garden City, NY, p. 12.
4 Quoted in Seymour Martin Lipset and Earl Raab, 'The election & the evangelicals', *Commentary*, March, 1981, p 27.
5 Lipset and Raab, p 27.
6 Theodore Kerrine and Richard John Neuhaus, 'Mediating structures: a paradigm for democratic pluralism', *The Annals of the American Academy of Political and Social Science*, 446, November 1979, p 11.
7 ibid., p 15.
8 Quoted in Judi Hasson, 'Grasping for power', *Patriot Ledger*, 10 October 1985, p 29.
9 Quoted in David Nyhan, 'Mr pray TV bombs in Michigan', *Boston Globe*, 10 August 1986, p 21.
10 Quoted in Higgins, p 90.
11 Quoted in Anthony J. Lukas, *Common Ground: A Turbulent Decade in the Lives of Three American Families*, Knopf, NY, 1985, p 402.
12 *New York Times*, 23 January 1983.
13 Quoted in Hasson, p 29.
14 William J. Bennett, 'Founders wanted religious values', *USA Today*, 12 August 1985, P 8A.
15 Quoted in Joseph L. Blau (ed), *Cornerstones of Religious Freedom in America*, Beacon Press, Boston, 1949, pp 200–1.
16 *Boston Globe*, 10 October 1985.
17 *Boston Globe*, 4 August 1986.
18 Quoted in David Nyhan, 'Another voice out of Virginia', *Boston Globe*, 9 September 1984, p 93.
19 Quoted in Perry Deane Young, *God's Bullies*, Holt, Rinehart & Winston, NY, 1982, p 102.
20 Quoted in Nyhan, 'Mr pray TV bombs in Michigan', p 21.
21 Quoted in Young, pp 330–2.

Gillian Peele

Women's issues in American politics

The last part of the Reagan years found the American women's movement in a somewhat depressed mood. Although the 1986 mid-term elections saw the election of a number of additional women to Congress and to significant state-wide offices, women's groups were adjusting to an environment in which they were having to fight to preserve hard-won advances rather than adding to their agenda of issues. The loss of the Equal Rights Amendment had underlined the extent to which there was a grass roots opposition to the feminist cause and the way in which issues related to women's social, economic and political status had become part of a wider conflict about family values.[1] The concern with budget deficits and the general approach of the administration to domestic spending made the political climate hostile to attempts to alleviate poverty in American society – a poverty which was increasingly seen as particularly likely to affect women. The nomination of William Rehnquist to be Chief Justice of the United States was a reminder of the fact that the ideological impact of the Reagan years was likely to outlast the period of the Reagan presidency and would leave a legacy of judicial appointments calculated to be antagonistic to the women's lobby. Even if it is impossible in the space of a short article to do justice to the complexities of the debate about women's issues in contemporary America, it may be possible to present an over-view of the women's agenda and to outline some aspects of the political strategy which the women's lobby has adopted. Before identifying the key issues of concern to the various women's groups in 1986, however, it is necessary to say a little about the Equal Rights Amendment both because that issue polarised the debate about women's issues in America and because its defeat created

great uncertainty about the future agenda of the women's
movement.

The defeat of the ERA

The Equal Rights Amendment is one of six constitutional amendments (and only the second in this century) to fail to be ratified by
the states after passage through Congress.[2] For its proponents it was
the 'heart and soul of the contemporary women's peaceful revolution' and the 'legal bedrock' on which all other changes were to be
inscribed.[3] For its opponents, the ERA threatened the family unit
and its ambiguity appeared to offer an invitation for a new round of
judicial activism.[4] Yet the degree of the polarisation – while clearly
visible from the perspective of the mid-1980s – was not apparent
when the ERA was passed by Congress in 1971–72. Then it seemed
that the proposal was based on consensus and indeed this view was
seemingly confirmed by the quick ratification of the amendment by
the legislatures of 35 of the 38 states necessary for passage. After
the easy first stage, however, the amendment ran into difficulty and
even after a controversial extension of the time limit for state
ratification in 1978, it died in 1982. Although this was not the first
effort to secure a constitutional guarantee of female equality – and
will certainly not be the last – the experience revealed much about
the changing character of American politics and about some of its
structural constraints.

The period during which the battle for the ratification of the ERA
was fought out was one of deep and fundamental change in
American politics – change which went beyond the simple oscill-
ations of party support and administrative turnover. It was a period
when the familiar issues of economic policy were complemented by
ones of morality, lifestyle and culture. Initially the impetus for this
expanded agenda came from the left, with its emphasis on such
'post-material' themes as environmentalism. In the mid-1970s,
however, the activity on the right was at least equally pronounced as
groups mobilised to fight permissiveness in American society.
Political parties found themselves unable to control forces they
were used to mediating, as issues such as the war in Vietnam, black
power, abortion and gay rights produced activists intent on using
the parties primarily for the pursuit of a single cause. And, in this
environment of decentralised politics, the new right honed its

organisational skills, cultivated issues which might be exploited by such new techniques of electioneering as direct mail, and developed a plausible alternative to the liberalism which had dominated American political thought for so long.

The issue of the Equal Rights Amendment offered conservative groups an opportunity to mobilise at the grass roots around the 'family values' that formed a central part of their coalitions and their fund-raising. It also helped cement the alliance between the political new right and the emergent force of the religious right. Phyllis Schlafly's 'Stop ERA' and 'Eagle Forum' organisations gained much of the credit for preventing the ratification of the amendment but these were part of a much larger crusade – a struggle for what they called 'the soul of America' in which liberals, universities and secular humanists were lined up on one side and traditional, religious middle America lined up on the other.[5]

Debate about the responsibility for the defeat of ERA will doubtless continue. Apart from the changed political situation which has meant that appeals to egalitarian values will no longer automatically be persuasive, some commentators have emphasised the difficulty of passing any constitutional amendment in the United States.[6] Article V of the Constitution requires that a proposal must first be passed by two-thirds of both houses of Congress and then be ratified by the legislatures of three-fourths of the states – a requirement which by 1972 meant 38 states had to ratify if an amendment was to be successful. (Alternatively the legislatures of two-thirds of the states may ask Congress to call a convention to consider constitutional amendments, although this procedure has never yet been used). In a political system whose procedures are designed to preclude hasty initiatives based on transient majorities, the requirement demands a breadth and depth of consensus that is hard to achieve. Of course, some amendments have been passed, and not all of them with the unusual form of persuasion exerted by the federal government after the Civil War.[7] However, it remains true that the process is a difficult one, which requires lobbying at both the federal and the state levels. In the case of ERA the speed with which the proposal, having passed Congress, was ratified by the first batch of states may have deceived the women's groups into a false sense of complacency just as the apparent absurdity of many of the views of their opponents – who suggested *inter alia* that ERA would prohibit separate toilet facilities for men and women and make women subject to precisely the same military obligations as men – may have led them to underestimate those opponents' political support.

There was a strong regional quality to the opposition to the ERA. It was in Southern legislatures that the amendment was stalled, although some non-Southern states – notably Utah and the crucial state of Illinois – also failed to ratify it. In the South, cultural conservatism combined with political structures which the pro-ERA lobbyists found difficult to penetrate. Thus, one female lobbyist in Virginia found that the legislature was dominated by senior politicians who were determined to prevent the issue from coming to a floor vote. Virginia was one of the key states needed for ratification of the ERA, but the entrenched power of a small group meant that it was kept in committee. Supporters of the ERA might claim that had the issue come to a floor vote they would have won and that it was undemocratic to allow the hangovers of an earlier age to impede full discussion of the amendment; the ERA went unratified in Virginia.[8]

Finally, some scholars have emphasised the extent to which the ERA was affected by the onset of the debate about abortion.[9] In 1973 the Supreme Court affirmed the constitutional right of women to have an abortion in the first trimester of pregnancy, although the decision sparked off a major political conflict.[10] For the women's movement, freedom to control reproduction was essential and the Supreme Court's decision had to be supported. For many church groups, however, the abortion issue was morally sensitive and the equation of female equality with abortion rights was damaging. Inevitably, the increasingly strident new right and new religious right linked the two issues in a way which brought more enemies to the cause of the ERA.

The failure of the ERA meant that a number of laws which treated women differently from men remained on the books within the several state jurisdictions. Although some 16 states had inserted equal rights provisions into their constitutions, as the Civil Rights Commission pointed out in a study designed to encourage ratification, there were still a number of anomalies and inequities in the various states' handling of such matters as inheritance, divorce and domicile.[11] At one point it had seemed that the Supreme Court might itself declare sex discrimination unconstitutional but the fact that sexual equality was a live issue within the political process in the form of the ERA may have discouraged the Court from elevating sex discrimination to a 'suspect category' which would demand strict judicial scrutiny. The failure of the amendment also seemed to preclude judicial innovation in this area because it showed that the political process gave no warrant for such change.[12]

The determination of the Reagan administration to use its power to appoint federal judges to secure a bench which was tilted towards the ideological right and away from the egalitarian liberalism of the Warren era makes it increasingly unlikely that the courts will fashion new tools for erasing sexual inequality from American law. Nevertheless, no groups can afford to overlook the power of the judiciary in the American political system, and the organised women's movement has strongly criticised the Reagan approach to judicial nominations. In 1986 the National Women's Political Caucus testified against the selection of William Rehnquist as Chief Justice because of his insensitivity to women's issues. Rehnquist's attitudes were said to be epitomised in a memorandum which he had written on the topic of the ERA in 1970 for the Nixon administration. He had noted that the basic objection to the ERA was that it was not designed to confer any 'benefits or privileges' on women. On the contrary, it would invalidate those laws which had been enacted on the theory that in some areas women deserved privileged and favourable treatment. 'Such a doctrinaire insistence on rigid equality' Rehnquist wrote, 'seemed almost certain to have an adverse effect on the family unit as we have known it'.[13] Such remarks suggested that Rehnquist's jurisprudence was unlikely to be greatly concerned with sexual discrimination.

The opposition to the ERA had in part relied on the argument that such an amendment was unnecessary. When the 1980 Republican Convention abandoned the party's long-standing commitment to the ERA, Reagan had been forced to articulate some alternative proposals. Two initiatives which he announced seemed calculated to achieve the goals of the ERA by other means. In fact these alternatives – a 50-state project to survey state laws and a task force on legal equity for women – were feeble efforts which received little funding and little political support from the top of the administration. Indeed, far from actually developing alternative routes to equal treatment for women, the Reagan administration seemed to many to be unwilling to enforce those laws which had already been passed on the subject. Thus there was much criticism of the extent to which the Reagan administration was enforcing Title IX of the Education Act Amendments of 1972, which had been designed to guarantee equal treatment for women with regard to higher and professional educational opportunities.[14]

The women's agenda after ERA

The Reagan administration was generally unsympathetic to claims for special treatment for minorities or disadvantaged groups and, as has already been mentioned, the agenda of the conservative movement covered a wide range of cultural and moral issues. While the women's movement was not necessarily opposed to all features of cultural conservatism (it was, for example, at one with the conservatives over pornography), to the extent that the new right and its allies wanted to assert the traditional roles of women and to impose their own moral views on American society as a whole, the women's movement had to resist it. In addition, it was a central part of the Reagan platform that the role of the federal government should be reduced and that the route to renewed prosperity lay in a combination of tax and budgetary cuts. In consequence, this meant that many of the programmes designed to protect the poor were threatened. Women were hit unusually hard by this development both because many of the poorest groups in the United States were families where the woman was the single wage earner, and because in the absence of federal intervention women tended to work in the least well-paid jobs. Thus the women's agenda for the years was necessarily two-fold: it had to defend the rights of individuals against any attempt to put the clock back and it had to campaign against policies which were contributing to the 'feminisation of poverty'. The arguments about the proper method of dealing with the poorest groups in American society are complex, but two broad approaches developed during the 1980s. The Reagan administration and its conservative supporters believed that the only way to combat poverty was to raise the general level of wealth in American society. Others, however, believed that there were reasons why some of the poorest families in America would not be touched by general increases in prosperity without specific policies aimed at the poor. As Michael Harrington has written:

. . . if women are locked into welfare dependency not because they are lazy, but because there is no child care, then even the existence of job openings for them is not going to change their situation. A significant number of AFDC families, (families on welfare), then, might be immune even to prosperity.

Increasingly, therefore, the women's movement found itself opposed both to the cultural dynamics of the Republican Party under Reagan and to the implications of the Reagan administration's social and economic policies.

The women's movement was not, of course, entirely united on strategy. Indeed, it is important to remember that the women's movement is not monolithic and that, although some groups such as the National Organization of Women (NOW) and the National Women's Political Caucus may generally be found in the liberal camp, other groups are less easy to categorise politically. Thus the League of Women Voters maintains a studied political neutrality and the Women's Equity Action League (WEAL) is generally less liberal than either NOW or the NWPC. In addition there are groups with specialist interests. Thus the Women's Legal Defense Fund – which was founded in 1971 – encourages litigation attacking sex discrimination. Despite this *caveat,* however, it is convenient to examine the concerns of the contemporary women's movement by looking at the issues which the NWPC identified as key issues for rating Congressmen and Senators as well as by examining those issues deemed to have priority by NOW in its lobbying efforts.

Sixteen issues were identified as important to the NWPC in the first session (1985) of the 99th Congress – nine votes in the Senate and seven in the House.[16] The issues of abortion and family planning were high on the agenda since there were frequent efforts in Congress to eliminate federal funding for both. Part of the opposition to these programmes was doubtless religious in origin; but part of it reflected the symbolic politics of the new right: those who were in favour of family planning tended to be associated with other aspects of the permissive society – abortion on demand, homosexual equality, sex education and secularisation. The issues were not therefore something to be treated equally on their merits but rather as competing visions – one secular, one religious – of American society. At its most extreme, family planning was seen as part of an evil design of state-minded secular humanists who were aiming at nothing less than the subversion of the American family and even, through such bodies as the International Planned Parenthood Federation, the destruction of family values throughout the world.

The women's movement found itself defending not just abortion rights and family planning from the attacks of the new right, but to a limited extent also the status quo with regard to prayer in schools. Here the motivation may have been rather more than a simple desire to rebut the advocates of school prayer, which might not in itself have been obnoxious to the majority of Americans. Rather, the problem was that many of the advocates of reintroducing school prayer had wanted to achieve their aims by limiting the jurisdiction of the federal courts. Such an effort, if it were ever to succeed, would have profound implications for other constitutionally protected rights – most notably abortion where, although subject to perpetual political and legal challenge, the 1973 decision remains intact.[17]

Of the remaining votes, all except one related to the funding of programmes of particular concern to women. The programmes which the NWPC wanted to save from the budgetary axe included *Headstart*, developmental disability and handicapped education programmes, school lunch programmes, the work incentive programme, student aid and food stamps. In addition, the NWPC gave high priority in restoring cuts made to the *Medicare* and *Medicaid* programmes.

The remaining issue of concern to the NWPC – that of comparable worth – arose from a bill to establish a commission to oversee a study of the federal workforce to see whether differences in pay and classification had arisen as a result of discrimination based on sex, race or national origin. This bill (which was introduced by Mary Rose Oakar, a Democrat from Ohio) underlined the extent to which there were still pay disparities in the United States despite the promise of the 1963 Equal Pay Act. This study was the kind of inquiry which might have been the proper task of the Civil Rights Commission, However, given the reconstitution of the Commission in 1983 and the lack of faith in it among civil rights groups thereafter, many groups sought to bypass the Commission. Although the issue of equal pay for jobs of comparable worth remains an important issue on the agenda of women and many Democrats – and was emphasised before the Senate in its 1984 hearings on the impact of an equal rights amendment – it seems unlikely that much will be done about the situation of pay inequities in the present climate, a situation which has been estimated to involve women receiving 60 cents to every dollar earned by a man.[18]

Key votes in Congress may be reactive rather than initiating. Thus, many of the votes singled out by the NWPC were responses to cuts in the federal domestic budget. The whole issue of the treatment of women within the social security system remains high on the agenda since the complex system was designed in a period when fewer women worked outside the home and when there were fewer marital breakdowns. Also of major importance is the issue of child care. Groups such as NOW are anxious to promote better facilities for the care of children of working mothers, although there is little prospect at the moment that the federal government would bear the cost of this. Job security and maternity leave are also major issues, since there is no general legal entitlement in the United States to paid maternity or temporary disability leave.

Two observations may be made about the issues taken up by the women's movement in the United States at the moment. First, because of the weakness of the women's groups when acting alone it is important that they be able to operate within broader coalitions – for example, the Leadership Conference on Civil Rights. Secondly, it is prudent to identify issues which enable the women's lobby to reach out to the majority of ordinary American women who may be unmoved by the theoretical issues of equality contained in the ERA or even repelled by the commitment to abortion rights or homosexual equality. Issues such as child care – which has a large constituency – and job security offer an opportunity for women activists to consolidate their support as well as being important issues in their own right. On the other hand, the themes of gay rights and reproductive freedom are in a sense 'non-negotiable issues' for many women's groups. Organisations such as NOW acknowledge that gay rights will always be on their agenda because as one spokesperson said, 'an important part of the NOW constituency is the lesbian community'.[19] Similarly, access to abortion and contraception is crucial to any defence of women's freedom of choice. Even so in the climate of the 1980s it makes sense to try to concentrate on issues which can be won rather than to exacerbate further the ideological, moral and cultural divisions within Congress.

Women in politics

The prospects for social legislation in which women have an interest depends greatly on the presence in Congress of women who can alert their colleagues to the significance of an issue and craft legislative provisions to deal with the matter. While it is not the case that only women can give such a sympathetic hearing to women's issues, organisations such as NOW do look to women legislators when they want to advance a cause.

The numbers of women elected to Congress have risen since 1971, but not spectacularly. In 1971 there were 15 female members of Congress; after the 1986 elections there were 25, including two female Senators.

Women have done better at the state level, where the total number of women legislators rose from 362 in 1971 to 1,102 in 1985.[20] In addition, the number of women mayors has risen dramatically. Whereas only seven women were mayors of cities of over 30,000 inhabitants in 1971, by 1985 there were 80 women in such positions. Although at the gubernatorial level only Kentucky (Martha Layne Collins) and Vermont (Madeleine Kunin) could boast female incumbents, the 1986 race in Nebraska turned into an all-female one.

One of the features of American elections in recent years has, of course, been the huge rise in costs and expenditures and the growth in the importance of Political Action Committees (PACs). To the extent that women are less likely than men to be independently wealthy, they are handicapped in the new electoral environment and perhaps they are also less likely than men to be seen as candidates to be favoured with corporate PAC money. The National Women's Political Caucus and other women's organisations do endorse candidates, but by no means all the candidates they endorse are women. Conversely, not every woman will be endorsed by a woman's organisation. The amounts of money at the disposal of the women's groups are relatively small. Thus NOW/PAC spent $212,284 altogether for the primary and general elections of 1984 on Congressional candidates and NOW/Equality PAC spent a total of $102,080 in 1984 state races. At the Congressional level the amounts varied, with some candidates for the Senate getting the maximum contribution of $5,000 and others getting a token donation of $500. At the state level in 1984 the average contribution given to women candidates was $762, to minority candidates $571 and to male candidates $275.[21]

One change which emerged in 1984 as far as NOW's political activity was concerned was the proportion of money going to female candidates. In 1984 the proportion of money from NOW going to support female candidates was 55 per cent, as opposed to a mere 27 per cent in 1982. At the state level, the number of NOW/Equality PAC endorsed candidates who were women increased from 40 per cent in 1982 to 73 per cent in 1984.

The results of the expenditure in 1984 were not very encouraging, at least at the Congressional level. All six of the women backed by NOW/PAC for its Senate were running for the first time, and all lost. Their races took up 52 per cent of NOW/PAC's Senate contributions. NOW's preference for challengers was reflected in the fact that 82 per cent of the Senate contributions went to challengers. Two of those challengers won, as did the three incumbents backed by NOW/PAC and two of the three NOW/PAC-backed candidates for open seats. In House races there was an initial difference in that the women backed by NOW/PAC were more likely to be challengers than incumbents, and they were therefore more likely to lose. In fact none of the fourteen women challengers backed by NOW/PAC were elected, although seven NOW/PAC-supported female incumbents were re-elected. Of the 80 men backed by NOW/PAC for the House 46 were incumbents, 28 were challengers and six were running for open seats, and there was a predictable difference in the success rates of these categories. Of the 43 male winners who had NOW/PAC support 40 were incumbents, one was a challenger and two were running in open seats. As NOW recognises, the big difference between men and women candidates politically as far as the House of Representatives is concerned is that women are more likely to be challengers. In seeking to spread their support NOW and other female organisations are often in the unenviable position of having to support either women, who are likely to lose, or men, who are likely to win.

The fact that NOW/PAC gave support to no Republican candidates for the Senate and only eleven Republicans for the House (out of 123 candidates supported) underlines the extent to which the women's organisations are still firmly in the Democrat camp, tempered only by the occasional support of a liberal Republican. Although some of the older groups dedicated to the advancement of women – such as the League of Women Voters – and feminists within Republican ranks may regret the development, the politics of the 1970s and 1980s have created a sharp partisan division, with the Democrats taking up the issues associated with the women's movement. At the electoral level many commentators seem agreed that the United States is unusual in having a 'gender gap' in its electoral behaviour which results in women being more liberal in outlook and voting patterns than men. To what extent this is the result of specific issues – such as the 'peace issue' – and to what extent it is the result of other factors, including Reagan's style, is debatable.[22] What is clear is that, while the Democratic advantage was not sufficient to secure the election of a democratic candidate in 1984 even with the first female vice-presidential candidate – Geraldine Ferraro – on a presidential ticket, that discrepancy and the size of the female vote means that it cannot be written off by Republicans, any more than liberal women's groups can write off the federal government simply because it seems to under 'opposition' control. The interesting question in the immediate future is how American women and party strategists will trade off their ideological preferences and their pragmatic concerns.

Notes

1 For a general account of the rise in importance of family issues in the context of the politics of the 1970s and 1980s see G. R. Peele, *Revival and Reaction: The Right in Contemporary America*, OUP, Oxford and New York, 1984.

2 There are a number of useful works on the history of the ERA. See especially Mary Frances Berry, *Why ERA Failed: Politics, Women's Rights and the Amending Process of the Constitution*, Indiana UP, Bloomington, 1986 and Jane J. Mansbridge, *Why We Lost The ERA*, University of Chicago Press, 1986. Also Janet K. Boles, *The Politics of the Equal Rights Amendment: Conflict and the Decision Process*, Longman, New York, 1979, and the excellent study by G. Y. Steiner, *Constitutional Inequality: The Political Fortunes of the Equal Rights Amendment*, Brookings, Washington DC, 1985.

3 Bella Abzug, *Gender Gap*, Houghton Mifflin. Boston, 1984, p 18. Also E. Smeal, *Why and How Women Will Elect the Next President*, Harper Colophon, New York, 1984.

4 For a statement of the doubts about ERA see *Hearings on the Impact of the Equal Rights Amendment*, United States Senate, Committee on the

Judiciary, Sub-committee on the Constitution, (98th Congress 1984), especially the opening remarks by Senator Orrin Hatch (Republican-Utah).

5   On Phyllis Schlafly's rôle see Carol Felsenthal, *The Biography of Phyllis Schlafly: The Sweetheart of the Silent Majority,* Doubleday, New York, 1981 and J. Mansbridge, *op.cit.*

6   G. Steiner, for example, talks of the amendment process as a 'stacked deck' and quotes Professor Paul Brest's opinion that the Article V procedures are 'designedly obstacle-ridden and anti-majoritarian'. G. Steiner, *Constitutional Inequality,* p 28.

7   On this see Mary Frances Berry, *Why ERA Failed*, pp 4–10, also J. Mansbridge, *op. cit.* For more detailed discussion of the post-Civil War debates see Harold H. Hyman and William M. Wiecek, *Equal Justice Under Law: Constitutional Development 1835–1875,* Harper & Row, New York, 1982.

8   Interview with Catherine East, Legislative Director of the National Women's Political Caucus, Washington DC, 10 September 1986.

9   This point is made by G., Steiner, *Constitutional Equality.* See also the testimony of Representative Henry Hyde (Republican-Illinois) in *Hearings on the Impact of the Equal Rights Amendment.*

10   *Roe v Wade* 410 US (1973).

11   United States Commission on Civil Rights: *Statement on the Equal Rights Amendment,* Washington DC, 1978. The Civil Rights Commission first endorsed ERA in 1973 and in 1981 it published a further endorsement designed to counter some of the myths associated with the proposed amendment. See United States Commission on Civil Rights, *The Equal Rights Amendment: Guaranteeing Equal Rights for Women under the Constitution,* Washington DC, 1981.

12   'Strict scrutiny' in the most active form of judicial review under the Fourteenth Amendment and applies where a 'suspect classification' or 'fundamental interest' is involved. The burden is placed on the state to show that the classification serves a compelling state interest and makes challenge relatively easy. For an overview of cases see P. G. Polyviou, *The Equal Protection of the Laws*, Duckworth, London, 1980.

13   See Judy Mann, 'A Justice for all? Not for women', *Washington Post,* 12 Sept. 1986.

14   For a useful discussion see the testimony of Donna E. Shalala in *Hearings on the Impact of the Equal Rights Amendment.* Also of importance is the case of *Grove City College v Bell* 104 S. Ct 1211 (1984), which restricts the extent to which federal funding may be denied to an institution which discriminates against women and in certain other circumstances.

15   Michael Harrington, *The New American Poverty,* H. Holt & Co., New York, 1984, p 202.

16 I have taken this material from the National Women's Political Caucus, *1985 Voting Record.*

17 The abortion issue may be traced in J. T. Burtchaell (ed), *Abortion Parley,* Andrews and McMeer, Kansas City, 1980, and A. Merton, *Enemies of Choice: The Right to Life Movement and Its Threat to Abortion,* Beacon, Boston, 1981. Also helpful is G. Y. Steiner, *The Abortion Dispute,* Brookings, Washington DC, 1983, and K. Luker, *Abortion and the Politics of Motherhood*, University of California Press, Berkeley, Cal., 1984.

18 The figures vary, but see prepared statement of Senator Tsongas *Hearings On The Equal Rights Amendment* in which Senator Tsongas draws attention to the facts that 'The Equal Pay Act has not changed the fact that working women still earn only 60 cents for every dollar paid to men, the same ratio that existed a century ago'.

19 Interview with Lois Reckitt, Executive Vice-President, National Organization for Women, September 1986.

20 I have taken these figures from the National Women's Political Caucus publication *National Directory of Women Elected Officials 1985* Washington DC, 1985.

21 I have taken these figures from two documents prepared for internal use 'NOW/PAC Election 84 Summary' and 'NOW/Equality PAC Election 84'.

22 A useful overview of the political salience of women's issues in Ethel Klein, *Gender Politics*, Harvard University Press, Cambridge, Mass., 1984. For more detail on the 1986 elections see *Public Opinion* Jan/Feb. 1987.

IV

Economic and social policy issues

Fredric A. Waldstein

The economics of health care policy

Health care and its provision as a public policy issue is not new in the United States. As early as 1769 New York City adopted licensure requirements for those who wished to practise medicine. In 1798 Congress created the US Marine Hospital Service to care for ill and disabled sailors, and in 1809 Massachusetts passed the first law making vaccination for protection against smallpox compulsory. During the late 19th and early 20th centuries there was a flurry of activity calling for government-sponsored health insurance as well as the establishment of both preventive and treatment-oriented health care facilities. As the Progressive Era came to an end, however, the demand for a comprehensive health care programme waned. Legislation in the 1960s creating *Medicare* and *Medicaid* programmes suggested that some type of uniform health care programme for all citizens might no be far away. Indeed, in the early 1970s the prospects for passing such legislation appeared to be quite good. Even Republican Presidents Richard Nixon and Gerald Ford advocated the creation of national insurance plans to cover the costs of at least some medical bills.

Yet if one looks at the landscape of health care policy in the middle of the 1980s, one is confronted with very divergent and seemingly contradictory patterns of behaviour. For example, the field of public health, defined generally as community responsibility for health-care policy, has been limited primarily to sporadic diagnostic and educational services. On the other hand, the field of personal health care, as defined by individual responsibility for diagnosis and treatment, is littered with countless health care programmes provided by the private, public, and not-for-profit sectors for targeted populations within society. But this highly

competitive and segmented system leaves a relatively large proportion of the population without adequate preventive, diagnostic, or
curative health care. Children of the rural and central city poor are
especially likely to fall within this category.

The purpose of this chapter is to outline briefly the history of
health care provision in the US, examine the current state of health
care policy within this historical context, and speculate about what
the immediate future may hold in this critical issue area. Much of
one's ability to understand health care and its provision as a
contemporary public policy issue in the United States is dependent
upon an understanding of the socio-political parameters which have
defined the issue historically.[1] It is to this which we first turn our
attention.

Historical traditions and expectations

At least some of the debate surrounding the quality of and
accessibility to health care in America today can be traced to
differences in perspective about health care as a right of citizenship
to be protected and promoted by government *versus* health care as a
privilege afforded to those private individuals who have the means
to secure it. That such debate could exist at all, at least within a
societal context, was unthinkable in the early 19th century. Access
to a provider of health care was considered no more a right than
access to the pedlar or blacksmith, and the medical practitioner
enjoyed a rather comparable status.

Those who practised the healing arts were first and foremost
entrepreneurs who to stay in business relied as much on their skills
as salespersons as they did upon their knowledge of medicine.
There was no uniform educational curriculum, and scientific knowledge about the causes of and cures for diseases was extremely
limited. There was a broad spectrum of competing and frequently
contradictory schools of thought about how best to diagnose and
treat disease. For example, homeopathic practitioners treated
diseases by administering small doses of drugs which produced
symptoms similar to those produced by the disease itself.
Osteopathic practitioners treated ailments by attempting to reduce
the pressure of displaced bones and nerves. Allopathic practitioners
treated diseases by administering drugs which counteracted its
effects, and eclectic practitioners claimed to take the best methods

from all schools. The consumer had a wide variety of options from which to choose, and there was fierce competition among those who called themselves doctors.

Thus, the physician existed in an economic environment where market forces played a decisive role. There was a great deal of elasticity in both supply and demand. Doctors charged for those services they performed, and anyone able to earn a reputation as a successful practitioner could attract a wealthier clientele that was willing to pay more for the services provided. This fee-for-service formula continues to be the principal means used by medical doctors in the United States to generate income.

Changing the health care environment

In 1847 the American Medical Association (AMA) was estab-lished to do three things, all inter-related: to create an orthodoxy of procedures and practices; to promote orthodox standards as legitimate and necessary in the minds of both the public and members of the profession; and to generate greater control by the profession over the market environment. In the beginning the efforts of the AMA were only marginally successful at best. But by the first quarter of the twentieth century the practice of medicine had been transformed into one of the most respected and well-paid professions. This was accomplished through a combination of factors, some of the more important of which are discussed below.

The discoveries of anaesthesia, which made surgery relatively painless, and antisepsis, which greatly reduced the risk of infection during surgery, were of fundamental importance to the develop-ment of the medical profession for at least two reasons. First, they allowed surgeons to treat patients more successfully, which enhanced the prestige of the medical profession as a whole. This increased public confidence, which led to an increased willingness on the part of the patient to defer to the knowledge and skill of the physician. Second, because the hospital was the most efficient setting for performing surgery it was transformed from an instit-ution for the poor, and where the chronically ill went to die, into a centre which successfully treated a more affluent clientele, making it economically more important to physicians. But access to hos-pitals was controlled by those who administered them. The power to grant or deny physicians access to hospitals was a tool that was used to promote conformity with medical orthodoxy.

Another major development was the dissemination of a report in 1910 commissioned by the Carnegie Foundation which proposed major reforms in medical education.[2] It helped to accelerate the decline of small, private medical schools of dubious quality by calling for a standardised curriculum, and promoting the importance of linking medical education with teaching-hospitals based on the model established by Johns Hopkins University.

These developments contributed to public acceptance of the medical profession as being scientifically based, which allowed the profession, primarily through the AMA and its local affiliates, to assert its authority over who should practise medicine and how. State licensing boards and oversight committees came to be considered the private domain of the profession by physicians and the general public alike. The medical profession effectively used its increased legitimacy to protect and promote the socio-economic status of its members by controlling entry into it, and to impose sanctions on those who might stray from orthodox procedures and standards. In many respects the market in which physicians have practised throughout most of the twentieth century is opposite to that in which their professional antecedents practised during much of the nineteenth century. What has remained constant is the desire for professional independence by physicians as individual practitioners which has been sustained by the fee-for-service means of payment and the strong psychological bond that the modern patient has traditionally exhibited toward the physician who treats his or her illness. Any attempted third-party intervention in this relationship – especially by the state – has been strongly resisted by the medical profession. These factors are important when contemplating the state of health policy in the US.

Government and the field of health

As the prospects for improving health and curing illness increased, new issues beyond provision of basic sanitation services, enforcement of sanitation regulations, and meeting the health care needs of disabled or aged soldiers and sailors began to be introduced on local, state, and federal policy agendas. The emphasis was on measures that would prevent or contain the outbreak of epidemics or similar health problems; or simply to educate targeted populations about causes of disease and means of prevention.

But the medical profession was extremely wary of any government intervention in the health care field that might compromise the professional independence of physicians, and by the 1920s the AMA was able to wield sufficient political power to check potentially significant government efforts in the field of health care. For example, the sociological section of the American Public Health Association was organised in 1910 to help low income patients coming to hospital outpatient departments and dispensaries. By 1922 this section had disbanded in the wake of strong AMA opposition to all proposals that might extend the health care role of government. The Sheppard-Towner Act, passed in 1921, established the first federal grants-in-aid for local child health clinics. But, as Milton Roemer reports, 'Many local health departments . . . declined to accept these grants for fear of alienating private practitioners. The AMA and local medical societies opposed the programmes vigorously, and in 1928 Congress allowed it to terminate.[3] The medical profession was adamantly opposed to any kind of government-sponsored health insurance programme, and President Franklin Roosevelt excised such a programme from early discussions of the Social Security Act for fear that it would jeopardise its enactment by Congress. Subsequent efforts to promote a government-sponsored health care programme for targeted sections of the civilian population were defeated until the passage of *Medicare* and *Medicaid* in 1965.

Physicians, on the other hand, successfully encouraged government subsidies to build hospitals, provide for the most modern medical equipment, fund medical research, and bear at least part of the cost of training medical doctors. Government involvement in health care was supported, or at least tolerated, if it was consistent with the interests of the profession and did not threaten the doctor-patient relationship, including the fee-for-service payment system.

Why was the medical profession so successful in the political arena from the 1920s through the early 1960s? Several factors contribute to an explanation. First, the profession was extremely well-organised through the efforts of the AMA and its affiliates. Through journals, newsletters, and local and national meetings the membership was kept very well-informed about issues that were relevant to physicians and the positions on those issues that were in their best interests. Second, mobilised organisations or groups able to effectively counteract the highly-organised efforts of the medical profession were slow to evolve. Organised labour and the elderly have been most successful in filling this gap, but this is a relatively recent development. Third, as members of the socio-economic élite physicians had financial resources and personal contacts with individuals in positions of power that gave them influence beyond what their numbers might suggest. And they proved willing and able to use their influence to protect their professional interests very effectively. The AMA has traditionally been recognised as one of the most effective lobbying organisations in Washington. Fourth, physicians were able to mobilise public support on their behalf by successfully linking their position on an issue to its impact on the provision of health care for the public. Thus, public health insurance was linked to 'socialised medicine' with an implied decrease in the quality of health care delivery.

However, there exists an inherent conflict of interest between the public's desire to maximise the provision of health care at minimal cost and the physician's desire to maximise payment from the patient on a fee-for-service basis. These are mutually exclusive goals.

Health insurance

This conflict of interest may be alleviated in part by subscribing to some form of insurance programme that can help defray costs of at least some medical expenses. Several governments in Europe, beginning with Germany in the 1880s, undertook this responsibility. But for reasons already discussed, this was not a viable option in the US. The field was left to private insurance companies, hospital-sponsored nonprofit prepayment plans, such as Blue Cross, and subsequent hybrids. Although wary of such plans, physicians accepted their existence as long as they were able to bill the patient directly, there was no attempt to regulate physicians' fees, and the plans were voluntary.

The proliferation of private health insurance and prepayment plans during the twentieth century may have contributed to the dominance of a curative rather than a preventive health care orientation because of the types of protection they have traditionally offered. This is logical given their function and goals. Hospital-sponsored plans such as Blue Cross are treatment-oriented because that has been the principal mission of hospitals. A curative orientation is consistent with the history of private insurance practices where policies are marketed as a means for protection against some catastrophic event. And the broad range of costs for treating illnesses allows for a large number of insurance options that can be marketed to a wide range of income groups.

Increases in the costs of medical care created increased demand for health insurance for all segments of society. This demand was met through a variety of means with the individual, employer, or some other entity paying the premiums. Those left most vulnerable in this environment were those too poor to afford insurance, and those who had difficulty getting insurance because they were in a high health risk category. The elderly were vulnerable on both counts. As individuals retire from the work force they see a substantial reduction in their income at the same time as their need for health care is on the rise. The elderly spend about three and a half times as much per capita for health-related expenses as do the young. The problem is compounded by the fact that the number of individuals aged 65 and older increased from 3.1 million in 1900 to 16.7 million by 1960, with projections of 34.9 million by the year 2000. In addition, the percentage of the population that is aged 65 years and older almost tripled between 1900 and 1983 (4.1 per cent to 11.7 per cent).[4] Thus, not only are there more older people, but they also constitute a growing proportion of the population.

As an increasing number of elder citizens and their families began to experience the impact of increased medical expenses and foresaw the potential for the cost of medical care to cause financial ruin they were forced to consider two alternatives: to go without costly medical care; or to seek some type of government intervention to provide for those who could not get adequate health care insurance. By the 1950s and into the 1960s the first option was not acceptable. Belief that the US was the wealthiest and most advanced nation in the world led an increasing proportion of Americans to conclude that society had an obligation to ensure adequate health care for all its members - especially the elderly.

But the AMA remained strident in its opposition to government intervention in sharing the burden of costs associated with medical care. This attitude is reflected in an article written by the president of the AMA in 1961 which predicts what will happen to the physician's professional and personal life when government intervention occurs.

> He no longer collects from his patients for his services, he submits his bills (in triplicate or quadruplicate) to the government for payment. And the government, because it inevitably must control what it subsidizes, will eventually tell him how to practise, where to practise, how many patients he can see, how much money he can make – and in effect dictate what his home life shall be.
>
> Exaggerated picture? Not on your life. This is what doctors' wives in countries where medicine has been socialized have found to be true.[5]

In spite of AMA opposition the federal government enacted two health insurance programmes in 1965, *Medicare* and *Medicaid,* under the Social Security Act. Medicare is funded by Congress with a uniform eligibility and benefit structure throughout the US. It is composed of two parts: the mandatory 'Hospital Insurance Program' which is financed by payroll taxes and concerns hospital care; and the voluntary 'Supplementary Medical Insurance Program' which covers specified physicians' services and is financed through monthly premium charges to enrollees. Medicare is administered through the Department of Health and Human Services (HHS).

Medicaid is a federally-aided, state operated and administered medical assistance programme for low-income individuals. Within federal guidelines the states are given substantial latitude to determine eligibility requirements, range of services offered, and reimbursement policies. States are required to provide certain hospital and physician services, but they are permitted to establish limits on the amount of care provided under a service category. The federal government pays from 50 per cent to 78 per cent of medical expenditures. Like Medicare, the federal government's responsibilities for Medicaid are administered through HHS.

The rising cost of health care

Medicare and Medicaid legislation did not place any constraints on the traditional fee-for-service payment structure other than to stipulate that physicians' fees and other costs be 'reasonable'. Since the government was subsidising a large proportion of the costs for the specified target populations, an individual's financial resources were much less relevant as means to check increasing medical costs, which rose sharply. While Medicare and Medicaid are not the sole reason for the surge in costs they have nonetheless contributed to it. In 1965 the federal government spent $11 billion in health expenditures, or $54 per capita, which accounted for 26.2 per cent of total health expenditures in the US. In 1983 the federal government spent $148.8 billion on health care, or $611 per capita, which accounted for 41.9 per cent of total health expenditures in the USA. Thus, while private funding continued to account for the majority of total health care dollars the percentage increase by the federal government has been dramatic. This coincides with a total increase in health care expenditures from $41.9 billion ($207 per capita) in 1965 to $355.4 billion ($1459 per capita) in 1983. In 1965 health care expenditures accounted for 6.1 per cent of the Gross National Product. By 1983 it had climbed to 10.8 per cent.[6]

This growth trend has been conspicuous enough to receive much attention in the media and as an issue on the policy agenda of the federal government. The focus on health care has shifted from concern about insurance coverage for the poor and elderly to assure some minimal standard of health care protection to concern about containing the skyrocketing cost of health care in general. The Reagan administration has taken the lead in formulating policies that have slowed the increase in government expenditures for health care, and various segments of the private sector – especially the insurance industry – have followed its lead.

Cutting the cost of health care and its impact

The Reagan administration's efforts to reduce the growing cost of medical care to the federal government is consistent with its general philosophy of cutting the domestic portion of the federal budget and reducing the government's role in providing social welfare programmes. Between 1981 and 1986 more than $30 billion in cost savings were rendered from Medicare, and changes in Medicare proposed by the Office of Management and Budget (OMB) would save an additional $23 billion from 1987 through 1989.[7] These are major changes indeed for a programme whose expected outlays in 1986 were projected to be $74 billion.[8] But it must be re-emphasised that savings are calculated according to a reduction in the rate of growth rather than as an actual decrease in the budget.

The single most important change in the Medicare Program occurred in 1983 amid a crisis atmosphere that the Medicare Hospital Trust Fund was in serious financial trouble. The effort to keep the fund solvent included legislation which ended cost-based reimbursement for treating Medicare patients and started a prospective payment system. In other words, rather than automatically paying the hospital bill that was submitted, as was normally true under the old formula, the federal government established fee schedules that it would pay for the treatment of various categories of illness identified as Diagnostic-Related Groups (DRGs). Hospitals that hold the cost of treatment below the DRG rates are permitted to keep the difference, while those that exceed the rates must absorb the costs. Thus, hospitals have a major incentive under the schedule to increase efficiency and economise their operation. The new prospective payment plan was phased in over a transition period which ended in October 1986.

The Department of Health and Human Services released statistics which suggest that the prospective payment plan is having the intended effect. Admissions to hospitals fell from 36.3 million in 1983 to about 35 million in 1984. 'The average length of a hospital stay for medicare patients was reduced by about 20 %, from 9.6 to 7.4 days. The average for patients covered by other insurers fell from 7 to 6.7 days.'[9] This has resulted in hospitals experiencing an increasing number of empty beds. For example, Hospital Corporation of America, the nation's largest operator of for-profit hospitals, saw its business decline by 20 per cent from 1983 to 1985.[10] To counter this trend Hospital Corporation has joined the ranks of other hospitals, insurance companies, and health-related institutions in developing and promoting their own prospective payment model, or some variant thereof, as a means to reduce the cost of health care.

Perhaps the most widely-known prospective payment system is the Health Maintenance Organization (HMO). The largest HMO, Kaiser Health Plans, was formed during World War II and has over 4 million subscribers. Under the typical HMO plan subscribers pay an annual flat fee for medical services through a particular corporation which employs physicians to treat them. The flat fee financing gives the HMO a strong incentive to minimise the cost of treatment by practising preventive medicine and keeping subscribers out of the hospital. The escalation of medical costs over the past twenty years has made HMOs highly competitive with traditional medical insurance plans. This has led to a rapid growth in the number of HMOs (estimates range from 7,000 to 18,000) and HMO subscribers (from fewer than 3 million in 1973 to 18,9 million in 1986). Some experts predict that half of all Americans will be enrolled in HMOs by 1995.[11]

Increasing the burden on the elderly

Savings from trends which show shorter hospital stays and a decrease in the number of hospital beds being used nationwide are spent on the increase in per diem costs of hospital care. The prospective payment system seems to have slowed the increase, but it continues to be a problem – especially for the elderly.

Medicare beneficiaries are expected to pay a deductible equivalent to the average cost of one day of hospitalisation for Medicare patients before the Medicare hospital insurance programme pays any bills. The fee has increased steadily from $40 deductible in 1966 to $492 deductible in 1986. This has placed an increasing burden on those with fixed incomes such as Social Security recipients, whose income increases only to compensate for increases in the general cost of living. Indeed, average out-of-pocket health care expenditures for the elderly increased from $300 in 1966 to approximately $1850 in 1986. These expenditures which accounted for 15 per cent of income in 1966 had climbed to 16 per cent by 1986.[12] Efforts to limit the deductible or to tie it to some other formula which would ease the burden on the elderly have not met with success at least in part because the Reagan administration disapproves of such changes. Opponents of the proposals point out that such limits will mean the government must make up the difference which will increase the cost of the Medicare Program.

Checking the costs of physicians' fees

Although Congress has dramatically changed the mandatory Hospital Insurance Program of Medicare, it has not altered the voluntary Supplementary Medical Insurance Program which covers physicians' fees. Under this system Medicare pays doctors or reimburses their patients for 80 per cent of what the Department of Health and Human Services determines is a 'reasonable fee' which is defined as the lowest of three charges: actual charge to the patient; the physician's customary charge for a given service; or the prevailing local charge for the service. While this formula gives some discretion to HHS, fees remain controlled by physicians. The remaining 20 per cent is paid by the beneficiaries. To help cover the cost of the programme beneficiaries pay a monthly premium and an annual deductible which was $75 in 1986.

Recent events suggest that physicians' fees may not be immune from the cost-cutting atmosphere which pervades government.[13] For example, in July of 1984 Congress blocked an increase in the fees Medicare pays physicians. Payments to physicians nevertheless increased by 11 per cent the following year due to an increase in the number of medical bills that were submitted. But the symbolic importance of efforts to freeze physicians' fees may be more significant than the immediate success or failure of those efforts.

Those who support legislative reforms that would change the physician reimbursement system of Medicare face a difficult challenge. First, the political climate is different from when the hospital payment system was changed. There is no sense of crisis regarding the funding for the Supplementary Medical Insurance Program, and efforts to curb fees are tempered by worries that physicians will not treat Medicare patients. In addition, there is no consensus regarding an appropriate alternative to the existing system. However, three different options have entered the discussion. The first option would be very similar to the prospective payment system for hospitals. Physicians could be paid according to a patient's diagnosis rather than for each service they perform. A second option is to formulate fee schedules for different services that physicians provide. A third option is capitation. Under this plan the government would pay a flat, per capita fee to insurance companies that would, among other things, pay physicians according to the number of individuals enrolled with specific practices. This is an option that has drawn favourable comment from Reagan's Secretary of HHS, Otis Bowen, as a means for reducing government involvement in health care.

At the state level Massachusetts took a major step in the direction of limiting physicians' fees when the legislature unanimously passed a law requiring physicians seeking to get or renew a licence to practise medicine to agree not to bill Medicare patients more than the fee Medicare deems reasonable.[14] This represents an attempt to limit the practice of 'balance billing'. As noted earlier, Medicare pays 80 per cent of what it determines to be reasonable and the patient is responsible for the remaining 20 per cent. But Medicare allows doctors to bill patients more than the 'reasonable charge'. This is what is meant by 'balance billing'. It remains to be determined if the statute will survive a legal challenge, but the fact that such a bill received legislative approval caused physicians' organisations and their members across the country to take notice.

Additional developments that will affect the incomes of physicians are taking place within the profession itself. The projected growth of HMOs will mean fewer doctors in solo practice and more working as salaried employees. The philosophy behind and structure of HMOs as described earlier requires them to keep costs fixed and predictable. Consequently, some experts predict that 50 per cent or more of the nation's physicians will be working for a salary by the end of the century. Perhaps more startling is the prediction by some authorities that physicians' incomes will actually decrease.[15]

What helps account for these trends? There is general agreement that three factors have had a significant impact on the practice of medicine and the health care industry in general: the pressure generated by society at large to hold down the cost of health care; the large surplus of hospital beds; and the increased number of physicians. The first two factors have already been discussed. But why is there an increase in the number of doctors – an increase that some call a surplus? Part of the explanation may stem from the increased use of HMOs and the decrease of hospitalisation. The greater efficiency of HMOs with their orientation to preventive medicine may simply mean that fewer MDs are needed to treat a given population. In addition, there are more doctors practising in the US than ever before. In 1960 there were approximately 250,000 physicians in the US compared to about 500,000 in 1986 with projections of more than 700,000 by the year 2000.[16] This increase is attributed to both large medical school enrollments in the 1960s and 1970s and the influx of physicians from foreign countries. Whether or not this increase constitutes a surplus is a matter of perspective. But it is true that the supply side of the health care market is much more competitive than a generation ago.

Decline of the health care industry's political influence?

Recent events and trends suggest that the medical profession and its allies may have lost some of the political power which they have wielded so effectively during most of the twentieth century. If this does prove to be the case to what can one attribute the decline? The answer may be related to several points worthy of mention. First, the very success of the health care lobby which protected hospitals and physicians from government intervention may be partly responsible. In return for the co-operation, if not support, of the health care industry, and especially physicians, the government was willing initially to sacrifice virtually any control over the costs of programmes to doctors and hospitals. The resulting rise in the cost of health care far outpaced average rates of inflation and created what appeared to be a potential crisis that demanded government intervention to control costs. Second, changes in the health care environment, a number of which have been discussed, have meant that physicians, hospitals, and insurance companies no longer necessarily share complementary goals, and in some instances their goals conflict. Thus, what was once a relatively unified lobby is in disarray. Concomitantly, the health care consumer lobby has organised itself into an effective political force. As one health care lobbyist put it, 'I don't care how good you are. If you have 6,000 hospitals and 450,000 physicians organized and trying to give a message , it means nothing if you're sitting on the opposite side of the table from 30 million elderly people'.[17] Finally, even according to the AMA the negative image of physicians is growing. Gone are the days when physicians could rally strong support for their position simply by saying it was in the public interest to do so.

These changes do not mean the political power of physicians can be discounted or that major changes in health care policy are inevitable. The history of health care in the US indicates that one should never underestimate the skill of the medical profession in protecting its perceived interests. But this does appear to be a period of transition, and the opportunity for substantive change may be ripe.

Postscript

Discussion about the health and well-being of the population has been intentionally omitted from this chapter to emphasise that health care policy in the US has focused on economic issues. Health care provision is business, and issues of health and well-being independent of their utility as business indicators have normally been secondary concerns. For example, it is instructive that discovering the impact of the health care received by the elderly as a result in the change to the DRG formula has not been a priority. Quite to the contrary, the Reagan administration, hospital officials, and others respond to complaints that the elderly are being discharged from hospitals 'quicker and sicker' with the position that no solid evidence exists to substantiate such charges. This suggests that the potential consequences to health do not appear to be deemed especially important in the formulation of health care policy.

However, it is possible that events surrounding the discovery of Acquired Immune Deficiency Syndrone (AIDS), its deadly effects, and evidence that the general population is contracting it at epidemic rates may help alter this attitude. The public appears to becoming less satisfied with the absence of a substantive national policy to address the AIDS menace, perhaps the greatest potential natural health threat to humans around the world. The lack of national leadership on this life and death issue has resulted in a hodgepodge of state and local initiatives that lack cohesion and are frequently contradictory. It would be sadly ironic if it took an international epidemic like AIDS to move the American public to demand that government give priority to the health of the population rather than the economics involved therein.

Notes

1 For a comprehensive and highly readable interpretation of the history of health care in the US see: P. Starr, *The Social Transformation of American Medicine,* Basic Books, New York, 1982.

2 A. Flexner, *Medical Education in the United States and Canada, Bulletin no. 4,* Carnegie Foundation for the Advancement of Teaching, New York, 1910.

3 M. I. Roemer, 'The politics of public health in the United States', in T. Litman & L. Robins (eds), *Health Politics and Policy,* John Wiley and Sons, New York, 1984, p 264.

4 Profile of older Americans: 1984', US Department of Health and

Human Services, Program Resources Department, Washington, DC, 1984.

5 E. V. Askey, 'If your husband's practice were socialized', *The Doctor's Wife,* March/April, 1961, p 20.

6 'Economic report of the president', transmitted to the Congress February, 1985, Government Printing Office, Washington, DC, 1985, p 134.

7 'Reagan's health Rx', *National Journal,* 8 Feb. 1986, p 324.

8 'Medicare budget facing triple jeopardy', *Congressional Quarterly Weekly Reports,*18 January 1986, p 115.

9 'Decline in Hospital use tied to new policies', *New York Times,* 16 April 1985, p 1.

10 'The Hospital Corp's. stumble', *New York Times,* 8 Oct. 1985, p Di.

11 'Health care', *Washington Post National Weekly Edition,* 5 May 1986, p 19.

12 'Protecting the Elderly', *National Journal,* 24 May 1986, p 1254.

13 'The next step: curbing physicians' fees', *Congressional Quarterly Weekly Reports,* 18 Jan. 1986, p 119.

14 'Medicare fight givers doctors a fright', *National Journal,* 1 Feb. 1986, p 281.

15 'Health care', *Washington Post National Weekly Edition,* p 19.

16 'Health care', *Washington Post National Weekly Edition,* p 19.

17 'Protecting the elderly', *National Journal,* p 1258.

Sandra E. Elman

Education: crisis, challenge and commitment

Introduction

Historians may view the 1980s as an unprecedented period of recognition, introspection and assessment for American education which could culminate in significant structural reform. Two seminal questions underscore the policy debates: what is the state of education today? and, where should we be going?

Recent national reports indicate that there is a far greater consensus with respect to the first query than the second: education – from kindergarten through college – is in a state of disarray.[1] That education is in a significantly worse condition than it was twenty-five or fifty years ago is somewhat uncertain. Nonetheless, both within the educational community and beyond, education is *perceived* as *not* accomplishing what it should be. Perceptions and attitudes toward education, as toward other public policy areas, are affected by the overall national political *gestalt* which in part is a manifestation of and takes its cue from the President and his administration. Harsh criticism of education is not shunned in an environment where the administration voices the least positive accolades. Unwittingly, perhaps, the administration is doing education a service: the educational community has been galvanised. The era of complacency has given way to a new wave of dynamic examination, a prerequisite for constructive action.

This chapter seeks to address two questions. First, what effect does the Reagan administration and the political process in general have on education? Second, how are two critical issues, testing and the recruitment and retention of teachers, affected by the political environment? The ensuing analysis may be best prefaced by a brief discussion of the basic structure, financing and operation of the educational system.

The structure of education

American education is distinctly decentralised. Public schools and colleges are under the purview of local and state authorities and not the federal government. The sanctity of the neighbourhood school remains an important part of the American tradition; one which, if tampered with, evokes much grass roots emotion and reaction. Whether it is because citizens feel that government regulation has become nothing less than ubiquitous, or whether it stems from a more fundamental belief that individual freedom is ultimately best protected if authority rests in the hands of small, self-governing communities, Americans are becoming increasingly concerned about who controls their schools. Implicit in this is the notion that if communities can maintain a certain degree of self-sufficiency and depend on local resources, the need for regulation decreases.

Local control of education is a tradition older than the Republic itself. As early as the 1650s. New England colonial schools wre supported by public funds and governed by public officials. Today, the major responsibility for operating and financing schools resides with local school districts. However, in so far as school districts are administrative units of the state, they share authority with it. The distinction is an important one. Such a dual authority structure calls for a state-local finance arrangement which does not always result in an easy partnership.

Financing of public education: who pays, who benefits?

As in most post-industralised societies, elementary and secondary education is financed differently from higher education. First, public elementary and secondary schools in all fifty states are tuition free. Moreover, elementary and secondary education is primarily supported by local and state taxes. The level of support generally depends on the level of tax revenues. If the amount of tax revenues generated in a specific locality decreases from one year to the next, as is often the case during a recession, then the maintenance of programmes may be threatened, or, at the very least, subject to serious review. In a majority of states, the property tax is the principal source of revenue for public schools. Despite the common funding source, the percentage of each tax designated for school support varies from one school district to the next and from state to state. Certain structural constraints pose difficulties in ensuring that schools throughout a given state are funded equally. Those variables that have a direct impact on financing education include: differences in the ability of school districts to raise their own money; the proportion of students requiring special needs programmes and, variations in costs among districts for providing equivalent services.[2]

While the states appropriate funds to support public education at all levels, public schools and colleges receive some federal support as well. The role of the federal government *vis-a-vis* education has evolved dramatically and may have had *the* major impact on the development of education over the last thirty years.

Toward interdependence or intervention? The changing role of the Federal government

Over the last three decades, the national government has expanded its role in areas traditionally reserved for state and local authorities: education, health, public welfare, and the environment. In contrast to fifty years ago, American federalism today is marked more by *mutual interdependence* of federal and state governments rather than by *mutual independence*.

The growing involvement of the national government in education has been the source of much controversy, not because it has created federal programmes that have replaced state activities or state control but rather as a consequence of two phenomena. First, the states and localities now operate a variety of programmes that are federally funded and accordingly are subject to varying degrees of federal control. Second, there have been numerous federal administrative acts, legislation and court decisions that impose nationally mandated guidelines and regulations which legally supersede those prevailing standards previously established by respective states.

Increased federal involvement in education is an outgrowth of two fundamental concerns: the need to ensure greater social justice by achieving, among other things, equality of educational opportunity; and the maintenance of America's economic and technological superiority among the superpowers.

Unlike its European counterparts, the federal government does not focus on who teaches what, when and how – its relationship is financial, not pedagogical. At the elementary and secondary school levels the concern has not been with what students should learn but with who has the opportunity to learn. Clearly, the federal government has had a significant impact on who may have access to the educational system, particularly to higher education through its various student financial aid programmes.

The concern with enhancing equality of educational opportunity was particularly evident during the era of the Great Society. The Headstart Program, for example, provided preschool education for the economically disadvantaged. Title I of the Elementary and Secondary Education Act of 1965 appropriated federal funds to improve the education of economically disadvantaged children. The passage of the Veterans 'G.I.' Bill of Rights after World War II provided tuition grants and subsistence allowances, and in so doing paved the way for universal access to higher education. Title IV of the Higher Education Act of 1965 provided federal assistance through various student loans and grant-in-aid programmes which enabled thousands of individuals from lower and middle-income families to pursue a college education.[3] The fate of these programmes such as the Educational Opportunity Grants – later named the Pell Grants after Senator Claiborne Pell – is presently under question, given prospects of the unprecedented budget cuts mandated by the Gramm-Rudman-Hollings Act. This will be further discussed below.

One of the difficulties in analysing the federal government's role in education is that there is not a coherent, clearly defined articulated federal policy. Instead, there exist a myriad of federal statutes, executive orders, regulations and judicial rulings. In 1976, the then US Office of Education administered over 130 separate programmes. Prior to the 1980s, policymakers and educators argued that the establishment of a separate independent national agency for education would eventually result in greater programme consolidation and co-ordination, and coherence of policy directives. A Department of Education (DOE) was created in 1979 under the Carter administration. Yet, the federal government's relationship with education has remained relatively unchanged. A consensual, well defined federal policy toward education has yet to be formulated. Nonetheless, shifts in policy initiation have occurred.

The executive branch and Congress: who leads? Who follows?

From the advent of Sputnik in the late 1950s to the reformist days of the Great Society, the executive branch was generally the initiator of federal educational policy (particularly as it pertained to higher education), Congress, the reactor. During the 1970s, however, the pattern was reversed. Policy formulation for the most part took place in the appropriate House and Senate committees, not in the Department of Health, Education and Welfare (HEW). Rather, the Office of Education in HEW was largely responsible for, and ostensibly satisfied with, guiding and monitoring the implementation of educational policies. That pattern has continued into the 1980s. Policy proposals usually flow from the congressional committees to appropriate offices in the Department of Education, rather than from the Department to Congress. Though the DOE's role has not significantly changed, the Reagan administration has injected its own thrust which is different from that of previous administrations.

The Reagan administration: its perceived and actual impact

Critics of the Reagan administration allege that there has been a concerted effort on the part of the President, Cabinet officials and other key advisers to get the federal government out of education; and, that this has had a negative impact on education. The administration's detractors further claim that education is one of several substantive areas which has been negatively affected by the 'Reagan Revolution'.

However, on balance the Reagan administration has not had a major impact on educational policy, in part because the federal government simply does not play a dominant role in this sector. As such, it does not make an extraordinary difference who is in the White House; although to be sure, the national mood and sentiment toward education, as in any other policy area, are certainly influenced by the stance of the Chief Executive's Office. What is important to recognise, as many critics seemingly have not, is that the educational reform agenda existed before Reagan, and, for the most part, it will probably exist after him. Part of the reason why the Reagan administration has had less impact than might be expected, is that, notwithstanding his predispositions toward prayer in school and tuition tax credits, none of which substantially affects either the DOE or the overall educational system, Reagan has had no educational policy which he seeks either to impose upon the system or to implement. Moreover, there is little evidence to suggest that the administration's position on those issues is grounded in their merit as means for enhancing the quality of education, but rather because they further certain ideological positions which have policy implications beyond education alone.

Thus, the agenda – undefined and uncharted as it may be – remains largely unchanged. What the Reagan administration, perhaps more than any other, has proved, is that the entire educational system, given its vastness and diversity, is relatively unresponsive to the federal government regardless of who is in power. This is not to imply that the Reagan administration's impact on education has been nil. Its effect is, as one long-time Department official put it, 'indirect', its approach 'passive'. By contrast, it is their perceived political constituencies who make the difference.

Many top-level positions in the DOE have been filled to accommodate conservative constituencies. Generally, these individuals serve as a subtle but ever-present means of pressure within the Department. Overall, their actions are more symbolic than substantive, which is consistent with the President's own commitment. They represent the administration by appeasing their constituencies, but they seem to have had relatively little impact on the agenda. This is especially interesting given the attention that has been focused on Reagan's criticism of the American educational system. Partial explanation as to why the rhetoric appears to lack substance is the fact that the American educational system, because it is so decentralised, does not automatically respond to shifts in federal policy.

Symbolism may be the hallmark of the Reagan administration *vis-à-vis* education. One could argue that the administration's choice of a teacher to be the first civilian astronaut in space demonstrates its commitment to strengthen education. That contention is debatable. It may very well be another example of artfully crafted politics designed to disguise with style and symbolism a lack of commitment to substance.

While the Reagan administration may not have gutted educational programmes, it has attempted to reduce the education budget. The administration has made it clear that education should contribute to budget cuts which are essential in dealing with the budget deficit, and, furthermore, that reduced funding is warranted and justified. But education has many supporters in Congress among both Republicans and Democrats. Likewise there are Republican governors, such as Kean of New Jersey and Ashworth of Missouri, who are outspoken proponents of a strong education system in need of federal support. They have worked to prevent the massive cuts advocated by the administration. Thus, fiscal years 1985–87 have witnessed level funding for education programmes. Given inflation, this means an actual decrease in terms of real dollars, but the decrease is much less than the administration would have liked.

Had the Senate approved the White House plan proposed in Spring 1986 which sought to terminate 43 federal programmes, FY87 might have been a financial disaster for higher education and would have had far-reaching negative implications. Rather surprisingly, however, the Senate, by a vote of 83 to 14, rejected the President's proposal to abolish such noteworthy programmes as State Student Incentive Grants, college-housing loans, aid to libraries, health-manpower training, and the Department of Agriculture's extension service. Instead, it adopted by a vote of 60 to 38 an amendment sponsored by Senator Mark Andrews, Republican of North Dakota, and Senator Ernest Hollings, Democrat of South Carolina, which aimed at ensuring that all federal education programmes except Guaranteed Student Loans served the same number of students in 1987 as in 1986 and provided the DOE with an increase for FY87 of $1.2 billion.[4] Thus, another reason for less substantive change than the rhetoric might suggest is the strong support that Congress has continued to provide to education.

Beyond FY87 the more serious concern is what impact Gramm-Rudman-Hollings (GRH) legislation will have on higher education. In FY85 the federal government spent about $15.7 billion dollars for higher education. If current policies continue, by FY91 that amount would rise to $17.5 billion, given an inflation rate of 4 per cent. According to one economic forecast, under GRH by 1991 spending for higher education could drop to $11.9 billion, or a 25 per cent decrease from current funding. Perhaps GRH legislation's most detrimental effect is the degree of uncertainty it will continue to generate within higher education and the unprecedented stress and strain individual institutions will experience.[5] Ultimately it may not be a question of whether a particular programme(s) is retained but rather who shall be afforded the benefits. These questions are normative and call into question the ideological underpinnings of many of the programmes established in the days of the Great Society. What is at risk then is not only the loss of funding but the dismantling of a tradition of affording students equal educational opportunity.

Contrary to prevailing liberal notions, there has been no revolution *vis-à-vis* education: there has been reform. The difference is critical. If revolutionary – progressive or regressive – policies had been enacted, there would be a marked variance in the level and scope of change which would undoubtedly have a trickle-down effect: public schools and colleges across the country would not be functioning as they are now. There have been no overwhelmingly significant changes within the educational system as a result of the Reagan administration.

Policy formulation: uncertainty and complexity

Clearly, policy goals as well as policy solutions reflect both structural realities and normative concerns. What makes policy formulation difficult is conflicting notions among policymakers regarding critical issues such as decentralisation, federally-supported student aid programmes, academic freedom, standardised testing, and assessment of professional competence. The policy crisis is not over the ends, but the means to those ends. Policymakers and educators, regardless of partisan persuasions, seek educational excellence. There is far less unanimity, however, with respect to how that goal may be attained.

In spite of the lack of direction from the Reagan administration, a number of issues such as student performance and teacher competency, continue to beset the education policymaking community.

Student performance: to test or not to test

The policy debate over the validity and reliability of utilising standardised test scores to measure student competencies is as old as the testing movement. Proponents of standardised testing argue that in order to provide better quality education and improve instructional methods and materials it is necessary to know on the basis of some uniform comparative data how well students comprehend what they are supposed to be learning. They further maintain that these results are a means of monitoring educational standards over a period of time without which teachers and administrators would be hard-pressed to identify weaknesses in instruction and curriculum. Moreover, test results which show that there are significant gaps in the performance levels of white and minority students, for example, can be used as legitimate data by parents and others to pressure schools and to find ways to close those gaps.[6]

Critics of standardised testing have questioned why one should assume that 'equal opportunity should yield similar scores on similar tests for all subgroups in the US population'. To do so, they maintain, one may fail 'to consider the cultural backgrounds of the test developers, the manner in which such tests are standardized, and the variations in mental abilities that exist among different racial and ethnic subgroups'.[7] Detractors further contend that most tests have built-in biases which skew the results and ultimately produce misleading findings.

One area in which political actors – namely, state legislators – have had an impact on charting educational developments is competency testing, a rather new development within the testing movement. High school competency testing programmes were developed in the late 1970s in response to legislative concern that many students were being promoted on the basis of length of time of their schooling rather than their academic capacities. While state legislators hoped that competency testing programmes would at least ensure that students had mastered certain basic skills, educators have been fearful that programmes which test for minimal capabilities will undermine curricula. It is unproven, but feared by some, that minimum competency examinations, now required in 37 states, result in a lowering of educational standards for everyone. The states that have these programmes do not agree that the 'minimum' becomes the 'maximum', and inasmuch as only they have the power to rescind such programmes, their survival appears secure.

The use of minimum competency tests and average scores of cohorts of students on standardised tests to assess student performance reflects the public's and policymakers' preference for relying on 'scientific' standardised test results rather than a teacher's judgement. Furthermore, it has led to increased centralisation of school management; and increased legitimacy of more objective, certain, neutral data for assessing educational performance – a trend which legislators welcome.

Recruitment and retention of teachers

Elementary and secondary schools enroll approximately 45 million students. Of those, almost 10 per cent attend private schools. The enrollment declines of the 1970s were not immediately followed by staffing decreases in the number of teachers employed, in part because of the new needs of special and bilingual education programmes. However, because of stringent budgetary constraints, the number of public school teachers fell to 2.2 million in 1980 and dropped another 2 per cent between 1980 and 1983. Private schools, however, witnessed a 12 percent increase in the number of teachers employed between 1980 and 1983. Recent projections indicate that during the late 1980s and early 1990s the number of teachers in public and private schools will rise by 11 per cent, and by 1993 reach an historical high of 2.7 million. Between 1990 and 1993 the demand for additional teachers is expected to climb as high as 200,000 each year.[8] Such demand partially explains the widespread concern over the quality of teachers in general and on the perceived decline of quality in teacher training in particular.

The role and status afforded teachers is both perplexing and regrettable. Teachers are expected to do far more than simply meet the educational needs of their students, and this often in a debilitating physical environment. Schools, particularly in large urban areas, are overcrowded, asbestos-ridden, have inadequate instructional and physical facilities, and are in total disrepair. It is not surprising that not enough academically able students are being attracted to teaching. Consequently, a serious shortage of teachers exists in key fields. Unlike most other professionals, teachers are deeply concerned not only about salaries but also about their loss of status, the bureaucratic pressures, a negative public image, and the lack of recognition and rewards.[9] Traditionally, teaching has been a woman's profession, but as opportunities for women have expanded in various other fields many women have sought non-teaching careers.

Teachers' salaries are low in relation to other professions, and almost nine in ten indicate that inadequate compensation is the primary reason why teachers leave the profession. The shortage of teachers is becoming increasingly problematic, particularly in regions of the country where there is a strong economy and the number of college graduates is declining overall. Shortages are even more critical in the areas of mathematics and science.

Economic determinants notwithstanding, teachers are facing demands for greater accountability from a variety of sources ranging from state education departments to parents' committees. Stringent state-mandated assessment mechanisms and copious curriculum guidelines have, perhaps inadvertently, afforded teachers less discretion and autonomy in determining what instructional materials should be used and how much time should be allocated to specific activities. Teachers' discretionary powers are also becoming increasingly limited. For the most part, teachers have no decision-making authority regarding either the physical space or instructional time they are allocated. Increasingly, they have less authority over the choice of textbooks used in their classes. In as many as 17 states – mostly in the South and Southwest regions – a centralised office selects textbooks for all students in all grades.[10] The trend toward increased centralisation and accountability is likely to have a significant impact on policy outcomes over the next decade.

Policy options

Concerns about poor student performance have prompted numerous policy proposals. These include:

(1) Lengthening the present 5 1/2 – 6 hour school day by at least an hour; lengthening the school year, which on the average consists of 180 days compared to 220–260 days for most other industrialised nations. The effective implementation of such structural changes depends upon the support of teachers who, unless provided with adequate incentives, may not lend their endorsement.

(2) Granting teachers' salaries on the basis of performance rather than on seniority. The present system of equal pay limits both incentives for doing one's best and opportunities for advancement.

(3) Lower class loads

(4) Increase class preparation time and exempt teachers from non-instructional duties

(5) Increase average teacher salaries by 25 per cent above inflation over the next three years, and

(6) Continue allocation of resources for inservice teacher renewal.

Clearly, policy proposals abound; adequate solutions need to be found.

Conclusion

According to Clark Kerr, former President of the University of California, the federal era may be over for colleges and universities in particular, less because of the Reagan administration's policies, more as a result of the economic consequences of federal budget deficits, the national debt and planned new weapons systems.[11] Inasmuch as education at all levels has been appropriated a greater share of state budgets, it is not surprising that the states have not only become more interested in what the education sector does, but in insisting on greater accountability than twenty years ago.

Education, perhaps more than other policy areas, is greatly affected by demographic patterns and economic and social trends that occur independent of the Reagan or any other administration. Academe competes with the marketplace in attracting and retaining faculty, particularly in such professional fields as business, law and engineering. The profile of the average elementary school student as well as that of the college student is affected by the increasing numbers of single parent households, the number of women re-entering higher education, declining birth rates and the need to retrain workers. The Reagan administration may be a disconcerting force and may deter the momentum of the education sector in so far as so much time is spent by educational leaders fighting funding battles and in finding means to increase economic efficiency at the institutional level.

Ironically, though, the Reagan administration may have unintentionally given education the impetus it needed to reassess its performance and perspectives. In the face of uncertainty, instability and an unsupportive environment, the education community has exhibited a sense of urgency and spirit toward improving and reforming from within as much as possible. Ultimately, if real structural and pedagogical breakthroughs occur, the *esprit de force* has to emerge internally.

Although there is little doubt that educational excellence is a desired goal, educational problems remain exceedingly complex. But what may be unique about this policy issue, unlike others such as national security, arms control and tax reform is that the people –educators and non-educators alike, parents, teachers, community leaders – can become directly involved in and have a direct impact on the development of policy innovations.

Whether America responds to the challenges depends on the extent to which the nation is intent on translating rhetoric into reality. The 1990s may hold out the 'last chance' for America to reform public education in ways that ensure children and adults an education of value which is distinctive of a progressive, democratic society.

Notes

1 Ernest L. Boyer, *High School: A Report on Secondary Education in America,* Harper & Row, New York, 1983; National Commission on Excellence in Education *A Nation At Risk: The Imperative for Educational Reform,* US Department of Education, Washington, DC, 1983; Select Committee of the Project on Redefining the Meaning and Purpose of Baccalaureate Degrees, *Integrity in the College Curriculum: A Report to the Academic Community,* Association of American Colleges, Washington, DC, 1985; Study Group on the Conditions of Excellence in American Higher Education, *Involvement in Learning: Realizing the Potential of American Higher Education,* National Institute of Education, Washington, DC, 1984.

2 Walter I. Garms, James W. Guthrie & Lawrence C. Pierce, *School Finance. The Economics and Politics of Public Education,* Prentice Hall, Inc., Englewood Cliffs, New Jersey, 1978 pp 211–12.

3 These included the Basic Educational Opportunity Grants; Supplemental Educational Opportunity Grants, the State Student Incentive Grants Program which provides for federal matching grants to the states 'to assist them in providing grants to eligible students in attendance at institutions of higher education'; Guaranteed Student Loan Program designed to encourage states and nonprofit organisations to establish adequate student loan insurance programmes, and to provide loan insurance for students who do not have access to a state or private nonprofit programme; College-Work Study Program designed to stimulate part-time employment of students, especially those in financial need; and the Direct Student Loan Program which stimulates and assists in the establishment and maintenance of funds at colleges and universities to provide low-interest loans to students.

4 *The Chronicle of Higher Education.* 'Senate Bars Reagan Plan to Curb Aid; Votes $1.2 Billion Extra for Education', 30 April 1986, pp 11,13.

5 Arthur M. Hauptman, 'Gramm-Rudman-Hollings: its potential impact on higher education', *Higher Education & National Affairs*, XXXV, Number 7, 21 April 1986, pp 5–8.

6 Gregory R. Anrig, 'Educational standards, testing and equity', *Phi Delta Kappan*, LXVI, 1985, p 624.

7 Charles V. Willie, 'The problem of standardized testing in a free and pluralistic society', *Phi Delta Kappan*, LXVI, 1985, p 626.

8 Demand is based on the number of teachers needed to respond to increased enrollments, improve teacher-student ratios and replace teachers leaving the profession. National Center of Education Statistics, *The Condition of Education, 1985*, Government Printing Office, Washington, DC, 1985, p 137.

9 Boyer, *High School*, p 155.

10 Beatrice and Ronald Gross (eds), *The Great School Debate*, Simon & Schuster, New York, 1985, p 129.

11 Jean Evangelauf, 'Kerr says federal era has ended for colleges; governors now the key', *The Chronicle of Higher Education*, XXX, Number 5, 3 April 1985, pp 1. 11.

Fredric A. Waldstein

Crime and criminal justice

Introduction

The criminal justice process – from crime prevention to imposing sanctions on the guilty – throughout the history of the United States has been the responsibility primarily of the states, by virtue of the general police powers reserved for them in the Constitution. State and local jurisdictions account for more than 90 per cent of all funds spent on the criminal justice system, and employ over 90 per cent of those who work in it, including police, judges, lawyers, corrections officers, and various support personnel. But the federal government has played an increasingly important role in terms of organising, administering, and funding interstate law enforcement activities. In addition, we look increasingly to the federal government for leadership in establishing priorities and policies respecting crime and how it is treated. This chapter, therefore, will focus on crime as a national policy issue and how federal government leaders respond to it.

As the chief executive of the government the President is in a unique position to determine how much visibility will be given to the issue of crime, and what kind of priority different types of criminal activity will have. In addition to his legal authority as chief executive, the President, as well as his top political aides and allies, also sets a moral standard for the country through his actions and associations. How a President and his team conduct themselves both influences and reflects the moral tone of America. In this chapter we will examine how the Reagan administration views crime, ethical misconduct, and morality in both word and deed, with the hope that it will provide insight into how American society at large views these activities. We begin with a general discussion of criminal trends reported in recent years and governmental response.

Crime

Crime has been defined as a 'positive or negative act in violation of penal law: an offence against the State or United States'.[1] The public has always exhibited strong concern about crime and its impact on society. Whether the rate of crime is rising or dropping is a perpetually contentious issue, especially for politicians who attempt to invoke statistics that support their respective positions. It is difficult to get an accurate picture of crime in America because there are so many studies and surveys that offer different perspectives. This is due in part to the fact that patterns of criminal activity vary significantly, depending on the crime categories and demographic reference points one uses. For example, a study released in 1985 by the Bureau of Justice Statistics suggested that crime fell 4.1 per cent in 1984 to its lowest point in twelve years. The number of violent crimes excluding murder, however, rose 0.9 per cent in 1984 to more than 5,950,000.[2]

The importance of demographic reference points can be illustrated by using statistics which show that most 'street' or violent crime is committed by males between the ages of 15 and 35. Therefore, as the post-World War II 'baby boom' generation moves into middle age, one might expect a drop in these types of crime. However, demographics for the nation as a whole may not be relevant or accurate for specified areas composed of minorities or poor whites, where crime has traditionally been a greater problem.

Compounding the measurement problem is evidence which suggests that as many as 65 per cent of crimes go unreported. Thus, increases or decreases in crime statistics may reflect only changes in the percentage of people reporting crimes and not the actual amount of criminal activity taking place. In addition, police agencies which provide much of the data used in crime statistics may have their own political or budgetary agendas which cause them to define and report the data to meet their own needs.

Another problem for those who wish to measure the impact of crime is society's attitude toward different types. Defining an act as criminal is a subjective moral and ethical judgement by government claiming to represent society at large. As social mores change from place to place and time to time, so do attitudes about what constitutes a crime and what penalties should be imposed upon those who commit criminal acts. The criminal law, like all law, is dynamic and in a constant state of transition. For example, laws against the possession of marijuana vary significantly from one state to the next, and laws are enforced differently from one community to the next even within one city. In several Southern states possession of a marijuana cigarette could result in the offender spending years in prison. In a few communities efforts were made in the 1960s and 1970s to decriminalise possession of small amounts of marijuana. It was treated as an ordinance violation which required the offender to pay a fine similar to that required for a parking violation. Another example involves the use of capital punishment, or the death penalty. A crime committed in one state might mean the offender could be put to death. The same crime committed in another state might not include the possibility of execution. In 1972 the Supreme Court decision rendered in *Furman v. Georgia,* 408 US 238, had the effect of temporarily proscribing capital punishment throughout the US. However, 35 state legislatures enacted new death penalty statutes that passed judicial scrutiny. In addition, there has been an increased willingness on the part of the states to impose the death penalty since it was reinstated by the Supreme Court in 1976. Of the 57 executions that took place in the US from 1976 through June 1986, only 10 occurred before 1983. And as of June 1986 another 1,714 persons were awaiting execution nationwide.

Even though the definition of crime and what might be considered an appropriate penalty are subject to change, there nevertheless remains a general consensus within society that certain types of behaviour such as murder, rape, robbery, and other forms of violent crime, are inherently harmful to society, and those who commit them are social deviants. Less consensus exists about what response to deviant behaviour defined as criminal is appropriate, but the options can be divided into three general categories that may be mutually reinforcing or contradictory, depending upon one's point of view. These are 1) treating or rehabilitating the offender to prevent future recurrences of the deviant behaviour; 2) punishing the offender as a warning to him or her and others in society that such behaviour will not be tolerated; and/or 3) remove the deviant from society for a specified period to proscribe further danger to society during that time.

While experts may debate the relative merits of the different responses to crime, the politicians and the public they represent understand that someone who is behind bars is not an immediate threat to society. During the past decade the federal government and states throughout the nation have taken steps to increase the number of people incarcerated and the length of time they must serve upon conviction of a crime. In 1950 the number of federal and state prisoners serving more than one year in custody was 166,123. Twenty years later that figure had risen to 196,429. Since then the increase has been tremendous. By 1975 the number had reached 240,593, and in 1984 there were 445,381 people incarcerated for more than one year.[3]

The increase in the prison population has not been matched by increases in the amount of prison space necessary to house it, partly because the cost of building and maintaining correctional institutions has risen dramatically. In 1982 prisons, jails and other correctional facilities cost federal, state, and local governments almost $8 billion in direct expenditures, and employed more than 290,000 individuals. This was an increase of approximately $2 billion and 30,000 employees since 1980.[4]

Because taxpayers and legislators have other priorities, the resources to accommodate adequately the increased number of inmates have not been allocated. This has resulted in overcrowding so serious that some institutions are under court order to reduce the number of inmates or face contempt for human rights violations. To reduce overcrowding many institutions have resorted to early release programmes. Also, some criminal court judges, sensitive to the problem, are forced to sentence convicted felons to nonprison sentences or shorter prison sentences than they would if space were not a serious constraint. However, this behaviour stimulates political demand both to reduce the sentencing discretion judges have, and to increase the penalties for the commission of crimes so that criminal deviants cannot evade their debt to society. But this merely compounds the problem, and the cycle repeats itself.

Unfortunately we know little about what causes a particular individual to commit a particular criminal act, let alone the degree of effectiveness that the response mechanisms noted above have in terms of limiting future deviant behaviour. The one obvious exception to this generalisation is that we can be quite certain execution removes the possibility that an individual will pose any future threat to society. But this option is not without costs. It engages the state in an activity that it condemns, and thus raises questions of its credibility and the standards it sets. Also, when the state takes a life it destroys any potential positive contribution to society the individual may have had to offer. The finality of death symbolises a sense of failure and loss of hope that we like to imagine is repugnant to the human spirit.

The Reagan response to violent crime and street crime

The Reagan administration has cultivated a 'get tough' image with respect to crime and law enforcement. The administration has been especially concerned about what it perceives to be too much lenience toward criminals and not enough freedom for the police to bring them to justice. Attorney General Edwin Meese reflected this attitude when he publicly supported the use of the death penalty for those under eighteen years of age who commit capital crimes. Regarding the establishment of a minimum age for executions Meese said, 'fourteen seems to me to be pretty young, but it would depend on the circumstances, I guess, of what a state's overall legal context was'.[5]

The administration has been especially anxious to see a reversal of the so-called 'exclusionary rule' which prohibits the use of evidence illegally obtained in a court of law. Critics of the exclusionary rule have long argued that criminals are too often released because law enforcement officials inadvertently or unknowingly violated some right of the suspect that excluded crucial evidence from the trial proceedings. The exclusionary rule was made applicable to the states by the Supreme Court's 1961 decision in *Mapp v. Ohio,* 367 US 643. But the exclusionary rule was under critical review throughout most of the tenure of Warren Burger as Chief Justice of the Supreme Court. During that time the Court narrowed the scope of the exclusionary rule so that it no longer applied when law enforcement officers made a 'good faith' effort to comply with the suspect's guaranteed protections. What constitutes a good faith effort is subject to court interpretation, and the Court seems inclined to assume good faith effort unless proven otherwise. Further reductions in the scope of the exclusionary rule are likely to occur under the leadership of Reagan's appointee as Chief Justice, William Rehnquist. However, it appears that the administration will be satisfied with nothing short of an outright reversal of the *Mapp* decision.

Because most crime is principally the responsibility of state and local government, the federal government is limited to giving advice and taking a position on what response it believes is appropriate. But there are federal criminal statutes that give federal law enforcement personnel pre-eminence in certain area. One of these is immigration law.

Illegal aliens

It is illegal to enter the US without permission, and those who do so are subject to detention and deportation back to their country of origin. There are twelve detention centres across the United States which operated at or above capacity for a total of 1,273,850 days of alien incarceration during the fiscal year 1985. Just under 1,350,000 individuals were deported in fiscal 1985. In spite of these efforts, the Immigration and Naturalization Service (INS) appears to be fighting a losing battle. According to estimates of the INS, between 3 million and 6 million illegal aliens now reside in the US, and from 100,000 to 300,000 enter the country each year in search of a better life. The vast majority are from hispanic America, with approximately 85 per cent coming from Mexico alone. They slip across the 2200-mile border between Texas and Mexico.

The Reagan administration has given visibility to the problem of illegal aliens, and in the fiscal year 1985 the INS budget was increased to permit the agency to hire an additional 512 agents. But the issue is complicated by both economic and political factors. The immigrant labour population, both legal and illegal, contributes to the economy and helps keep labour costs down because it works for less money than the indigenous labour population. In addition, while it is illegal for aliens to work without a permit, there have been few sanctions against those who hire them. Thus, many Americans in management positions with agribusiness have no incentive to reduce the supply of cheap labour. Indeed, they have economic reasons to oppose more aggressive law enforcement, and they count themselves among Reagan's conservative coalition. Harold Ezell, Western Regional INS Commissioner, has complained about Republicans who say that low-paid workers from Mexico help limit inflation and contribute to economic growth. Nonetheless, Congress passed an immigration bill in 1986 which imposes sanctions on those who employ illegal immigrants after May 1988. The bill also has an amnesty provision which allows some illegal immigrants to stay legally.

Taking a different perspective on the issue, people like John Tanton believe that illegal immigration poses a serious threat to the fabric of American society because of the dominant hispanic cultural characteristics most immigrants share. Tanton founded both the Federation for American Immigration Reform (FAIR) and US English to support efforts to curb respectively, illegal immigration and bilingualism.

Foreign policy has also played a role in US response to immigration from hispanic America. Mexico is sensitive about ill-treatment of its citizens in addition to seeing the US as a source of employment for the many workers who cannot find jobs in their economically distressed homeland. Also, immigration policy is used as a tool to promote US foreign policy in Central America. Immigrants from countries perceived to be unfriendly to the US are much more likely to be granted refugee status than those from countries perceived to be allies. Refugee status allows one to petition for asylum on the assumption that such an individual would be subject to prosecution upon return to his or her homeland. Thus, those fleeing war in Nicaragua are more likely to be accepted as political refugees than those fleeing war in Guatemala or El Salvador, who are treated as economic refugees unless they can prove otherwise.

Disagreement with US foreign policy has led to the creation in the United States of something akin to the underground railroad of the nineteenth century for those fleeing war in Central America. Called the 'sanctuary movement', it consists of approximately 270 churches and synagogues which have defied government policy to shelter approximately 3,000 people. In 1984 the INS, in an effort to halt spread of this type of civil disobedience, began legal action against members of the movement and has won several convictions. But such tactics may lead to greater support for sanctuary workers by publicising their cause as an act of faith. If the public perceives the legal activity against the sanctuary movement as a form of harassment and persecution, the government will have miscalculated the effect of criminal prosecution.

'Drug wars'

In the late summer of 1986 a national war on drugs was launched with all the fanfare one associates with efforts by governments to mobilise their populations to support military campaigns. Several factors help account for the sudden attention paid to this issue. Nancy Reagan spearheaded over a number of years administration efforts to raise the issue to the top of the national agenda. Also, drug use was perceived to be filtering out of the inner-city ghetto and into middle-class neighbourhoods, which made it a much more salient issue. This was reflected in public opinion polls and statements by members of Congress returning to Washington after the summer recess. As Republican Representative Jerry Lewis of California put it, 'People were generally fat and happy. They had nothing really bothering them except some esoteric matters about the deficit. The one issue they talked about with emotion was drugs'.[6] Of special concern was a rise in cocaine use among teenagers and young adults. Recently-published studies indicate that cocaine and a potent derivative known as 'crack' are highly addictive and potentially life-threatening.

Perhaps the single most important event that proved to be the catalyst for mobilising the anti-drug crusade was the death of a University of Maryland basketball star from cocaine intoxication a day after he had been selected as the first draft pick of the professional champion Boston Celtics team. The death of this successful young man from a middle-class background seemed to touch the conscience of the country. Republican Representative Robert Dornan of California said, when attempting to explain the rapid government response to the issue, 'I think it comes down to one young man not dying in vain'.[7]

The political response was both rapid and comprehensive. the President and Mrs Reagan went on national television to take their case against drugs to the American public. The administration outlined a four-point plan to reduce drugs in America: 1) the government would spend about $1.7 billion to reduce the supply of drugs both at home and abroad, where much of it is manufactured; 2) more money would be used to treat drug addicts; 3) more effort would be made to educate the public about the dangers of drugs; and 4) the use of urinalysis and other measures that would allow detection of drug users would be employed for some federal officials.

Congress was not about to be left out of the campaign, and bipartisan efforts were mounted in both chambers to pass stiff, new anti-drug legislation that would impose severe sanctions on those selling drugs and provide more appropriations to stop drug use. In the stampede to push legislation a number of amendments were inserted with little debate, which gave some critics cause for concern. Included among these was the death penalty for murder involving drugs (at the time there was no federal death penalty statute), abandonment of the exclusionary rule in drug-related cases, and use of the armed forces to combat drugs. These proposals and the President's call for mandatory drug testing of certain federal employees have significant implication for our individual commitment to civil liberties. Yet the politicians appeared to accept those proposals with little question. It seemed as though no one dared to raise objections for fear of being labelled 'soft' on drugs.

Whether or not all of the rhetoric will be matched by substance is open to question. The Reverend David Else of Pittsburg, Pennsylvania has been working with drug and alcohol abusers for sixteen years, and he has succinctly expressed mixed feelings about the government's efforts to limit the use of illegal drugs. 'I think it's good we're getting a focus,' he said, 'but I fear we're falling into the same sort of trap drug abusing people are into: looking for a quick fix'.[8]

Whatever symbolic gestures are employed, the fact remains that the federal government has steadily cut funding for those already fighting the war on drugs. The House Select Narcotics Abuse and Control Committee reported that block grants awarded to the states for drug abuse treatment and education were reduced by 40 per cent between 1982 and 1986. In addition, the National Institute on Drug Abuse saw its publishing budget, which was used for drug education programmes, cut from $2 to $3 million in the decade prior to 1981 to $600,000 in the fiscal year 1984.[9] Also, research on drugs, their effects, and how to curb their use has suffered from severe budget cuts under the Reagan administration.

One reason for the scepticism about the government's commitment to this issue is that it is too easy to jump on the 'drugs wars' bandwagon. It makes everyone look like a 'good guy'. After all, who could publicly be against the effort to rid society of an obvious social liability? But was this the primary motive for focusing so much attention on the crusade against drugs? Perhaps the following observation is instructive on this point:

(Early in September 1986) most of Reagan's senior political advisors –

more than a dozen prominent Republican strategists – held a dinner meeting in Washington. The consensus of the group was that between (then) and election day (November 1986), the president should concentrate exclusively on drugs, avoiding all other, more controversial issues.[10]

White collar crime

On the same day that the *Boston Globe* reported Edwin Meese's position regarding the use of capital punishment for individuals under eighteen years of age it also reported that Meese had reacted defensively to congressional criticism that the Justice Department had been soft on so-called 'white collar crime', which has been defined as 'an illegal act or series of illegal acts committed by nonphysical means and by concealment or guile, to obtain money or property, or to obtain business or personal advantage'.[11] Meese said that 'some people are misinforming the public or distorting things in the press'.[12] His remarks were delivered as the Senate was about to begin hearings on anti-fraud legislation that was more punitive in some areas than the administration wanted.

Americans have always had a double standard when it comes to comparing and responding to street crime and white collar crime. There are at least two reasons for this. First, white collar crime rarely imposes a direct, physical threat to the victim. Indeed, victims may not even know about the crime until long after it has been committed, if they find out at all. Second, those who commit white collar crime tend to be 'respectable' individuals with attributes that members of society at large identify as positive. For both reasons white collar criminals may appear less threatening to the public. But white collar crime is a serious problem in the US. Although exact figures are difficult to determine, there is general agreement that it costs the public many tens of billions of dollars. Estimates from the late 1970s indicate that fraud and embezzlement alone cost more than $35 billion annually.[13] These figures are probably higher for the 1980s.

The impetus for tougher anti-fraud proposals came in part from what many regarded as unreasonably lenient penalties against the respected brokerage house, E. F. Hutton. Hutton was engaged in illegal activities that allowed it to collect millions of dollars in interest on money that technically no longer belonged to the firm. After one of the largest criminal investigations the federal government had ever undertaken and 2000 felony counts had been lodged against the firm, no individuals were indicted and nineteen potential indictees were granted immunity by the Justice Department.

Another source of white collar crime is 'insider trading' – the practice of buying or selling stocks, bonds, and other securities based on important, nonpublic information – which erodes confidence in investment markets. Three incidents garnered especially widespread media attention. In 1985 R. Foster Winans, a journalist for the *Wall Street Journal,* and others were found guilty of insider trading. Winans was fined $5000 and sentenced to eighteen months in prison for his part in the scheme. In 1986 First Boston Corp., a major investment banking firm, was charged with taking advantage of confidential information about one of its clients. First Boston agreed to pay approximately $400,000 in fines and penalties. In perhaps the biggest scandal to hit Wall Street this century, respected arbitrager Ivan Boesky and several top brokerage house executives shocked and investment community with a series of guilty pleas in 1986 and 1987 to insider trading. The shock was accompanied by public anger regarding the perceived lenient action taken by the government against Boskey and others, such as allowing them to keep much of their ill-gotten wealth.

The Securities and Exchange Commission (SEC), the Federal Trade Commission (FTC) and a host of other agencies that have responsibility for monitoring business practices have found themselves in something of a paradoxical position during the Reagan years. Their statutory mandate runs counter to the Reagan philosophy that business is overregulated which causes inefficiency and slows the economy. Whether or not this has led to the abrogation of government responsibility to deter illegal business practices has been a topic for debate. But even without this dilemma the task of identifying white collar crime is made difficult by the fact that the line between which practices are illegal and which are not is unclear and subject to change.

Organised crime

Perhaps the strongest link between street crime and white collar crime is provided by what we call 'organised crime'. The 1967 President's Commission on Law Enforcement and Administration of Justice defined it as follows:

Organized crime is a society that seeks to operate outside the control of the American people and their governments. It involves thousands of criminals, working within structures as complex as those of any large corporation, subject to laws more rigidly enforced than those of legitimate governments. Its actions are not impulsive but rather the result of intricate conspiracies, carried on over many years and aimed at gaining control over whole fields of activity in order to amass huge profits.[14]

An example of this link came into the public view in 1985 when the highly respectable Bank of Boston pleaded guilty to federal charges of failing to report $1.22 billion in cash transactions and was fined $500,000. There was substantial evidence that at least some of the money involved in the transactions was being 'laundered' for New England organised crime. That is, money from the sale of illegal drugs and other illicit activities was transferred to foreign bank accounts without reporting the transactions to the federal government, to disguise where the funds originated. Many organised crime figures perceive themselves as business people who meet a public demand for goods and services, such as drugs and prostitution, that the government prohibits. For these individuals the profit margin is the sole determinant of what type of business to pursue.

Perhaps the most publicised ties between organised crime and what we normally assume to be legitimate organisations are those with labour unions. Partial explanation for this can be attributed to the fact that the concept of organised labour does not fit neatly into American ideology, with its emphasis on individualism, and this has historically generated suspicion about the motives of union members and their leaders. But it is also apparent that organised crime has infiltrated a number of unions and used them to serve their own ends. In 1986 the President's Commission on Organized Crime identified four major unions with a combined membership of almost 3 million, or about 17 per cent of all union members in the US, as being controlled by organised crime.

The ties between organised crime and a labour union are probably best recognised in the history of the International Brotherhood of Teamsters. The 1.6 million-strong union bills itself as the largest union 'in the free world'. But its size, wealth, and centralised power structure have made it a target of organised crime. In 1986 Jackie Presser became the fourth Teamster president of the lst five to be indicted, and the third to be elected while facing criminal charges. Perhaps the most famous Teamster president, Jimmy Hoffa, was identified with organised crime early in his career, eventually served a federal prison sentence, and is widely presumed to have been killed by a criminal element closely associated with the Teamsters.

What makes the link between the Teamsters and organised crime especially interesting in the 1980s is the additional link between the Teamsters and the Reagan administration. The Teamsters was the only major union to endorse Ronald Reagan for President in both 1980 and 1984. Teamsters president Jackie Presser was named to the Reagan transition team in 1980. And the head of Reagan's 1984 re-election campaign, Senator Paul Laxalt of Nevada, asked President Richard Nixon in 1971 to pardon Jimmy Hoffa, the union's former president. He called Hoffa 'a political prisoner' of Kennedy-era investigations. Laxalt, a close political ally of Reagan's, with political ambitions of his own, has long been associated with people suspected of having ties with organised crime.

The important question to come out of this is whether or not such connections influence political decision-making to the detriment of the public interest. The evidence leaves room for suspicion. Allegations that Jackie Presser was engaged in illegal activities led a government strike force to recommend that the Justice Department seek indictments against him. The Justice Department initially rejected this recommendation and found itself the target of much criticism. Even the President's Crime Commission, in an interim report, scolded the administration for the 'appearance of impropriety' that had been created. In another incident the *Washington Post* reported that the Army, at the request of the White House, intervened to help the Teamsters union win a hotly contested election between it and the National Federation of Federal Employees (NFFE) over who would represent civilian employees at the Fort Sill military base.[15] A meeting was held at the White House between Army personnel and Teamster officials, and this meeting was used by the Teamsters to demonstrate their effectiveness in representing their members. The White House meeting was a 'political payoff' according to a leader of the losing NFFE. The intervention at least gave the appearance that the administration had broken the federal law requiring the government to maintain neutrality in such situations.

The 'sleaze' factor

The appearance of illegal activity, misconduct, or unethical behaviour, whether true or not, has been a problem for the Reagan administration since it first took office. This so-called 'sleaze' factor has not touched the President himself, leading some critics to label him 'teflon-coated'. While few question the personal honesty and integrity of the President, a number of his close aides and high ranking subordinates have been the centre of legal and ethical controversy. Attorney General Edwin Meese has been the subject of investigation by a special prosecutor for conflict of interest activities on two occasions. Raymond Donovan, Reagan's first Secretary of Labor, was under investigation for illegal business activities almost from the day he took office. In October, 1984 he was indicted on 137 counts for scheming to defraud the New York Transit Authority of more than $7 million. The President never asked Donovan to step down, and he waited until March 1985 before he resigned. A number of high ranking officials in the EPA were linked to illegal or questionable practices.

One of the most widely publicised allegations of potential misconduct by an official or former official of the administration involves former White House deputy chief of staff, Michael Deaver. An old family friend of the Reagans, Deaver left his post and organised his own lobbying firm, apparently marketing his close relationship with the Reagans as a major asset. But Deaver's aggressive style has left observers wondering whether or not he violated laws governing ethical conduct proscribing senior officials who leave the government from lobbying their former departments or agencies for one year. Especially questionable was his willingness to lobby for the Canadian government about acid rain, an issue which he was involved in while at the White House. Deaver is only one of more than a dozen former high-ranking officials who became lobbyists after leaving the administration in an official capacity. The President, seemingly seeing no potential for conflict of interest, does not discourage such activity, and he has staunchly defended Deaver.

Other administrations have had their share of unsavoury activities that raised questions about ethical standards and legality. And none of the examples noted is by itself enough to taint the integrity of the entire Reagan presidency. But these and other incidents, when considered collectively, reveal a pattern of behaviour that give one pause to wonder about the administration's commitment to promoting honesty and integrity in government.

The Iran-Contra Affair

The honesty and integrity of the President and his administration have been most severely tested to date by the revelation of secret negotiations with Iran to trade arms for hostages and money, and allegations that at least some of that money was used to purchase illegally military equipment for rebels fighting against the Nicaraguan government. Testimony before congressional committees indicates that White House, State Department, and CIA officials were intimately involved in the planning, financing and operation of the affair. What role President Reagan played remains an open question. Regardless of what that role was, his credibility has been irreparably damaged. It appears that members of the administration did serious harm to Ronald Reagan personally and to the office of the presidency in their disregard for at least the spirit of the law to promote their controversial policy agenda.

Conclusion

The Reagan administration is headed by a man who is widely perceived to have great personal integrity. The President and his aides have taken a strong public stand against street crime and they have declared war on illegal drugs. Yet the administration has been associated with individuals and engaged in activities that suggest a high tolerance for behaviour that is ethically and morally questionable, at the very least. This does not necessarily mean the government consciously applies a double standard in responding to potential wrongdoing. It does help demonstrate that what constitutes crime and how it should be treated are matters of personal bias as well as public debate. It is the responsibility of the citizenry to demand that government officials suppress personal bias and fairly execute the laws which are born from political debate.

Notes

1 Henry Campell Black, *Black's Law Dictionary*, 5th Edition, West Publishing Co., St. Paul, Minn., 1979, p 334.

2 'Criminal victimization 1984', Bureau of Justice Statistics. US Department of Justice, Washington, DC, 1985.

3 Table 321. 'Federal and state prisoners: 1950 to 1984', *Statistical Abstract of the United States, 1986,* Bureau of Census, US Department of Commerce, Washington, DC, 1986, p 184.

4 Table 302. 'Criminal justice system – public expenditures and employment by level of government: 1980 to 1982', *Statistical abstract, 1986,* p 175.

5 'Meese backs death penalty for young in capital crimes', *Boston Globe,* 17 Sept. 1985, p 10.

6 'The political pulse', *Washington Post National Weekly Edition,* 29 Sept. 1986, p 10.

7 'The political pulse', *WPNWE,* 29 Sept. 1986, p 11.

8 'A quick fix or a war on drugs?', *Boston Globe,* 21 Sept. 1986, p 1A.

9 'Who's winning the national war on drugs?', *National Journal,* 13 Sept. 1986, p 2200.

10 'The political pulse', *WPNWE,* 29 Sept, 1986, p 12.

11 Herbert Edelhertz, *The Nature, Impact, and Prosecution of White Collar Crime,* Government Printing Office, Washington, DC, 1970, p 3.

12 'New rules proposed on white collar crime', *Boston Globe,* 17 Sept. 1985, p 10.

13 'White collar crime: the problem and its import: US Chamber of Commerce', cited in *The Criminal in Society,* vol.1, Leon Radzinowicz & Marvin Wolfgang (eds), Basic Books, New York, 1977, p 317.

14 The President's Commission on Law Enforcement and Administration of Justice, *Task Force Report: Crime and Its Impact – An Assessment,* Government Printing Office, Washington, DC, 1967, p 205.

15 'The Army helps win one for the Gipper', *WPNWE,* 8 April 1986, p 29.

Fredric A. Waldstein

Environmental politics

Introduction

1976: An explosion at a pharmaceutical plant in Seveso, Italy caused the release of the deadly chemical dioxin into the atmosphere which contaminated at least 700 acres of land and affected more than 5,000 people.

1977: A toxic waste dump that had been filled and turned into a housing development came under scrutiny for its adverse affects on the population's health, and eventually the Love Canal site had to be abandoned.

1979: The first reported nuclear power plant accident occurred at Three Mile Island outside Harrisburg, Pennsylvania.

1982: The entire town of Times Beach, Missouri was evacuated and condemned after dangerously high levels of dioxin were discovered in oil that was used to spray city streets as a dust suppressant.

1984: More than 2,000 people were killed and approximately 200,000 injured when lethal gas escaped from a plant located in Bhopal, India.

1986: A Soviet nuclear power plant at Chernobyl experienced at least partial meltdown and caused a marked increase in radiation levels throughout much of Europe. Death and the potential of contaminating the agricultural heartland of the Soviet Union were attributed to the accident.

These are some of the most publicised events over the past ten years that have heightened public sensitivity to the potential for widespread environmental pollution that may threaten the existence of humankind. But they are by no means the only events that have occurred. A government survey revealed that in the first half of this decade nearly 7,000 chemical accidents which killed 135 people and injured 1500 others occurred in the US alone.

Perhaps even more sinister than the disasters which command blockbuster headlines are the more subtle alterations to the environment whose cumulative effect may be even more damaging and present a greater threat to human survival. Deforestation, soil erosion, depletion of the ozone layer, acid rain, contamination of the air and groundwater are examples of this more insidious type of pollution because either we are largely unaware of it or we feel we can worry about it at a later date.

This chapter will focus on US government policy pertaining to the protection of the environment and controlling pollution. For our purposes the environment is defined as 'the sum of all external conditions and influences affecting the life and development of organisms'.[1] Pollution is defined as the 'direct or indirect alteration of the physical, thermal, biological or radioactive properties of any part of the environment in such a way as to create a hazard to the health, safety, or welfare of any living species'.[2]

Protecting the environment against pollution is an extremely complex issue from both a scientific and technological perspective. Because of the intricacy of the environment it is difficult for scientists to draw unambiguous cause and effect relationships among pollutants, their sources, and their impact. Even if these relationships are not ambiguous, it is often beyond our technological capability to do much about it. Decontaminating land, water, and air on a large scale is not something we know how to do as a response to many, if not most, forms of pollution.

But even when the causes of pollution are known and the means exist to purge the environment of it, there is no guarantee that the political will to take action can be mobilised. This is true for several reasons. One of these is the cost and who should bear it. Pollution normally results as a by-product of activity that is perceived by those who derive benefit from it as desirable. Beneficiaries may include corporate investors, managers, employees, and consumers who are willing to accept varying degrees of risk from pollution if the only alternatives are to stop the activity altogether or allow it to continue at a higher cost to the beneficiaries. In addition, those who derive benefit from whatever activity causes pollution may not be affected by its consequences. For example, the pollutants from the tall smoke-stacks of the industrial midwest seem to cause the greatest damage to the eastern states in the form of acid rain. Determining what trade-offs will be made to protect the environment is becoming an increasingly important part of the political decision-making process in terms of both the career goals of individual politicians and the health and well-being of future generations of life on earth. Our goal in this chapter is to describe how this issue has fared in the political arena, and perhaps offer some partial explanations about why.

Protecting the environment prior to the 1960s

In the first 170 years of the nation's history very little attention was paid to the environment other than as something to be conquered and exploited for the wealth it could bring to individuals and glory to the country. The natural resources seemed boundless, so there was little need for thoughts of preservation. As the industrial revolution reached its zenith however, some concerns about the environment and the need for government intervention began to appear. These had to do mostly with promoting cleanliness and health in urban centres both at home and at work. The provision of clean water and sewage disposal became standard government services, for example.

While most governmental intervention in environmental affairs of this type was by state and local governments, the federal government was also taking steps to promote public health. The Food and Drug Administration was created in 1907 to ensure the safety and effectiveness of food, cosmetics, and pharmaceuticals. Additional consumer protection measures were added with the Food, Drug, and Cosmetic Act of 1938.

In 1886 Congress passed the Rivers and Harbors Appropriation Act to address the problem of dumping refuse into the harbour of New York City. A much more comprehensive piece of legislation was passed as the Rivers and Harbors Act of 1899. This legislation, which remains relatively unchanged to this day, defined what types of behaviour pertaining to navigable waters were unlawful, and set forth penalties for violation of the act. Although not primarily an environmental statute, the Supreme Court, in a series of decisions during the 1960s and 1970s, interpreted the Act to make it unlawful to discharge material into a navigable stream without a federal permit.

The Congress played a direct role in preserving the natural beauty of the environment with the creation of Yellowstone National Park in 1872. Federal forest reserves were established in 1891, and the Forest Service was created in 1905 to manage them.

The National Park Service was created in 1916 to 'promote and regulate the use of National Parks, monuments, and reservations and to conserve the scenery and natural and historic objects and the wildlife therein . . . for future generations'.

Other federal legislation passed in the first half of the twentieth century with an environmental component included the Antiquities Act of 1906, the Mineral Leasing Act of 1920, the Federal Power Act of 1933, the Fish and Wildlife Coordination Act of 1934, and the Water Pollution Control Act of 1948. But for the most part, environmental protection and preservation was a relatively low priority even in many of these legislative measures. Development of resources was the main priority, and if development projects were not unnecessarily inconvenienced conservation practices were encouraged. In addition, agreement about what constituted conservation and environmental protection was not always readily forthcoming.

The development of the atom bomb ushered in the era of nuclear energy with its vast potential for positive and negative consequences. The Atomic Energy Act of 1946 created the Atomic Energy Commission to control and develop the uses of nuclear power. In 1954 the Act was modified to permit private development of atomic energy for industrial purposes. Congress abolished the Atomic Energy Commission in 1974, transferring its licensing and regulatory function to the Nuclear Regulatory Commission (NRC), and its research and development function to the Energy Research and Development Administration (ERDA). Both the NRC and ERDA were created in 1974. Also pertinent to nuclear energy was the Price-Anderson Act passed in 1957 to attain two objectives: to provide funds to meet public liability claims in case of nuclear accident; and to remove the threat of unlimited liability which was perceived to be deterring private industry from engaging in nuclear research and development. While these measures were not primarily concerned with environmental protection, they nevertheless acknowledged the potential for nuclear accident and the responsibility of government in that event.

From 1960 to 1980: the environmental era

The 1960s and 1970s witnessed increasing public sensitivity to the concern for the environment, broadly defined, and threats to its stability. Reports on the extinction or rapid dimunition of various plant and animal species attributed to pollutants or loss of habitat received prominent media attention. Pictures of seabirds covered with oil struggling hopelessly to survive, and the reported 'death' of Lake Erie as a natural ecosystem, for example, caused many people to examine the gravity of threats to traditional environmental stability and led to questions about what implications this had for the health and well-being of *homo sapiens* as a species. Funds for environmental research became available and led to studies that confirmed the dangers of ignoring threats to the environment. Some environmental scientists, perhaps most notably Barry Commoner, went beyond experimentation and analysis to take a leading role in advocating the importance of protecting the natural environment. Symbolic gestures of solidarity with the environment such as Earth Day stirred public consciousness, and 'environmentalism' became a policy issue that political figures could not ignore.

Responding to public demand for an active governmental role in environmental protection, a spate of public rules and regulations were enacted at the local, state, and federal levels to form the corpus of environmental law, defined as follows:

> Environmental law can be defined as those statutes, administrative regulations, executive orders, and court decisions which pertain to the protection of nature and human beings from the consequence of unwise production or development and the procedural means by which these 'laws' can be invoked by citizens and government.[3]

Between 1960 and 1980 the federal government alone passed more than twenty five pieces of environmental legislation spanning a broad range of activities that fell into one or more of three general categories: pollution control laws; conservation laws; and laws requiring agencies to co-ordinate their projects with the goal of promoting pollution control and conservation. Among the measures enacted were: the Wilderness Act (1964); the National Historic Preservation Act (1966); the National Environmental Policy Act, or NEPA (1970); the Geothermal Steam Act (1970); the Clean Air Act (1970); the Clean Water Act (1972); the Safe Drinking Water Act (1974); the Toxic Substance Control Act (1976); and the Comprehensive Environmental Response, Compensation, and Recovery Act, better known as 'Superfund' (1980). Some legislation was very narrow and specific, such as the Wild Free-Roaming

Horses and Burros Act (1971). So much activity led the Commission for a National Agenda of the Eighties to conclude, 'It may well be that no other domestic policy challenge of recent times has been addressed as forcefully and quickly [as environmental issues]'.[4]

However, successfully implementing environmental laws has proved to be far more difficult and costly than anticipated or acknowledged by advocates of environmental reform. In several instances new standards for pollution control were set that were beyond the technical capacity of polluters to achieve without closing their operations. But the absences of technical knowledge appears to have been largely ignored in the formulation of public policy. As Walter Rosenbaum put it, 'Congress resolutely pressed technology on the presumption that the requisite technologies could be summoned if only enough regulatory pressure were applied'.[5]

This is not to suggest that all environmental laws were ill-conceived and doomed to failure. Many positive and significant steps in the direction of environmental protection were taken, and a number of success stories are well documented. But the cost of environmental protection substantially exceeded early expectations, which may have led to a certain amount of public disillusionment with the environmental cause. Several factors help explain why the costs were not more accurately predicted at the outset. More data on the ecosystem showed that pollution damage was greater than expected, and eliminating it from the environment was much more difficult than anticipated. Also, those sectors of the economy that anticipated higher costs of operation as environmental laws took effect engaged in litigation and used whatever political pressure they could bring to bear on their behalf to modify, if not halt, original timetables and pollution control projects. Delay coupled with inflation greatly increased the costs beyond original estimates which tended to be conservative at the outset to make them more appealing.

As the 1970s wore on, the economy slowed and both inflation and unemployment continued to rise. This state of affairs was attributed to a number of factors, not the least important being the increase in the costs of energy and the regulatory burdens imposed on business by the government. In both instances the environmental movement was perceived as contributing to the stagnation of the economy. The energy production industries argued that they were so overburdened with potential liability for damage to the environment that they could not afford to seek domestic sources of energy to meet the rising price of oil that resulted from the cartel established as the Oil Producing and Exporting Countries (OPEC). This argument was made repeatedly to the American public, even in the face of record profits by oil companies, utilities, and other segments of the energy industry in the 1970s.

Environmental legislation was blamed for the rising costs of production in other industries as well. Pollution control and environmental protection laws were cited, among other factors, as reasons why the cost of production had risen to a level where American producers were no longer competitive with their foreign counterparts. And many businesses made good on threats to close their American production facilities and go abroad. Organised labour increasingly became identified with the position that environmental reform had to take a back seat to job preservation, particularly in the construction industry. In the face of these events the environmental movement lost much of its momentum and constituency. Those who continued to espouse the environmental cause were disparagingly labelled 'nuts and berries freaks', who, if successful, would cost more in taxes and jobs than the public could afford to pay. This position was openly advocated by Ronald Reagan in his bid for the presidency. Environmentalism was cast as one of the factors keeping the country from attaining its potential and recapturing its rightful position as the dominant economic force in the world. Reagan's election clearly put the environmental movement on the defensive, where it remains.

Environmental protection under Reagan

While some environmentalists took comfort in the legislative measures that had been formulated and passed during the previous two decades and the pro-environmental inertia that had been mounted within the federal bureaucracy, the more pessimistic were fearful that implementation of those laws would be halted or severely curtailed. Reagan's initial appointments to key government positions did nothing to alleviate those fears.

James G. Watt was nominated and confirmed to the post of Secretary of the Interior. Established as a cabinet level department in 1845, the Interior Department is responsible for environmental issues in several critical areas including: the protection and management of approximately 550 million acres of public land; the administration of lands and programmes concerning American natives; the enforcement of federal surface mining regulations; the conservation and management of wetlands; and the preservation and protection of wildlife.

While Secretaries of the Department under recent administrations were perceived to be compatible with,, if not always overtly supportive of, environmental concerns, Watt was perceived by many to be an enemy of conservation who brought with him an agenda that would promote private sector use of public lands at the expense of the environment. Prior to his appointment Watt headed the Mountain States Legal Foundation, which represented corporate and state government interests opposed to federal environmental regulations.

Watt brought individuals into the Interior Department and initiated policy changes that confirmed the fears of many of his critics. And even though he was forced to resign in 1983 because his abrasive style and insulting demeanour finally made him a liability to the Reagan administration, his substantive policy positions continued to be implemented by his successors, albeit in a more subtle manner.

The Environmental Protection Agency (EPA), created by President Nixon in 1970 through an executive order, is the most important government entity concerning environmental issues and policies. Among the major programmes for which EPA is responsible are: the Clean Air Act; the Clean Water Act; the Safe Drinking Water Act; the Toxic Substance Control Act; and the Federal Insecticide, Fungicide, and Rodenticide Act. The Agency's proposed operating budget for Fiscal Year (FY) 1987 was down slightly from the record $1.36 billion requested by the Reagan administration in FY 86. These levels reflect approximate parity with the EPA budget at the time President Carter left office. In the first two years of the Reagan administration the Agency's budget was slashed by more than $300 million from Carter's last budget request.

Until Reagan took office the administrator of the EPA had always been an individual acceptable to environmentalists and generally sympathetic to the Agency's mission. Reagan's first choice to head the EPA was Ann Gorsuch (later to become Ann Burford through marriage), a corporate lawyer who numbered among her clients companies hostile to federal environmental regulations.

Environmentalists interpreted [Gorsuch's] appointment as a deliberate signal that the White House intended to move the agency's sympathies toward business and other regulated interests and away from the environmental groups that considered themselves the agency's natural constituency. Early on [Gorsuch] appointed to the agency's upper management individuals exclusively associated with past opponents of EPA programs . . .[6]

Under Gorsuch the Agency experienced reductions in personnel, and the number of court cases it recommended to the Justice Department for prosecution for violation of environmental laws dropped to 50 in the first nine months compared with 230 in the last year of the Carter administration. These and other signs suggested that the EPA simply would not fulfil its statutory mandate. Furthermore, there were indications that some EPA personnel were actively helping companies evade environmental protection regulations. In addition, there were allegations that funds to clean up toxic waste ('superfund') were being distributed in a partisan manner to aid Republican candidates running for office. Morale at the agency was extremely low among career personnel, and programmes were in an apparent state of disarray.

In October of 1982 John Dingell, chairman of the House Commerce and Energy Investigation subcommittee issued a subpoena for documents pertaining to the Agency's use of 'superfund' monies. In November of the same year the House Public Works Investigation subcommittee served a subpoena on Gorsuch requesting specific documents. President Reagan, invoking executive privilege, ordered Gorsuch not to comply with the subpoenas. She was subsequently cited for contempt of Congress, thus becoming the highest executive branch official ever so charged. Within six months the White House had backed down from its position, and Gorsuch (then Mrs Burford) and nineteen other high ranking EPA officials had been pressured to resign. Rita Lavelle, the person in charge of the toxic waste clean-up programmes, was dismissed by the President and eventually sentenced to prison after being convicted of lying under oath before congressional committees. Lavelle was found guilty, and became the only high-ranking official of the Reagan administration to be convicted of a crime in the performance of her duties.

The negative publicity generated by the inquiry into EPA activities and subsequent dismissals and resignations created a minor crisis of credibility for the administration regarding its commitment to environmental protection. It was one thing to modify EPA tactics and timetables. But it was quite something else to sabotage the EPA's central mission. To limit the political fallout on this issue the President needed to make a public demonstration of his commitment to the EPA and its goals. He was able to accomplish this by persuading the first administrator of the Agency, William Ruckelshaus, to return to his former post. Not only was Ruckelshaus strongly identified with the environmental movement by virtue of his previous work at EPA, he also enjoyed a reputation for honesty and being a man of his own convictions. But Ruckelshaus was also a pragmatic businessman who left a position with a timber company to take over EPA. The administration felt comfortable that he would be a 'team player'. In any case, Ruckelshaus stayed just long enough to boost morale within the Agency and reduce the political damage that had accrued to the President.

The events which transpired at EPA and the Interior Department were perhaps more spectacular as media events than other activities of the Reagan administration pertaining to the environment. But they reflected an attitude that was consistent throughout the executive branch, at least at the upper echelons of power. This attitude has had specific consequences on important substantive issues including acid rain, nuclear power and toxic waste.

The politics of acid rain

Precipitates with lower than normal pH levels have been collectively dubbed 'acid rain'. There is general agreement within the scientific community that the greater levels of acidity detected in rain, snow, lakes, rivers, and streams are caused at least in part by sulphur dioxide emissions and other pollutants, and that this is having a negative effect on both plant and animal life. Much of the blame for sulphur dioxide emissions has been placed on the burning of high-sulphur coal.

One of the factors that makes acid rain an interesting and complex political issue is that those areas most affected by it (the Northeast and Canada) are relatively distant from its causes (the smokestack industries of the Middlewest). Predictably, politicians in the Northeast support legislative measures to reduce acid rain.

Politicians in the Midwest, on the other hand, fear that efforts to halt acid rain will mean increasing the cost of production by imposing mandatory 'scrubbing' devices and other forms of pollution-control equipment on factory smokestacks; requiring plants to burn more costly, low-sulphur coal; or both. These individuals anticipate that placing additional cost burdens on industry will result in plants closing and increased unemployment in a region that has already experienced severe economic problems. Thus, the benefits of reducing acid rain would accrue to the Northeast while the costs would be borne by the Midwest.

There are essentially two positions on this issue. Those opposed to strict acid rain legislation say we simply do not know enough about its causes to undertake extremely costly measures that may be ineffective in solving the problem. Not surprisingly, perhaps, this is the position taken by the Reagan administration. Advocates of strict legislation claim there is ample scientific evidence demonstrating the causes of acid rain, and that the problem needs to be addressed immediately.

The politics of acid rain is interesting because it not only cuts across partisan lines, it also divides interest groups which normally enjoy great unity, and makes allies of those who usually find themselves on the opposite side of many issues. For example, both the coal mining and utilities industries are divided. Western low-sulphur coal interests find themselves in the same camp with the environmentalists in support of legislation, while their Eastern high-sulphur coal-producing brethren are allied with the United Mine Workers in opposition to legislation.

Although the outcome is far from decided, there does appear to be a growing sensitivity among members of Congress to the damage caused by acid rain and the belief that enough scientific data exists to take remedial action. Whether or not this can be translated into the formation of a winning coalition that can agree on how much money needs to be spent to alleviate the problem and who will pay for it remains very much open to question.

The future of nuclear energy

The accident at the Chernobyl nuclear power plant in 1986 has been universally acknowledged as an environmental disaster of major proportions with consequences that may be felt for decades to come. The Soviet Union will undoubtedly suffer the greatest short-term and long-term negative consequences. Scores of deaths will eventually be linked directly to the accident, and what it will mean for future Soviet agricultural production is a significant question. Chernobyl is located in the Ukraine, the Soviet Union's major food-producing republic. Contamination from radiation of livestock, crops, land and water could have long-term negative consequences for the provision of basic foods to the Soviet people.

The Soviet government also suffered serious political damage first for not alerting its neighbouring countries to the accident, and second for not being forthcoming about the seriousness of the accident once high levels of radiation were detected in other countries. But critics have maintained that some European governments also deliberately downplayed the potential dangers to their populations from radiation exposure for fear of mobilising strong antinuclear sentiments that could have negative political consequences for the parties in power. Most European countries rely much more heavily on nuclear power than the United States. Currently about 16 per cent of the electricity generated in the US comes from nuclear power, compared to 31 per cent in West Germany and 65 per cent in France, for example. Thus, the issue is potentially much bigger in those countries.

While there is little disagreement that Chernobyl was a disaster, there are two different responses in the US about what it means for Americans. Some opponents of nuclear energy argue that this is proof nuclear power is unsafe and poses too great a risk for use. Proponents of nuclear power argue that such an accident could never happen in the US because the reactor designs and types used are different from the one at Chernobyl precisely to maximise safety. Both proponents and opponents of nuclear energy cite the 1979 accident at Three Mile Island, Pennsylvania to support their positions. In that incident human error and design problems were blamed for the release of radioactive materials, but most of it was kept from entering the atmosphere by the plant's containment dome. A potentially serious but less publicised incident occurred at the Besse-Davis nuclear plant near Toledo, Ohio in June 1985. Although no radiation was released, the potential threat was substantial. An NRC investigation subsequently cited lack of attention to detail in the care of plant equipment as the cause. A 1985 NRC study concluded that there was a 45 per cent chance of a major nuclear power plant accident in the US over the next twenty years. While the nuclear industry disagrees with these figures, it has pushed hard for renewal of the Price-Anderson legislation which would cap liability for the corporation involved in any accident at $2 billion.

According to a CBS News poll, most Americans believe that the kind of accident that happened at Chernobyl could indeed occur in the US. And a survey by the Washington Post-ABC News in May of 1986, a few weeks after the accident, showed that 78 per cent of the public, an all-time high, opposed expanding the use of nuclear power. However, a majority opposed eliminating existing nuclear power plants.[7] So while Americans appeared to be becoming increasingly concerned about the risks of nuclear power, they remained ambivalent about an appropriate course of action.

Perhaps more important than public opinion in terms of its impact on the nuclear industry is the economics of nuclear-generated electricity. In the 1950s the hope was expressed that nuclear power would provide electricity 'too cheap to meter'. But costs have skyrocketed, and 1984 statistics provided by the Atomic Industrial Forum show that the total generating costs in cents per kilowatt hour for nuclear plants that went into operation in 1983 were 9.4, compared to 5.3 for coal-fired plants that went into operation during the same year.[8] No utility has ordered a new nuclear power plant since 1978, and no work has begun on those that were ordered in 1978. In addition, many orders have been cancelled. The Reagan administration has generally been a strong supporter of nuclear energy, but the poor economic outlook for nuclear power and the negative political climate created by the Chernobyl incident have severely constrained the political options that can be exercised to the benefit of the nuclear industry.

Hazardous waste disposal

Another problem with nuclear energy is the unanswered question of what to do with the radioactive waste that it produces. The Washington Post-ABC News poll cited earlier also noted this as a major public concern. 58 per cent of those asked believed that nuclear waste could not be disposed of safely. Even low-level radioactive waste which results from research and other types of activity is a political 'hot potato' that contributes to the so-called

NIMBY ('Not In My Back Yard') problem. People do not care where toxic or nuclear waste is disposed, as long as it is not in their community.

The amount of hazardous waste that is generated in the US each year is unknown, but we do know it is a staggering figure. The Congressional Budget Office (CBO) estimates that industry generates more than 266 million metric tons of hazardous waste per year, not counting smokestack emissions or some forms of water pollution. Furthermore, disposal of hazardous waste costs industry approximately \$5.8 billion annually.[9] Improper disposal can create a variety of health hazards, one of the most serious being the contamination of the water supply.

The government's efforts regarding hazardous waste disposal have been the source of controversy, primarily because there is so little agreement both about appropriate levels of risk from exposure, and what methods best attain those levels about which there is agreement. Even something as apparently straightforward as the 1984 Resource Conservation and Recovery Act (RCRA), which forbids the disposal of toxic waste in landfills, is a source of disagreement. The EPA has interpreted the statute to allow the dumping of toxic waste in landfills that do not pose a hazard to people because, for example, the dump site might be in an uninhabited locality. Two of the EPA-approved methods of disposal which are widely used are incineration and deep-well injection. Both methods have their environmental risks and critics.

Rather than concentrate on waste disposal, some environmentalists, government officials, and industry personnel are increasingly looking to the potential for waste reduction. That is, finding other uses for material that is currently treated as waste. A number of companies have found that waste reduction techniques save money. In addition, a reduction of hazardous waste output may reduce the threat of potential liability to companies. But for the immediate future, waste disposal will continue to be a more prominent issue because it will be much more extensively practised.

Cleaning up existing hazardous waste dump sites that have been deemed the greatest potential danger to public health is the responsibility of the EPA's Superfund programme. Four hundred and nineteen clean-up projects across the country are currently under way. But the success of Superfund is dependent in part on the huge allocations of money that gives the programme its name. Congress, however, has failed to pass reauthorisation legislation that will keep the programme in business. The bill has been stalled in conference committee as different factions argue about the most appropriate response to the hazardous waste problem. The issue is complex and the outcome important, with both money and lives at stake. Meanwhile, the Superfund programme has ground to a virtual standstill.

Conclusion

We have briefly touched upon a number of points that help demonstrate the complexity of environmentalism as a political issue in the US. What makes it so complex is disagreement about both short-term and long-term risk assessment, and what response is appropriate and effective, once some agreement on assessment has been reached. Compounding the difficulties are the high stakes involved. Environmental protection is a costly enterprise, and deciding how those costs should be shared is of fundamental political importance. But the alternative to facing the issue squarely is living with the risk of environmental disaster that may destroy us. This thought, perhaps, gives us a more sobering perspective on the importance of environmental protection and the partisan political and economic struggles with which we are normally preoccupied.

Notes

1 *McGraw-Hill Encyclopedia of Environmental Science,* McGraw-Hill, New York, 1974, p 175.
2 M. Allaby, *A Dictionary of ther Environment,* 2nd ed., New York University Press, New York, 1983, p 390.
3 J. R. Pfafflin & E. N. Zeigler (eds), *Encyclopedia of Environmental Science and Engineering,* 2nd ed., Gordon & Breach Science Publishers, New York, 1983, vol. 1, p 362.
4 President's Commission for a National Agenda for the Eighties, *The American Economy, Energy and Environment in the Eighties,* Prentice-Hall, Englewood Cliffs, NJ, 1981, p 89.
5 W. A. Rosenbaum, *Environmental Politics and Policy,* Congressional Quarterly, Inc., Washington, DC, p 8.
6 Rosenbaum, *Environmental Politics and Policy*, p 54.
7 'Nuclear energy: skepticism rises', *Washington Post National Weekly Edition,* 9 June 1986, p 37.
8 'The nuclear option', *National Journal,* 5 July 1986, p 1647.
9 'Drowning in waste', *National Journal,* 10 May 1986, p 1106.

V
Foreign policy issues

Jack Spence

The banana republics revolt: the US and Central America

The US viewed Central America, before 1978, as a sleepy group of 'banana republics' marked only by one anonymous military coup after another. In the 1980 Presidential election campaign, candidate Reagan and the Republican party mounted a steady drumbeat of criticism against President Carter's foreign policy towards Latin America. Carter had given away 'our' Panama Canal to a Panama headed by a 'tinhorn dictator'. Nicaragua had 'fallen' to a left-wing government during Carter's 'watch'. To Reagan, that mistake in turn gave rise to a leftist guerilla movement in El Salvador, threatening a friendly government already weakened by the Carter administration's criticisms of its human rights record. In Guatemala, cut off from almost all US military aid by Carter due to human rights violations, a leftist insurgency was thriving. With Reagan's election it became common to refer to the 'Crisis in Central America'. Suddenly, it had moved to the forefront of US foreign 'hot spots'.

By the time of his inauguration President Reagan saw Nicaragua sliding towards totalitarianism, a slide completed by the time of his second term. The 'cancer' of Nicaragua would spread throughout Central America. A 'Soviet outpost' in Central America could threaten vital sea lanes or even become a base for hostile missiles. Refugees, fleeing totalitarianism, would swarm over the borders of the US, addding to domestic employment problems.

The Reagan solution to this crisis was to organise and finance an army to fight agaisnt the leftist Sandinista government in Nicaragua and to provide military aid to governments threatened, in the eyes of the Reagan administration, by Nicaraguan-sponsored left insurgencies. Congress, pushed hard by Reagan, reluctantly granted his aid requests, so that by 1985 $400 million in aid was going to El Salvador and $27 milion in non-lethal military aid had been approved for the contra army, seeking to overthrow an elected, leftist government in Nicaragua. Throughout, public opinion polls showed Americans to be opposed to this excalating involvement.[1] This was Washington's crisis in Central America.

To understand the Washington crisis concerning Central America is not to understand the Central American crisis. Washington's crisis did not arise until political turbulence threatened anti-democratic governments friendly to Washington. The Central American crisis considerably antedates this point. To understand it we will trace recent developments exacerbating unequal distributions of land, political power and wealth and the growth of extreme poverty. These changes led to political actions against undemocratic governments in El Salvador, Guatemala and Nicaragua. Washington took notice when the local established orders of military and large landowners were severely threatened. Then we will step back in time to look at the nineteenth century formation of US interests in the area. We will conclude with an assessment of the post-Vietnam era in relations between the US and Cental America.

The 'other' Central American crises – El Salvador

El Salvador illustrates the crucial inter-relation of land, poverty and political power. Since the early 1930s the military had run the government. Electoral exercises occasionally punctuated this period, but the military victory was a foregone conclusion. Civilian political parties and trade unions were either outlawed or severely curbed. But rich landowners enjoyed the protection of the military. The peasant majority could not legally organise, and could not participate. In urban areas it was virtually impossible to conduct a legal strike. More important than the lack of a meaningful national suffrage, in short, was the total absence for the bulk of the population of any access to power.

Liberalising change came in the mid 1960s. Political patrties were given a chance to run for Mayor and seats in the legislature. Three civilian parties had some successes. These offices were not powerful, but it was a beginning, a forum, a chance to build an electoral political base. In 1972 the three parties coalesced to run for the Presidency against a military candidate.

Wholly ignored in Washington, this election fundamentally altered Salvadoran politics. The unified ticket of Napoleon Duarte of the Christian Democrats and Guillermo Ungo, a Social Democrat, won big in the early returns, but when the sun came up the next morning they had been defrauded through 'midnight balloting'. The military maintained its grip and wealthy landowners had staved off a threat of land redistribution.

During these same years the perpetual land shortage for peasants worsened dramatically. The numbers of landless grew. For those who maintained access to land, through renting or owning, the average size of a piece of land shrank, for many, below a size which could produce in successive years a crop sufficient to feed the family. Full-time rural employment also shrank, as landowners sought to evade the one piece of reform legislation the new civilian parties had managed, a minimum wage law, by reducing the number of full-time employees. Some peasant families migrated to cities looking for jobs that were not there. Most, including many with access only to tiny parcels, fell into part-time, migrant labour.

El Salvador became a nation of migrant farm workers following the seasons of export crops. Population increase, El Salvador's small size, increasing lands put into export crops by large landowners, the forced return of 300,000 Salvadorans from Honduras following the 1967 War between those two countries, increased land costs and downward pressure on wages all resulted in an acute and growing land crisis.[2]

These two developments, all important to El Salvador, went unnoticed in Washington. The intersection of these two forces – a political opening followed by increased repression, and rural landlessness – led to more militant politics. Contributing to this were grass-roots church leaders, influenced by Vatican II and the new liberation theology, who saw their role as helping the poor to organise. Organisatons asking for runnning water, higher wages or more land cropped up in neighbourhoods, workplaces and villages. Requests became demands. The government and landowner-controlled military units broke up demonstrations, and by the late 1970s grass-roots leaders began to be arrested, tortured and 'disappear'.

In October 1979, shocked by the Sandinista victory over Somoza in Nicaragua, a young faction of the Salvadoran military overthrew the government and promised progressive reforms. In the next five months civilian members of the government resigned *en masse* three times because they had no control over right-wing military forces, in league with landowners, who were escalating violence against the grass-roots groups and 'disappearing' their leaders. Centrist and left civilians were going underground, fleeing the country, and increasingly joining guerilla forces in the mountains. In March 1980 Archbishop Oscar Romero, who had spoken out against military abuses, was assassinated by a right-wing death squad while saying Mass, and three days later the army attacked his funeral procession. The country moved to civil war, with a swelling guerilla army threatening the third military dominated junta government, supported by the US.[3]

Seen in the context of Salvadoran history, the civil war was the domestic product of the failure of the political system to expand grass-roots and electoral political participation and the failure of the economic system to be able to maintain even the precarious subsistence economy for major sectors of its poor majority.

But El Salvador's conflict was pulled by the reach of US power into the web of domestic US political rivalries and transformed from a question of corn, beans and land into a question of superpower politics, magnified by the most serious election-year bid for power the conservative wing of the Republican party had made in two generations. Carter, running on a weak economic record, was under attack from the right for ceding operational control of the Panama Canal, and for leftist Sandinistas in power in Nicaragua. To the GOP, Nicaragua had been 'lost' to communism, and El Salvador would be the next 'domino'. Carter attempted to shore up the new Duarte-military government with aid and an agrarian reform programme which was systematically attacked by Salvador's oligarchy and some of their military allies. Carter, sensitive to the 'domino' charge, threw his support to the Salvadoran government, despite the vast escalation in human rights violations between 1978 and 1980. Human rights groups estimate that 147 citizens were killed by assassination in 1978, 1030 in 1979 and, as Carter support was increasing, 8024 in 1980 (this in a country of five million). A roughly equivalent figure in Great Britain for 1980 would have been some 88,000 assassinations. By mid campaign, the US was poised to massively escalate its military involvement in El Salvador.

Crises in Guatemala and Nicaragua

Roughly similar dynamics of land and power inequities leading to a challenge to the established order followed by US efforts to restore order can be seen in Guatemala and Nicaragua, though the dynamics unfolded in different historical spaces. In Guatemala, a political opening came when the Dictator Ubico was overthrown in 1944 and replaced by Guatemala's first democratically-elected government headed by President Arevalo. He was succeeded, following another election, by Jacobo Arbenz. Arbenz followed up on Arevalo's initiatives, expanding the rights of trade unions, and legislating an agrarian reform bill that would take through a kind of eminent domain proceeding large unused landholdings, and distribute them to poor peasants. Arbenz, though not a communist, included a small number of Communist Party members in low-level positions in cabinet ministries.

The US based United Fruit Company had extensive banana holdings, 80 per cent of which lay fallow. It owned the only port on the Caribbean, controlled all railroads and electrical power in the eastern part of the country, and was the largest employer. Angered by the reforms, and the legal presence of the Communist Party, United Fruit and the Eisenhower administration determined to overthrow Arbenz, and did so in 1954 with the help of CIA-organised and financed army, and bombing runs over the capital.[4]

The US intervention was decisive in ending the threat to the old order. Agrarian reform was rolled back and the military moved into unchallenged political power (and by the 1970s very considerable economic power) for the next generation. Electoral political change and economic reform was closed off. In the 1960s guerilla warfare broke out. Defeated with the help of US Green Berets, the guerillas regrouped in the 1970s, organising among the highland Indians who suffered the severest land shortages and double discrimination. As in El Salvador, grass-roots organisations sprouted. Though their system was again challenged, previous years of US military aid enabled the Guatemalan military to exercise brutal, scorched-earth campaigns and massacres in areas sympathetic to the guerillas. By 1986, though the guerillas were not defeated, the old order restored by US intervention in 1954 still stood.

In Nicaragua the Somoza half-century dynasty began to be challenged in the 1970s. After the massive 1972 Managua earthquake Somoza channelled international relief funds into companies he owned. Rival sectors of the economic *élite* were being squeezed out of economic opportunities, and urban dwellers could see Somoza's National Guard *selling* black market international relief goods. Meanwhile, peasants were being displaced from lands by commercial cotton and coffee growers associated with the Somoza family. These conditions gave the Sandinistas, who had decided in 1966 that Somoza would never leave unless forced out, opportunities for organising. Somoza met their challenges with increasing repression, inflicted upon both Sandinistas and poor people suspected of helping them. In 1978, for the first time, brutal repression was used against Somoza's middle-class opposition with the assassination of opposition newspaper editor Chamorro. This provided the impetus to galvanise the opposition first into massive demonstrations, then into Sandinista-led military offensives. In July 1979, Somoza fell. Among the first acts of the new Sandinista-led coalition government was to confiscate somocista lands, some 25 per cent of the nation's total, and employ on them landless peasants. Though the US used diplomatic means to attempt to keep the Sandinistas out, in this case the US intervention to eliminate a radical challenge came after the leader of the old order had been thrown out.[5]

In each of the three countries patterns of increasing barriers to political participation combined with reduced access to land for the already-exploited peasants to result in political militancy and insurgency. Only the last stage of this process was sufficient to gain the attention of Washington. Each of the insurgencies threatened to alter dramatically the pattern of land ownership in these agrarian economies, and the power structure.

Why would this turbulence be regarded in Washington as such a threat to US foreign policy interests, if it simply meant that large landowners, in the main not US firms, would be the losers in a social revolution? The answer, and the deeper roots of the revolts, particularly in Nicaragua, can be found by looking back a bit further in history.

Roots of the banana republics

The US had territorial and commercial interest in Mexico, Central America and the Caribbean in the first half of the nineteenth century. In the 1830s and 1840s, the US conquered from Mexico, first Texas and then what is now California and the southwestern portion of the US. Driven by the self-justifying concept of manifest destiny – a doctrine holding that the grandeur of the US made it obvious that it was meant to expand, the US cast its eyes further south to Cuba, Central America and the isthmus of Panama. In this region, however, it had to confront the declining empire of Spain (in Cuba), and the world's most powerful nation, Great Britain, which had developed considerable economic activities throughout Latin America following its independence from Spain.

Both Great Britain and the US desired to build and control a canal from the Caribbean to the Pacific. There were two proposed routes, one through the narrow strip of Panama, then a territory of Colombia, the other route through the mouth of Nicaragua's San Juan River, across Lake Nicaragua and through a short canal, cut through relatively easy terrain, to the Pacific.

In the 1850s William Walker, a US-based buccaneer, invaded Nicaragua with an eye toward controlling the San Juan – Lake Nicaragua transportation route frequented by many bound for California. He took over Nicaragua, but, after two years was ousted by the combined forces of Nicaragua and Costa Rica, financially aided by the North American railroad tycoon Cornelious Vanderbilt, whose steamships had controlled the route before Walker.

This episode, until recently forgotten, or treated as a comic footnote in US history, was never forgotten in Nicaragua. The US had actually recognised the Walker government of Nicaragua, and Walker had been able to gain supporters from Nicaraguan political figures willing to take their chances with the foreign pirate.

Though Britain controlled much of the Atlantic Coast of Central America, and exploited its timber resources, it came to recognise that the US was to be a power in the region. In the Clayton-Bulwer treaty, the two agreed in 1850 that, were there to be an Atlantic-Pacific canal, they would build it jointly. Between 1850 and 1900 the US underwent a period of unprecedented industrial growth. It became a great naval power which rivalled Great Britain and, in the Caribbean basin, surpassed it. Like the imperial powers in Europe, the US was in search of territory to provide raw materials for its industries and of military outposts to protect its shipping. It captured Puerto Rico, Cuba and the Philippines from Spain. By the turn of the century, the US had gained sufficient force that it was able to abandon the Clayton-Bulwer agreement and construct a canal on its own. Able to wrest the isthmus of Panama from Columbia by fomenting and controlling a revolt in the area, it completed the canal in 1906 and imposed a treaty on Panama, which gave the US sovereign control in perpetuity over the canal and a fifty mile-wide strip.

By the eve of World War I, US commercial investment in the Caribbean basin almost equalled that of the leader, Great Britain. Great Britain had invested in Central America by building railroads for transporting agricultural goods and minerals to ports, and in government bonds. Though these bonds frequently lost value, they gave Britain, and later the US, the commercial power to control the national treasuries of a number of nations. US corporations also invested in railroads and in agricultural production, initially bananas. United Fruit bought large tracts of land, and built feeder railroads, ships and ports for the bulky crop.

Coffee also became a major export crop in the latter half of the nineteenth century. Lower capital costs made it possible for coffee to be controlled largely by Central American agrarian capitalists, not huge foreign corporations (though in Costa Rica and Guatemala there were significant pockets of Germans invested in coffee). These families formed the backbone of the economic *élite* in the Central American countries. The new coffee barons acquired land from poor peasants and Indians, in some cases by changing the legal structure to abolish Indian communal landholdings and then buying up parcels of land as the poverty-stricken peasants and Indians fell into debt. Unlike the peasants, the coffee entrepreneurs had the capital to sustain the initial five-year growth period before the first harvest. Coffee did not require the transport technology necessary for bananas, but it was labour-intensive, particularly at harvest time where each bean was (and still is) picked by hand. The newly landless peasants supplied the first labour pool.

None of the countries developed more than tiny industrial bases. They became suppliers of agricultural products and minerals, mostly to the US. The landed *élite* either invested its profits in further agricultural production, frequently displacing peasant land holders in the process, invested them outside the country, or spent them on luxury, imported consumer goods. Much of the *élite* was either associated politically or economically with the US (or British) foreign corporations, or was dependent on entry into US markets (and therefore low tariffs). Those Central Americans with capital and an interest in industrial investment were hindered by a lack of consumers (the coffee barons and banana companies wanted cheap labour) and the daunting prospect of foreign competition from the more technologically-advanced and capital rich countries. For most of the *élite,* therefore, it was easier and safer to invest abroad, find more coffee land, consume, and maintain friendly alliances with the US.

Maintaining political stability

During this era of expansion, the US justified its controlling economic position with self-congratulatory doctrines that included clear overtones of racial superiority. It saw itself as civilised, in contradistinction to its Latin neighbours. President Theodore Roosevelt's Secretary of State observed that Latins were so cheerful they found happiness in their existing, though poor, condition of life. But they had less 'of the inventive faculty which serves continually to increase the productive power of men.'[6] When revolts broke out in the impoverished nations of the Caribbean Roosevelt found it the duty of the US to put them down, These were 'small bandit nests of a wicked and inefficient type'.[7]

The US had by 1932 backed up these notions of moral superiority with dozens of military interventions in Central America and the Caribbean to protect US investments, bank loans or to insure that no government would come into power that would chart a course not in the self-perceived interests of the US. The most extensive of these interventions was in Nicaragua where the US Marines overthrew Presidents in 1909 and 1910 and militarily defeated a nationalist movement in 1911. From then until the Somoza era the US directly controlled national finances and elections and, through a forced treaty, future canal developments in perpetuity. From William Walker through the Somoza era American intervention and influence in Nicaragua was facilitated by pliant Nicaraguan political factions which saw US intervention working to their advantages.

Augusto Sandino, in the late 1920s, organised a guerilla force to challenge the US Marines in Nicaragua. Fighting against considerably greater forces for six years, he fought the US Marines to a standstill, and eventually negotiated with the head of the

Nicaraguan military, Somoza, over terms of the Marines' removal. Somoza had been singled out by the US to control Nicaragua after the Marines left. Betrayed during the negotiations, Sandino was assassinated in 1932 by Somoza's men, and his guerilla army slowly dissolved.[8]

In El Salvador in 1932, an uprising of peasant and Indian coffee workers, whose wages were cut and jobs lost during the Depression, took over the western highlands, the coffee growing region. Poorly armed, the peasants were defeated by the army with the aid of US destroyers off-shore. Then, after the battle, the army systematically slaughtered suspects. In a country of 2 million, 17,000 to 30,000 were killed in a few weeks after the uprising. The military took over the government.[9] In Guatemala, the Ubico dictatorship came to power.

Thus, the Depression ushered in military-supported dictatorships in Central America. Franklin Delano Roosevelt was elected in the US. The Roosevelt administration established the Good Neighbour Policy toward Latin America, a policy which in effect meant friendly support for the dictatorial regimes in Central America. As Roosevelt remarked, after a visit of Somoza to the US, 'He's a son of a bitch, but he's our son of a bitch'.

Following World War II, the stable political systems in each of the countries were shaken, but, with the exception of Guatemala and Costa Rica, the political and economic systems remained in place. The changes in Guatemala came in the midst of the Cold War and anti-communist fervour that the McCarthy era spawned in the US. As we have seen, the US would not tolerate the changes. In Costa Rica a reform government was successfully implanted which eventually provided social welfare policies beneficial to the middle class and sectors of the poor. But it was clear that the new Costa Rican government was sufficiently anti-communist and was not moving to expropriate the property of US multinational corporations so that the US did not attempt to overthrow it, as it did in Guatemala in 1954.

By then, the twentieth century picture of the US and Central America could be summed up as a period in which the US completed its ascension over Great Britain as the dominant superpower in the region. The US protected with military force and friendly clients what it saw to be its commercial and geopolitical interests in the region. The countries developed agroexport economies based on sugar, bananas, coffee and, after World War II, cotton and cattle. These agroexport economies rested on poorly-paid labour, extensive poverty and increasing incursions on the land worked by subsistence peasant farmers. Local economic *élites* controlled some crops; and US firms invested in crops, transport and finance.

Stability challenged

Sandino was the first major challenge to this system, a challenge directed more against US political control than against the predominant economic patterns. It is no accident that the challenge came in the Central American country with the most overt US intervention. Guatemala, under the elected governments of Arevalo and Arbenz from 1944–54 can be seen as the second challenge. The Guatemalan challenge addressed the land question and certain rules of the political game set by the US, e.g. no left-wing participation. In the short run, the US defeated each of these two challenges, in Guatemala, with considerable ease.

The next major challenge came in the Caribbean with Fidel Castro's military defeat of Batista, a US supported dictator. Castro expropriated large farms, including US-owned sugar plantations, cleaned up Havana gambling and prostitution controlled by US-based mobs, and expropriated US refineries when they refused to process oil purchased from the Soviet Union. The US moved to militarily remove the Castro government with a Miami-based anti-Castro Cuban army in the 1961 Bay of Pigs operation, but, unlike Arbenz in Guatemela, Castro had a strong army and an organised population. While the US succeeded for the most part in diplomatically and economically isolating Cuba in the hemisphere (a success which became less thorough over the years since 1961), it had not been able to displace the government. In 1965, fearing another Castro, the US met a small scale uprising in the Dominican Republic with 25,000 US troops.

Post-Vietnam Central America

The post Vietnam era brought challenges from Central America. The Panamanians successfully pressured for more control over the Canal. Insurgencies in Guatemala, Nicaragua, and El Salvador fought to change fundamentally the political and land tenure systems. In each of these countries, a previous challenge had been defeated by the US or with its help – Sandino in Nicaragua, the Salvadoran peasant uprising in 1932, and Arbenz in Guatemala. Each defeat ushered in a military-dominated dictatorial government pledged to maintain the power structure of the agroexport economy and to have friendly, loyal relations with the US. And each of these governments was met, by the late 1970s, with major grass-roots political and military efforts to change the land system and its tradition of political dictatorship. The US viewed each as a threat.

The outcome of these conflicts was unclear by mid-1987. Seen in a broader historical context, US power in the region seemed to have declined considerably from what it was before the end of the Vietnam War.

In Nicaragua, the leftist Sandinistas succeeded in taking over the government when belated US diplomatic efforts failed to achieve a non-Sandinista solution to Somoza. The Carter administration first cut off most aid to Somoza, under its human rights policy, then relaxed the ban when Somoza made a symbolic gesture. For nine months, while the Sandinistas gained ground militarily, Carter attempted to persuade Somoza and non-Sandinista opponents to agree to an election formula which would preserve Somoza's party and the National Guard. Not until days before Somoza fell did the US propose a formula that would allow one Sandinista representative in the new government. As the military balance shifted against Somoza emboldened Sandinista peasants invaded Somoza's lands, presaging the agrarian reform that was soon to come after his fall.[10]

The US sought to meet the guerilla challenge in El Salvador with massive amounts of military aid and several dozen advisers. The escalation of military aid staved off defeat, but after six years was not able to gain more than a stalemate. In Guatemala, the Carter human rights doctrine survived to the extent of minimising US military aid, but the Guatemalan military had by the mid 1980s pushed the guerillas back and crushed grass-roots organisations once again.

Nicaragua by 1986 was besieged by US military and economic pressure. The Congress voted $100 million in direct military aid to the contra army attacking Nicaragua and authorised the CIA, through use of its discretionary funds, to expand that to half a billion. But by mid 1987, the US had not sent in the Marines to

Nicaragua or El Salvador, though the threat to perceived US interests was, in each of the countries, given the historic reasoning of the State Department, manifestly greater than in 1965 when 25,000 troops went to the Dominican Republic and even though the Nicaraguan army was 1/20th and the Salvadoran guerilla 1/100th the size of the army the US had been willing to engage half-way around the world in Vietnam. And the resilience shown in the face of US pressure from an impoverished country of three million, and from the anti-government forces in El Salvador stood in sharp contrast to Guatemala of 1954. The Sandinistas stood, the guerillas in El Salvador and Guatemala had not been defeated, and the social causes which gave rise to the insurgencies in El Salvador and Guatemala had not been overcome.

Beginning in 1982 four Latin American nations – Panama, Mexico, Colombia and Venezuela – began a diplomatic effort to resolve the Central American conflicts. Called Contadora, this process was without precedent and, seen in historic perspective, was an additional challenge to US power because it represented an independent, Latin American effort to control events. By the middle of Reagan's second term, the Contadora process had been pronounced near dead many times, but was haltingly working its way toward a regional agreement to limit arms, foreign advisers and military manoeuvres, and to promote democracy.

Though publicly claiming to support Contadora, the US refused to sign a protocol agreeing to end support of the anti-Sandinista contra army attacking from Honduras and, on more than one occasion, manoeuvred to prevent an agreement suitable to Nicaragua. The US heavily influenced its allies – El Salvador, Honduras, and Costa Rica – to veto treaty proposals. By 1984 it was providing nearly half the military and balance of payments budgets of these three countries. But two of the countries, in 1986, showed signs of independence – the new President of Costa Rica publicly spoke out against aid to the contras, and the President of Honduras had informal talks with Nicaragua and played down the importance of an incursion of Nicaraguan troops into areas of Honduras militarily occupied by the contras. The foreign ministers of the Contadora countries, supported by four additional countries (Argentina, Brazil, Peru, and Uruguay) formally requested US Secretary of State Schultz in March 1986 to withdraw from Congress the aid to the contra army legislation, but the US refused.

The resilience of the Sandinista, the continued operations of the guerillas in Guatemala and El Salvador, and the increasing signs of Latin American diplomatic independence, may be attributed to the defeat of the US in Vietnam. The Vietnam Syndrome had become the popular name for a very strong reluctance of the US people, manifested time and again in public opinion polls, for the US to become militarily involved in Central America, or other foreign conflicts in which US interests were unclear and US soldiers might die. This opinion had not changed despite a steady barrage of speeches from President Reagan warning that Nicaragua was much closer to home than Vietnam.

This view of declining US power had been shared in a general sense by the political forces that brought Ronald Reagan to power. There were dominant elements in his administration that sought to go on the military offensive, to roll back what it saw as gains by allies of the Soviet Union, or at the very least, to prevent consolidation and economic growth of such governments.

By 1986 President Reagan had had considerable success in going on the offensive. Though there had been a fight in Congress over military appropriations to Central America every year, appropriations to El Salvador increased from $9.5 million in 1979 to $578 million in 1986 without strings. Aid to the contras had proceeded in four years from secret aid unapproved by Congress to $100 million of open military aid, quite in violation of an explicit June 1986 decision of the World Court. But despite gains by Reagan, his exercise in military and political power in Central America from 1980 to 1986 remained less, after protracted struggle with Congress and public opinion, than Lyndon Johnson's virtual overnight thrust of 25,000 troops into the Dominican Republic in 1965. His effort remained bogged down by surprisingly strong military capacity in the Sandinista army and among guerrilla groups in El Salvador, increasing Latin American diplomatic independence, and US public opinion.

Notes

1 A *New York Times*/CBS News Poll published in the *Times,* 15 April, 1986, (p 6), had 62 per cent opposed and 25 per cent in favour of the US providing the Contra army fighting the Nicaragua government with $100 million in aid. The poll followed eight weeks of intense debate on

the issue in the Congress and in the media. Despite this debate only 38 per cent knew which side the US was supporting in Nicaragua. However, once the pollsters asked more questions, respondents recalled and had a more distinct image of the issue. Though 59 per cent believed Nicaragua would provide the Soviet Union with a base (Nicaragua had strongly denied this for six years), 62 per cent of them opposed the aid, as did a 52 per cent majority among those who generally approved of President Reagan. Support for the aid shrank from 25 per cent to 16 per cent when asked if US military advisers be included.

2   For more details see, James Dunkerley, *The Long War: Dictatorship and Revolution in El Salvador,* Verso Books, London, 1983.

3   See Tommie Sue Montgomery, *Revolution in El Salvador,* Westview, Boulder, Colorado, 1982.

4   See Stephen Schlesinger & Stephen Kinzer, *Bitter Fruit,* Doubleday, Garden City, New York, 1982.

5   See George Black, *Triumph of the People: The Sandinista Revolution in Nicaragua,* Zed Press, London, 1981.

6   Walter LaFeber, *Inevitable Revolutions: The United States in Central America,* Norton, New York, 1984, p 36. LaFeber's is the best account of US foreign policy in the nineteenth and twentieth centuries.

7   *op. cit.,* p 37.

8   See, Gregorio Selser, *Sandino,* Monthly Review Press, New York, 1981.

9   Thomas P. Anderson, *Matanza: El Salvador's Communist Revolt of 1932,* University of Nebraska Press, Lincoln, 1971.

10 Shirley Christian, *Nicaragua: Revolution in the Family,* Random House, New York, 1985, pp 3–118.

Paul Watanabe

Giving peace a chance: the anti-nuclear movement

Public activism and foreign policy

One of the most often repeated axioms in America is: 'Politics stops at the water's edge'. The notion is that the partisan skirmishing and public activism that characterise domestic policymaking are inappropriate and, indeed, dangerous in the hostile confines of external affairs. Foreign policy is considered a special area in which the nation must speak with a clear, united voice and in which the complexities of diplomacy require the ascendancy of experts centralised within the national government and especially within the executive branch.

The axiom about politics halting at the water's edge has not, of course, wholly manifested itself in the history of American foreign policy. The Vietnam era, for example, provided ample evidence of widespread public participation and considerable wrangling over the conduct and consequences of American policies. Here the dominance of the executive in foreign policymaking was challenged, the alleged 'experts' were discredited and, regardless of what one believes about its desirability, the public's influence was substantial.

The Vietnam experience, however, did not diminish and, indeed, may have reinvigorated the view long held by many students of American politics and policy practitioners that democratic processes and public activism in foreign affairs are, if not unavoidable, certainly undesirable. Over a century and a half ago, for example, Alexis de Tocqueville in his masterful treatise on *Democracy in America* observed:

Foreign politics demands scarcely any of those qualities which are peculiar to a democracy; they require on the contrary, the perfect use of almost all those in which it is deficient. . . a democracy can only with great difficulty regulate the details of an important undertaking, persevere in a fixed design, and work out its execution in spite of serious obstacles. It cannot combine its measures with secrecy or await their consequences with patience.[1]

The concerns about democratic foreign policymaking reveal a deep-seated uneasiness about widespread public activism in the hostile and demanding confines of external politics. According to this view, citizen activism may be a blessing for domestic politics, but it is the bane of foreign policymaking. A generally untutored and undisciplined public serves as a serious impediment to the development of careful, consistent, and successful policies. Walter Lippmann, for example, echoed de Tocqueville's mistrust of the public's preparation and performance:

> The unhappy truth is that the prevailing public opinion has been destructively wrong at the critical junctures. The people have imposed a veto upon the judgements of informed and responsible officials. They have compelled the governments, which usually knew what would have been wiser, or was necessary, or was more expedient to be too late with too little, or too long with too much, too pacifist in peace and too bellicose in war, too neutralist or appeasing in negotiation or too intransigent.[2]

The United States in the 1980s has assuredly reached a 'critical juncture'. Momentous issues crowd the foreign policy agenda, and, reminiscent of the activism of the 1960s and early 1970s, a growing number of Americans have been stirred from their traditional lethargy to address them. Thousands of Americans, for example, have trekked down to their local town halls and from one end of the country to the other to express their concerns about the mounting nuclear arms race. College graduation ceremonies throughout the United States have been marked recently by students calling for their universities to divest themselves of stocks in companies operating in South Africa. Shanty towns have been erected on the college greens of several campuses to serve as vivid reminders of the prevailing injustices in South Africa. Large numbers of citizens have registered their opposition to the direction of United States policies in Central America through teach-ins, legislative lobbying, and the provision of sanctuary to refugees victimised by repression. In the summer of 1986, as the Congress was in the process of approving President Reagan's request for $100 million to assist anti-Sandinista 'Contra' forces fighting in Nicaragua, four Vietnam veterans returned their medals, including a Congressional Medal of Honor, and began a hunger strike to protest the rush toward a broader war in Central America. American society, in short, has been experiencing a level of citizen activism over foreign policy matters unmatched since the end of the Indochina War.

These peace movements assuredly have not been confined to the United States. The European anti-nuclear movement, for example, clearly has helped fuel its American counterpart. It does remain true, however, that no world power can match the potential of the United States to shape the prospects for nuclear armageddon or survival, the end or prolongation of apartheid, and the future of the nations of Central America. The movements in the United States that have emerged around these and other foreign policy issues, therefore, deserve to be watched closely for their success or failure will have telling consequences.

It should be kept in mind that these most recent manifestations of public involvement in the foreign policy realm operate in an environment in which the suspicions about this involvement shared by de Tocqueville, Lippmann, and countless others make it difficult to translate public concerns into policies. Doubts about the desirability of peace movements in particular have been raised. Four eminent American scholars, for example, have written:

> . . . the more civilized and non-violent a democratic nation becomes in its internal institutions and behaviour, the more peaceful and frank the outlook and conduct of its people, the more it may find it difficult, as a nation, to survive and prosper in the semi-anarchy of international affairs, in which secrecy, suspicion, and violence always lurk in the background.[3]

The people who have joined together to renounce the direction of United States policies in a number of arenas do not share the sentiments of their detractors. The powers arrayed against these activists are formidable. These peace seekers, however, may reflect a tenacity and an understanding that President Dwight Eisenhower recognised over a generation ago when he stated: 'People in the long run are going to do more to promote peace than our governments. Indeed, I think that people want peace so much that one of these days government had better get out of their way and let them have it.'

A close examination of the anti-nuclear weapons movement in

the United States will help illustrate some of the dilemmas posed by
aroused citizen activism on foreign policy issues. The inquiry will
focus primarily on the effort to promote the nuclear freeze initiative. It can be assumed that many of the concerns that have
motivated a public outcry over the direction of the arms race have
also been reflected in other endeavours such as the anti-apartheid
movement and the growing opposition to Reagan administration
policies in Nicaragua and El Salvador. It would be safe to predict,
therefore, that the Free South Africa Movement and the sanctuary
movement will be plagued, if they have not been already, by some
of the enormous demands that have accompanied the anti-nuclear
movement. The freeze experience offers ample evidence that any
effort to alter radically the direction of prevailing governmental
policy is an enormously arduous undertaking.

The nuclear freeze and the American peace movement

In the summer of 1982, nearly one million people came to New
York City to call for a halt to the burgeoning nuclear arms
competition between the Soviet Union and the United States. The
New York rally was the largest political demonstration in the
nation's history, eclipsing the numbers drawn to the numerous
Vietnam War protests of the 1960s and 1970s, and was part of a
growing movement principally sparked by an idea initially conce-
ived by Randall Forsberg. In 1980, Forsberg proposed a mutual and
verifiable freeze by the two superpowers on the testing, production,
and deployment of all nuclear weapons. The nuclear freeze has
served as a a rallying point for the anti-nuclear peace movement in
the United States much like opposition to the scheduled deployment of Pershing II and cruise missiles in Europe catalysed its
European counterparts.

The simple, but revolutionary, idea of the freeze drew support
almost immediately from across the United States. Hundreds of
local communities and counties and several states embraced the
freeze by voting for it in referenda or through legislative actions.
The United States House of Representatives passed a freeze
motion, although the Republican-controlled Senate defeated the
measure by a surprisingly narrow margin. Public opinion polls have
revealed consistently high and broad-based support for the

proposal. Throughout the 1980s around 80 per cent of the populace has regularly approved of a nuclear freeze.

The most important actor on the American scene, however, Ronald Reagan, has not favoured a freeze and has systematically campaigned to discredit the idea as unworkable and to portray its sponsors as generally well-intentioned but dangerously naïve. Reagan's opposition, of course, was anticipated. It was, in fact, concern about the Reagan administration's advocacy of unprecedented growth in America's nuclear arsenal, its unwillingness to pursue meaningful arms control, and its loose comments about the winnability of nuclear exchanges and the launching of nuclear warning shots that prompted a rash of public concern about the nuclear future. Reagan's tough talk has assuredly been music to the ears of many Americans who felt that the United States in the 1970s was failing to meet the challenge of Soviet might and who viewed experiences like the Iranian hostage crisis, the invasion of Afghanistan, and the fall of the Somoza regime in Nicaragua as manifestations of the decline of American power. On the other hand, if Reagan has been intent on putting a scare into the Soviets, he has also succeeded in elevating the fears of many Americans who had for various reasons suppressed thinking about the unthinkable. In a 1984 poll by the Public Agenda Foundation, 55 per cent of the respondents reported that they found themselves thinking about the possibility of nuclear war more often than they did five years before. In the same poll, 52 per cent felt that the United States has not done enough to reach serious arms reductions with the Soviets. A 1981 Gallup Poll revealed that 49 per cent of those interviewed believed that a nuclear war was very or fairly likely within the next decade.

The leadership of the anti-nuclear movement has been drawn from a broad spectrum of American society, although there has been a particularly dramatic response from professional groups. 'The profile of this latest of protests', according to *New York Times* writer Fox Butterfield, 'is a far cry from that of the powerful antiwar demonstrations of the late 1960s. The leaders are not bearded radicals but middle-aged and middle-class men and women, many accustomed to positions of responsibility and prestige. They include doctors, lawyers, nurses, scientists, teachers and priests. Their chief battles have been fought, not in street confrontations, but at sermons and lectures, in books and pamphlets'.[4]

The anti-nuclear message has been spread by an impressive array

of organisations active nationally, locally, and even internationally
– Physicians for Social Responsibility, Union of Concerned Sci-
entists, Physicians for the Prevention of Nuclear War, Social
Workers for Nuclear Disarmament, Social Scientists Against Nuc-
lear War, Freeze Voter, High Technology Professionals for Peace,
Lawyers Alliance for Nuclear Arms Control, Women's Action for
Nuclear Disarmament, Ground Zero, United Campuses Against
Nuclear War, Beyond War, and numerous others. Several religious
groups have also provided organisational and moral support to the
peace movement. The nuclear freeze proposal has been formally
endorsed by the United Church of Christ, the United Presbyterian
Church, the United Methodist Church, the American Quakers, the
Epispocal Church, and the Unitarian Universalist Church.

Several documents, letters, and resolutions have been issued by
these churches advocating a freeze and other initiatives for halting
the nuclear arms race. The Governing Board of the National
Council of Churches, for example, adopted two resolutions: 'Resolution on a Nuclear Weapons Freeze' in 1981 and 'Swords and
Ploughshares' a year later. The Episcopal House of Bishops issued
in 1982 a pastoral letter, 'Identity, Pilgrimage, and Peace', which
attacked the morality of nuclear deterrence and the arms race and
advocated a nuclear freeze and the constant pursuit of disarmament. A similar message was contained in a 'Pastoral Letter to a
People Called Methodist', written by the United Methodist Council
of Bishops.

The National Conference of Catholic Bishop's 'Pastoral Letter on
War and Peace', published in 1983, was the most publicised formal
statement by a major religious body denouncing nuclear weapons as
legitimate instruments of national policy. The letter offered a moral
justification for repudiation of nuclear weapons, condemnation of
their use, and a halt to their continued production and deployment.
The Catholic Bishops also questioned the morality of the strategy of
deterrence since it is based on the threat of unleashing massive
destruction on defenceless civilian noncombatants.

The peace movement's problems

The peace movement's success in enhancing public awareness of
nuclear issues and mobilising impressive organisational resources
has been tempered by several disappointments. One could argue,

for instance, that in the last few years the world on balance has crept closer to the nuclear abyss rather than backed away. The superpowers have undertaken aggressive weapons development programmes. No major arms control agreements have been consummated in over a decade. Instead, renewal of the Anti-Ballistic Missile Treaty and adherence to the SALT II guidelines on offensive systems appear to be in serious jeopardy. A new emphasis on active defense rather than disarmament has been the Reagan administration's response to the public's growing apprehension about continued reliance on deterrence and mutual assured destruction. Reagan's Strategic Defense Initiative (SDI, also called 'Star Wars') threatens to extend the arms race into the heavens. The Soviets have repeatedly indicated that the pursuit of a space-based missile defence system impedes progress toward arms limitations and accelerates the further deployment of offensive weaponry. All of these factors, and others, have contributed recently to a serious feeling of malaise in the anti-nuclear movement.

Although the public appears more fearful than ever of the likelihood of a nuclear apocalypse and is specifically nervous about Reagan's hand on the nuclear trigger, the peace movement has not been able to sustain the momentum of the early 1980s. The arduous journey of the 1986 Great Peace March for Global Nuclear Disarmament exemplified many of the movement's problems.

The 3,000-mile cross-country passage was billed by its organisers as a dramatic manifestation of citizen concerns with the dangers of nuclear war and the need for disarmament. The marchers had barely left Los Angeles when serious disagreements and problems emerged. Funds actually available to support the march fell significantly short of expectations. Dissension over strategies, the disbursement of money, and other matters accompanied a predictable decline in enthusiasm brought on by bad weather, Spartan accommodations, cold scrambled eggs and blistered feet. Within a very short time after the commencement of the peace journey, the ranks of the marchers had thinned to a hard core of no more than 500.

The biggest disappointment, however, centred around the inability of the movement to enlist an impressive cadre of activists from around the country to the anti-nuclear cause. The stop in Chicago, for example, two-thirds of the way across the country, was regarded as crucial by march supporters. Before entering Chicago, one of the march's board members stated: 'Chicago is going to tell us a lot. Either we are going to become a very large movement or we will leave Chicago a small group of dedicated people'. A small and disappointed group of people left Chicago. Advance teams had been assigned to make preparations for the marchers leading up to the anticipated celebration of what Mayor Harold Washington proclaimed as 'Survival Sunday in the city of Chicago'. The major event of the day was a rally in Lincoln Park in which numerous activists, movie stars, and notable Chicago-based personalities like author Studs Terkel appeared. The plan was for thousands of individuals to join in a massive rally. Instead, only a few hundred actually came. Terkel's faith in the march and the anti-nuclear cause remained solid. 'I know this march represents the deep-seated values of the great many', Terkel said. 'But when it comes to making the connection with daily life, we're up against banality, the evil of banality. The American society has to make up its mind if it has a life wish or a death wish. I've got a life wish. That's why I like this march'. The spirit of at least one participant, however, was severely shaken by the reception in Chicago and other stops along the march. 'We thought we were the darlings of the media. We were the spark. We were so arrogant', the marcher remarked. 'Chicago was a real humbling experience. We learned we've got a lot of work ahead of us. I think everybody came to the realization we weren't the cutesy-wutesy peace march that everybody thought we were.'

In an article entitled, 'Whatever happened to the freeze movement?', Thomas Halsted, director of public affairs for the United States Arms Control and Disarmament Agency from 1977 to 1981, declared that 'the nuclear-freeze movement is dead'.[5] Halsted identified five causes of the movement's death.

First, he maintained that the leadership of the movement was weak. Particularly harmful in this regard was the inability of a single figure like Martin Luther King or Robert Kennedy to emerge who could galvanise support and rally the public.

Second, the movement lacked mass appeal. It was too centred in the well-to-do, college educated, and predominantly white crowd. Professionals were effective in organising their peers. They were less successful or, perhaps, less interested in addressing the concerns of working men and women.

Third, the freeze movement did not match its success in depicting the horrors of nuclear war and the consequences of burgeoning nuclear arsenals with similar success in suggesting appropriate specific courses of action. The freeze, according to this criticism, was a powerful symbol, not a practical policy. Freeze advocates should have been better prepared, for example, to initiate and sustain opposition to specific weapons systems, to strive for small victories, and to determine dispassionately those initiatives that were truly possible and those that were largely pipe dreams. Along this line, United States Senator Charles McC Mathias Jr, of Maryland has suggested that, 'we try to freeze a few ice cubes before we try to freeze a whole 100-ton chunk of ice . . . What we need to do, if we are talking about freezing in a serious, mature way, is to talk about the various elements that could be frozen. We ought to be preparing ice cubes – of a usable, manageable, and practical size – that can be frozen quite easily individually. And then one by one they might gradually cool the nuclear arms race and bring it to a point where its direction could be reversed'.[6]

A fourth element that Halsted claimed went awry in the freeze movement was the tendency to favour big, splashy undertakings over nitty-gritty politicking. Large rallies and demonstrations and 'great marches' attract attention, but these 'one-shot, convulsive events', as Halsted called them, have little lasting impact. One freeze organiser has acknowledged: 'We were in a flat-out sprint when we should have realized we were running in a marathon'.

Finally, Halsted maintained that President Reagan skilfully circumvented the freeze movement. Reagan began to convey at least the appearance of an interest in arms control by suggesting alternative proposals such as 'build-down' and by agreeing finally to open dialogue with the Soviet leadership. Most important, the President offered SDI as the allegedly ultimate answer to dependence on nuclear armaments. In Halsted's words, 'No matter how costly, dangerous, unworkable and just plain nutty the idea seemed to be, it purported to be 'doing something' about the nuclear threat'.[7]

In response to the self-doubters within the freeze movement, many arms-control advocates believe that the movement has been wounded but has surely not been slain. 'The reported death of the freeze has been greatly exaggerated', Congressman Ed Markey, the principal supporter of the freeze in the United States House of Representatives, has maintained. 'This movement is a sleeping giant, not the corpse many would have us believe. It has had some notable political and legislative victories in its first few years, and it continues to have an organizational strength and broad political appeal that suggest the freeze will have a continuing impact on the course of US arms control policy'.[8]

The 'sleeping giant', Markey has admitted, badly needs a victory to awaken it. Anti-nuclear activists, therefore, must concentrate on winning some small battles and pursue a strategy consistent with Senator Mathias's notion of seeking little freezes rather than relying on a comprehensive freeze. Markey, for instance, has suggested that American policymakers should be encouraged to respond positively to Soviet initiatives to curtail nuclear test explosions. A testing freeze would demonstrate a mutual commitment to restrain the spiralling arms competition. A comprehensive test ban is also a notion that can rally support from both the grass-roots and the arms control 'experts'.

A smaller group of peace activists have argued that what is needed is not an incremental strategy but precisely the opposite. The problem with the nuclear freeze from this point of view is not its comprehensiveness but its fundamental narrowness. The freeze proposal does not adequately address the larger political, economic, and social context within which the arms race has been nurtured. The desire for quick victories, easy answers, and the impatience and panic that accompany inevitable setbacks tend to trivialise the forces that have brought the world to the brink of nuclear ruin. The requirements for success rely, therefore, much more on a demanding process of citizen education and on an expansion of the peace agenda rather than a hunkering down. Suzanne Gordon has noted:

> Unlike the more untidy Vietnam antiwar movement, the newly reborn peace movement's focus on legislation and electoral politics, rather than years of demonstrations and teach-ins, is said to be a sign of its political sophistication and maturity. Perhaps this is because many peace organisations have not fully come to terms with the fact that nuclear weapons and the ever-escalating arms race are not solvable single issues but are rather symptoms of a far deeper crisis in American economic and political life.[9]

Gordon has also anticipated the major criticism of her approach; namely that the nature and momentum of the nuclear arms race does not offer a great deal of time to check the rush toward oblivion. Gordon has written:

> Given the extreme urgency of the need to save the planet from a nuclear holocaust, such a long-term agenda, many peace activists would argue, is

a luxury the world can ill afford. What these activists do not understand – despite defeat after defeat – is that the arms race will never end until we change those governmental and corporate institutions that so relentlessly support it.[10]

Clearly, the anti-nuclear weapons movement in the United States has reached a critical point. The movement can be credited with building support for the idea of arms control and promoting awareness about the dangers of nuclear war and its consequences. Putting the aspirations of the public into concrete initiatives has been a more difficult undertaking. As we have noted, the public's views are complex and not always consistent. It is difficult to decipher the mixed signals emanating from the citizenry. Individuals, for example, yearn for peace and fear war, but they also appreciate national strength and are wary of being perceived as too weak in a dangerous world.

Many people would agree with de Tocqueville, Lippmann and others that the public's inconsistency is a good reason for suspicion about public activism in the complex realm of defence and strategic policy. Those in the peace movement, however, might regard dealing with the public's understandably varied views on issues of war and peace as challenges, not impediments. If fears about the Russians restrain the public's longing for an end to the arms race, it is essential that peace advocates address the foundations of these fears. If these sources of concern can be realistically appraised, the still difficult but at least identifiable goal can then be to determine how to overcome them. It is perhaps only in this way that the stigma attached to citizen participation in the foreign policy realm can be mitigated, and, more important, the way in which the dreams of those adventurous individuals who began the current peace movement by parading to their local town meetings to demand a halt to the arms race can be fulfilled.

Conclusion

The anti-nuclear movement raises acutely for the United States all the dilemmas of a democracy struggling with difficult foreign policy issues. Citizen activism in the sensitive area of nuclear weapons policy and arms control prompts all the traditional concerns of practitioners, policymakers, and expert technicians about the public's alleged shortcomings. Other Americans, however, have been drawn to the anti-nuclear cause precisely because of their belief that the traditional reliance on the centralisation of foreign policymaking power in a few hands has hastened the prospects of a senseless apocalypse. These activists, scared, scarred and angered by the unchecked growth of nuclear armaments, believe that greater openness and accountability must be instilled within the decisionmaking process. They maintain that an enhanced public role is the only effective means to challenge the prevailing nuclear dogma.

American opinion analyst and pollster Daniel Yankelovich began his discussion of the findings from a recent major study of public opinion on nuclear arms policy with the following observations that effectively summarise both the potential risks and rewards of citizen activism on nuclear issues.

> The heightened concern of the voter can be good, or it can be bad. It can be good if voters work to understand what our national options for action really are, and if they come to accept the trade-offs, risks, and sacrifices that will be associated with whatever option they choose. And it can be especially good if, in the exercise of democracy, a climate of understanding and political will is created that gives our political leadership the support it needs to diminish the rise of nuclear war.
>
> On the other hand, greater public involvement in the nuclear issue can be bad if it encourages demagoguery on this, the most fateful issue of our time. So deep is the concern about the nuclear arms race that if the country does not have a method for considering our options in a calm, mature fashion, the concern of citizens could erupt in overreaction, over-anxiousness, and support for action for its own sake. Our choice, in effect, is between democracy at its best or at its worst.[11]

The decisions made by the American public and policymakers will certainly have enormous consequences for the United States and, indeed, the planet. No issue demands democracy at its best more than the nuclear arms race.

Notes

1   Alexis de Tocqueville, *Democracy in America,* Knopf, New York, 1945, I, pp 234–5.
2   Walter Lippmann, *The Public Philosophy,* Little, Brown & Co., Boston, 1955, p 20.
3   William Ebenstein, C. Herman Pritchett, Henry A. Turner, & Dean

Mann, *American Democracy in World Perspective,* Harper & Row, New York, 1967, pp 645–6.

4 Fox Butterfield, 'Anatomy of the nuclear protest', *New York Times Magazine,* 11 July 1982, p 14.

5 Thomas Halsted, 'Whatever happened to the freeze movement?' *Boston Globe,* 6 June 1986.

6 Charles McC. Mathias Jr, 'Fire and ice', in Steven E. Miller (ed), *The Nuclear Weapons Freeze and Arms Control,* Ballinger, Cambridge, MA, 1984, p 159.

7 op.cit.

8 Edward J. Markey, 'A sleeping giant not a corpse', *Boston Globe,* 8 September, 1985.

9 Suzanne Gordon, 'The peace movement's malaise', *Boston Globe,* 9 June 1985.

10 ibid.

11 Public Agenda Foundation, *Voter Options on Nuclear Arms Policy: A Briefing Book for the 1984 Elections,* Public Agenda Foundation, New York, 1984, p 2.

Paul Watanabe

The new Cold War: foreign policy and Soviet-American relations

Introduction

In his first press conference as President in January 1981, Ronald Reagan was asked to assess his counterparts in the Kremlin. He unhesitatingly asserted that 'the only morality they [Soviet Leaders] recognize is what will further their cause: meaning they reserve unto themselves the right to commit any crime, to lie, to cheat.'

These comments prompted considerable discussion within the United States. Were these extemporaneous thoughts overly harsh and impulsive? Could the new President possibly negotiate in good faith with individuals cast in these dark terms? Reagan, while addressing a group of evangelicals in 1983, took great pains to make clear that his earlier assessment of his antagonists was genuine and had not been altered:

> . . . as good Marxists-Leninists the Soviet leaders have openly and publicly declared that the only morality they recognize is that which will further their cause, which is world revolution . . . they are the focus of evil in the modern world.

Walter LaFeber has succinctly and appropriately characterised the Reagan revolution in foreign affairs as the culmination of 'Cold War II'.[1] The Reagan administration's orientation toward the Soviet Union and international politics has consistently reflected three elements: the repudiation of central components of the Nixon, Ford, and, particularly, Carter foreign policies; the restoration of unchallenged American global hegemony guided by a vision of the world drawn from the 1940s and 1950s; and the considerable expansion of the American military arsenal at both the conventional and nuclear levels fuelled by unprecedented levels of defence spending.

From entanglement to defiance

A popular collection of essays, which examined United States foreign policy in the Carter years, was aptly entitled *Eagle Entangled: US Foreign Policy in a Complex World.*[2] The title conveyed the Carter administration's struggle to conduct foreign policy in an environment characterised by complex interdependence: a world in which the elements of power had become more diversified and less concentrated, the international agenda had been considerably broadened, and American dominance of economic and security affairs had eroded.

Flexibility and restraint marked the often painful adjustments called for by what Seyom Brown described as 'the changing essence of power'.[3] Commitments were narrowed while limits were imposed and identified. The Arab oil embargo of the mid-1970s, for example, made the United States and other Western powers especially cognisant of their sensitivity and, in some cases, vulnerability to disruptions in the supply of strategic resources. The consummate challenge for Jimmy Carter and his predecessors Gerald Ford and Richard Nixon was to exercise global leadership without hegemony.

Detente reflected a willingness in the strategic realm to recognise the attainment of essential parity between the United States and the Soviet Union. With this recognition the superpowers were able to concentrate considerable energy on defining areas in the arms competition where coinciding interests suggested the desirability of imposing constraints. The Anti-Ballistic Missile (ABM) Treaty, the Interim Agreement on Strategic Offensive Arms (SALT I) and the successful negotiation of the SALT II accord manifested the mutual willingness to seek meaningful arms control.

President Carter, as part of his attempts to seek adjustments to new or neglected international realities, strived to make the North-South dimension as central as the East-West dispute in the thoughts and actions of American leaders. In a similar fashion, he endeavoured to place the issue of human rights at the centre of United States foreign policy.

American policymakers throughout much of the 1970s, in short, seemed prepared to recognise the requirements of a changing world order and to restrain the quest for primacy. Their policies manifested some of the sentiments expressed by John F. Kennedy in his famous speech delivered at American University:

Let us not be blind to our differences, but let us also direct attention to
our common interests and to the means by which those differences can be
resolved. And if we cannot end now our differences, at least we can help
make the world safe for diversity. For in the final analysis our most basic
common link is that we all inhabit this planet. We all breathe the same air.
We all cherish our children's future. And we are all mortal.

Ronald Reagan's view of the United States and its role in the
world has differed markedly with his predecessors. Where others
saw the need for, and, indeed, the desirability of, the United States
adjusting to alterations in the international milieu, Reagan
regarded the changes as regrettable and unnecessary manifestations
of an American retreat from power. Reagan, consequently,
dedicated himself to a full restoration of American military and
economic predominance and to the eradication of the paralysis of
power symptomatic of the so-called 'Vietnam syndrome'.

Upon assuming the presidency, Reagan identified the debilitating
self-doubts, the erosion of American power, and restraints on
assertiveness as both causes and effects of setbacks for the United
States. The Reagan forces bemoaned 'losses' in Angola, Mozam-
bique, Ethiopia, Vietnam, Iran, and Nicaragua. In the United
Nations, the West was being assailed daily, and in the efforts to
negotiate an international regime for the deep sea beds the United
States presumably acquiesced too readily to Third World demands.
Arab oil sheiks brandished the oil weapon effectively, and a handful
of young Iranians held fifty-one hostages and the nation captive for
well over a year. The policy of détente allegedly offered the Soviets
a front for continued military expansion while the West retreated
unilaterally. The lesson to be learned was that we must resist rather
than accommodate 'the evil empire'.

Reagan's approach to international politics profited from the
perception held by many Americans that he was clear about his
objectives while his predecessor vacillated, and he exuded
confidence and strength while Carter conveyed weakness. Public
opinion analyst William Schneider, for instance, found that in 1980
a majority of the public believed that Reagan would do a good job
in bolstering America's military strength and standing up to the
Russians.[4] Unsurprisingly, therefore, Reagan's efforts to renew
United States power and to develop a strong national defence have
been politically appealing to a large group of Americans.

Although the public's regard for Reagan has generally been high and sustained, there has been from the very beginning of Reagan's presidency a certain uneasiness about Reagan's handling of foreign policy. The same 1980 poll, for example, indicated that the public feared that Reagan might be reckless in the exercise of military power and the one most likely to lead the United States into another major war. This element of doubt is important to identify because the line between perceptions of strength and provocation is narrow. A public appreciative of national strength can with little difficulty back away from actions deemed reckless and threatening to a peace it wishes to preserve with equal intensity.

The editors of *Eagle Entangled* appropriately entitled their collection of essays on the new Reagan administration, *Eagle Defiant: United States Foreign Policy in the 1980s*.[5] Since the Reagan team has come on board, defiance has been in and accommodation has been out. This administration has been inspired less by Kennedy's sentiments cited earlier than by President Woodrow Wilson's challenge enunciated seventy years ago during the First World War:

> The world must be made safe for democracy . . . We shall fight for the things which we have always carried nearest our hearts . . . the day has come when America is privileged to spend her blood and her might for the principles that gave her birth . . . God helping her, she can do no other.

Old ends and new means

The Reagan administration, in its drive to make the world safe for 'democracy' rather than 'diversity', has drawn its inspiration from the Wilsonian outlook and, in classic conservative fashion, has looked to the past to find a model for the present and the future. Reagan has conjured up images reminiscent of the world of the late 1940s and 1950s. His pronouncements have echoed those of George Kennan's famous 'long telegram', the Truman Doctrine, and National Security Council Paper No. 68 (NSC-68) in their depictions of an aggressive and implacable Soviet Union as the source of instability in the world.

While many argued then, and continue to argue now, that this view represents a simplistic assessment of the Russians, the Reagan administration has taken it to heart. In early 1983, for instance, Reagan described the confrontation with the Soviet Union as 'the struggle between right and wrong, good and evil'. As it has throughout much of the postwar period, this Manichean outlook has provided policymakers with a convenient and narrowly-focused lens through which to survey the international landscape. American interests have been defined overwhelmingly in strategic terms. Policy choices as a consequence have been radically simplified: friends of whatever stripe must be nurtured and maintained – no room for pious notions like 'human rights' – and enemies identified and aggressively opposed.

By calling the nation back to the posture of the early years of the Cold War, Reagan has offered not only explanations for present troubles but a blueprint for remedying them. The United States reigned pre-eminent in the early postwar decades. While most of the world was sick and shattered, the United States remained relatively healthy and unscathed. It enjoyed unrivalled strategic superiority, dominance in the global economy, unchallenged leadership of the Western alliance and a supportive, bi-partisan domestic consensus. Reagan has clearly looked upon this era as a lost ideal to be recaptured, as a norm to be re-established and not as an historical anachronism.

The contrast between the Reagan administration's fond embrace of the Cold War and its disdain for détente has been dramatic. In the words of Jeane Kirkpatrick, former United State Permanent Representative to the United Nations and a leading lieutenant in the Reagan revolution:

> Some critics of American foreign policy look back with dread on the 'dark years of the Cold War' and express morbid fear lest we reenter such a period. I must say that I have reservations about this view. In the context of the twentieth century, a century filled with horrors on a scale quite unprecedented in human history, the years of the Cold War were a relatively happy respite during which free societies and democratic institutions were universally secure.[6]

The Reagan administration's view of the Soviet Union has been marked by contrasting images. The Soviet Union has been portrayed on the one hand as a formidable power bent on aggressive conquest and possessing unequalled military might. While he campaigned in Chicago in 1980, for example, Reagan asserted that 'our principal adversary, the Soviet Union, surpasses us in virtually every category of military strength'. At other times, the administration has painted a picture of the Soviet Union as on the brink of collapse, torn asunder by ethnic discord, economic dissatisfaction, unpopular foreign adventures, and high-level political bickering. 'A new foreign policy', Jeane Kirkpatrick has stated, 'must begin from the . . . important, irreducible fact that the Soviet empire is decaying at its center'.[7]

The Reagan administration has skilfully and selectively invoked both images of the Soviet Union to justify the same response – the need to expand, strengthen, and diversify America's military arsenal. We must build our forces, the argument goes, because we cannot lag further behind the Russians. We must build as well to keep the heat on them. The sputtering Soviet economy and the presumably fragile hold of the leadership on the populace cannot sustain an intense, technologically sophisticated and expensive arms competition. In addition to an aggressive programme of military expansion, the administration has instituted a programme involving proxy competition in peripheral areas, e.g. Central America, and selective sanctions, e.g. efforts to derail the Soviet gas pipeline deal with Western European countries.

In dealing with the Soviet Union, Reagan has invoked other images from the past. Here, however, the experiences of the 1930s and Munich have been pointed to as warnings rather than as sources of inspiration and guidance. Clearly the ghosts of Munich have haunted Reagan as they have numerous other cold warriors. They have motivated his preoccupation with military strength. In a *Time* magazine interview, Reagan defended his ambitious military procurement agenda by observing:

> Not being strong, and not even having the means to be strong, which was true of us in the past, led to someone taking advantage to the point that whether we wanted it or not, we were in a war. Would World War II have occurred if the people of Europe and the people of England had listened to Churchill instead of ignoring him until it was too late? Would World War II have happened if Roosevelt's desire to enhance our armed strength had been heeded?[8]

Reagan has realised that President Carter was saddled with the charge of appeasing the Soviets by many powerful opponents of his policies. Senator Henry Jackson of Washington, for example, attacked Carter's decisions to go to Vienna to sign SALT II with Leonid Brezhnev along these lines. Carter, according to Jackson, would be retracing the footsteps of Prime Minister Neville Chamberlain's ill-fated journey to Munich in 1938. 'To enter a treaty which favors the Soviets as this one does . . . is appeasement in its purest form', Jackson charged. 'It is all ominously reminiscent of Great Britain in the 1930s. The failure to face reality today, like the failure to do so then – that is the mark of appeasement.'[9] Reagan has done all he can to avoid the invidious 'mark of appeasement'.

The process of restoring overwhelming American strength and 'facing reality' has so far emphasised substantially increased defence spending and procurement. In its first five years, the Reagan administration has increased military spending in real terms by about ten per cent per year with total outlays of more than $1.5 trillion. The development or deployment of sophisticated new hardware, including the B-1 and Stealth bombers, Trident submarines, aircraft carriers, tactical, intermediate and strategic nuclear delivery vehicles, nuclear warheads and anti-missile systems (notably the Strategic Defense Initiative [SDI or 'Star Wars']) have been vigorously promoted. The unprecedented military buildup undertaken by Reagan has been accompanied by loose talk by members of his administration about 'nuclear warning shots' and 'winnable nuclear wars'.

Reagan's enthusiasm for weapons development has not been matched by a similar interest in arms control. The Reagan administration has not successfully negotiated a single agreement in the arms control area. Instead, the ABM Treaty has been seriously jeopardised and the limits of the unratified SALT II agreement have been breached by the United States. In addition, Reagan declined Mikhail Gorbachev's invitation to halt further nuclear weapons testing.

Reagan's determination to proceed with development of the controversial Strategic Defense Initiative has considerably increased the stakes in the nuclear game and impaired any hopes for strategic arms control in the near future. By placing an emphasis on active nuclear defence as well as deterrence, the Reagan administration has entered a new and costly arena. Reagan has consistently asserted his desire to proceed with the programme. The Soviets, in turn, have indicated that they cannot accept any major accommodations with the United States as long as the threat of Stars Wars deployment persists. This combination is a recipe for deadlock, as was manifested by the breakdown of the Iceland summit.

The crisis in confidence

After the stunning forty-nine state sweep of the presidential election in 1984 by Ronald Reagan, supporters of the President began to talk about the possibility of his running for a third term. For Reagan to do so, of course, the 22nd amendment to the US Constitution, which limits presidents to two terms, would have to be overturned. The process of changing the Constitution is arduous and the prospects of succeeding fairly remote. The fact that a number of citizens felt that the possibility should be seriously explored, however, was evidence of Reagan's popularity.

Midway through his second term the speculation about a third term was abruptly shunted aside by a series of events that threatened to erode public confidence in the President. Instead of dreaming about a third term Reagan and his advisers were left with the challenge of trying to salvage the remainder of his second term. The Daniloff affair, the failure of the Reykjavik summit, the recapture of control of the Senate by the Democrats, and especially the Iran arms sales controversy will surely have a marked influence into the foreseeable future on the conduct and direction of American foreign policy.

The cumulative impact of these events may have harmed Reagan in at least two ways. They further confirmed the fears of Reagan critics that the administration was poorly equipped to deal responsibly with the Soviets and arrogant in its use of power and its unwillingness to talk straight to the public. Even more damaging, however, has been the way in which Reagan has undermined his own basic constituency. It was Reagan who was not going to play ball with the 'evil empire', and it was he that would not bow to 'terrorist thugs' or their sponsors. The administration that was so self-assured, indeed, cocky, was left squirming to explain the trade of an allegedly high-level Soviet spy for an allegedly innocent American journalist and to explain the regular shipments of American arms to the Ayatollah. Perhaps the most serious blow, however, was to the carefully cultivated image of Reagan as a man in charge and true to his own beliefs. In the words of *New York Times* columnist William Safire, Reagan was faced with the unpleasant prospect of being not simply a lame duck but a dead one.[10]

The costs of the Reagan administration's mishandling of the

Iranian secret arms deal and the diversion of funds to the anti-government Contras in Nicaragua became apparent very soon after the scandal emerged. A *New York Times*/CBS News poll taken in November 1986 indicated that President Reagan's overall job approval rating had plunged to 46 per cent from 67 per cent a month earlier. This decline in public approval was the sharpest one-month drop ever recorded by a public opinion survey in measuring presidential performance. The same poll revealed that a majority of the respondents believed that the administration was 'covering up' the facts of the arms deal and that the matter was at least as serious as the Watergate affair which ultimately toppled the Nixon administration in 1974. The Iranian affair raised particular public concerns about Reagan's ability to carry out foreign policy effectively. Only about a third (35 per cent) of the respondents indicated that they approved of Reagan's overall conduct of foreign policy, and 56 per cent of those polled said that they were 'uneasy' about Reagan's ability to deal with a difficult international crisis.

Although it is hard to gauge the full impact of the momentous events which unfolded in the latter part of 1986, one can note a certain irony in the fact that Reagan, who came to office determined to restore what he perceived as waning American power and stature, may find his final months as President preoccupied with the challenge of restoring the public's confidence in him.

Conclusion

In the early 1960s, psychologist Edwin Lawson devised a project to study the development of patriotism in children.[11] As a part of his study, Lawson asked eighty kindergarten students (primarily five-year-olds) in upstate New York to indicate which of twenty national flags displayed before them were the most attractive.

Perhaps surprisingly, but unremarkably, about three-fourths of these children included the American flag in their top five. The appeal of the United States flag as a symbol of their country was not lost upon these youngsters even though they had virtually no systematic exposure to civic education. More remarkable, however, was the finding that the flag of the Soviet Union was overwhelmingly judged least attractive by these students. A bare 10 per cent of the kindergarten children placed the Soviet flag in their top five. Furthermore, as the attractiveness of the American flag remained high among students in grades 1 through 12, the Soviet flag was deemed increasingly less attractive as students got older. The Soviet flag, for example, was listed in the top five of only one of the eighty twelfth-graders interviewed. The original Lawson study has been replicated many times, and the results have been consistent with the initial findings.

The impact of the Cold War has been pervasive. As manifested by the thoughts and actions of leaders of the so-called 'free world' as well as schoolchildren in cities, towns, and villages throughout the United States, the fear, distrust, and enmity toward the Soviet Union has been intense, persistent, and the single most important element guiding American foreign policy since the end of World War II.

American foreign policy in the 1980s under the tutelage of the Reagan administration, therefore, should not be understood as singularly combative or obsessed with an uncompromising view of the Soviet Union. As the Lawson study and the evidence of official American policy for decades unmistakably suggests, the Cold War mentality and cold warrior policies preceded Reagan and will most assuredly succeed him. What Reagan has done is to reinvigorate the vision of American hegemony and to intensify the habitual hatred of the Soviet Union, which has been transmitted to youngsters ignorant of the machinations of international politics but somehow prepared to separate the good guys from the bad guys. President Carter attempted to cope with an international milieu that was marked by increasing complexity, calling for policies sensitive to the new realities. He was abruptly turned out of office after a single term. The world from Reagan's perspective had become not so much complex as it had become hostile to American interests. Reagan, therefore, in a fashion unlike Carter, Ford, and Nixon, has concentrated on winning the Cold War rather than effectively managing it.

The world has grown so accustomed to the permanent competition between the Soviet Union and the United States that it is hard to remember a time when the rancour did not exist and the world was not shadowed by the threat of total destruction. Nevertheless, it surely must have been difficult for Alexis de Tocqueville, who travelled in the United States in the early nineteenth century, to imagine the infant nation as an important, much less super, power. Somehow, however, Tocqueville scanned his crystal ball and envisioned future greatness for the United States and Russia. He also envisioned with stunning clarity the awesome power of these combatants to shape the future of the planet.

> There are at the present time two great nations in the world, which started from difference points, but seem to tend toward the same end. I allude to the Russians and the Americans . . .
>
> All other nations seem to have nearly reached their natural limits, and they have only to maintain their power; but these are still in the act of growth. All the others have stopped, or continue to advance with extreme difficulty; these alone are proceeding with ease and clarity along a path to which no limit can be perceived . . . Their starting point is different and their courses are not the same; yet each of them seems marked out by the will of Heaven to sway the destinies of half the globe.[12]

Notes

1 See Walter LaFeber, 'Consensus and co-operation: a view of United States foreign policy, 1945–1980', in George Schwab (ed), *United States Foreign Policy at the Crossroads,* Greenwood Press, Westport, Conn., 1982, pp 3–26.

2 Kenneth Oye, Donald Rothschild, & Robert Lieber (eds), *Eagle Entangled: US Foreign Policy in a Complex World,* Longman, NY, 1979.

3 See Seyom Brown, 'The changing essence of power', *Foreign Affairs,* LI, 1973, pp 286–99.

4 See William Schneider, 'Conservatism, not interventionism: trends in foreign policy opinionm, 1974–1982', in Oye, Rothschild & Lieber (eds), *Eagle Defiant: United States Foreign Policy in the 1980s,* Little, Brown & Co, Boston, 1983, pp 33–64.

5 Oye, Lieber & Rothschild (eds), *Eagle Defiant.*

6 Jeane J. Kirkpatrick, *The Reagan Phenomenon – and Other Speeches on Foreign Policy,* American Enterprise Institute for Public Policy Research, Washington, DC, 1983, p 28.

7 ibid., p 35.

8 *Time,* 6 February, 1984, p 22.

9 Quoted in Strobe Talbot, *Endgame: The Inside Story of SALT II,* Harper & Row, NY, 1979, p 5.

10 William Safire, 'Enough already', *New York Times,* 24 November, 1986, p A19.

11 Edwin D. Lawson, 'Development of patriotism in children – a second look', *Journal of Psychology,* LV, 1963, pp 279–86.

12 Alexis de Tocqueville, *Democracy in America, Volume 1,* Vintage, NY, 1945, p 452.

The authors

Philip Davies is Lecturer in the Department of American Studies at the University of Manchester, and spent 1984–5 as Visiting Associate Professor at the University of Massachusetts/Boston, and Visiting Fellow of the John W. McCormack Institute of Public Affairs.

Kenneth M. Dolbeare has taught at Hofstra University, the Universities of Wisconsin (Madison), Washington (Seattle), and Massachusetts (Amherst), and currently is on the faculty of Evergreen State College, Washington. His many publications include the popular text, *American Politics: Policies, Power and Change*, D.C. Heath, Lexington, Mass., 1985 (5th edition).

Sandra E. Elman is Senior Researcher and Fellow in the John W. McCormack Institute of Public Affairs at the University of Massachusetts/Boston.

George Goodwin Jr recently retired as Professor of Political Science at the University of Massachusetts/Boston. His service to the University of Massachusetts, and to scholarship, was recognised with the presentation of an honorary doctorate. He now lives and works in Amherst, Massachusetts.

Linda Medcalf has taught at the University of Massachusetts (Amherst), and now teachers at Olympia (Washington) Technical Community College. she and Kenneth Dolbeare are co-authors of *American Ideologies in Transition: from Neopolitics to New Ideas and Beyond*, Random House, New York, 1987.

Gillian Peele is Fellow and Tutor in Politics at Lady Margaret Hall, Oxford University. She is author of *Revival and Reaction: the Right in Contemporary America*, OUP, Oxford & New York, 1984.

Jack Spence is Associate Professor of Political Science at the University of Massachusetts/Boston.

Fredric A. Waldstein is Assistant Professor of Government at Bentley College (Waltham, Massachusetts), and Fellow of the John W. McCormack Institute of Public Affairs.

Paul Watanabe is Associate Professor in the Department of Political Science, and Co-director of the William Joiner Center for the Study of War and Social Consequences at the University of Massachusetts/Boston.